TITHE LISTS FOR AMELIA COUNTY, VIRGINIA,

1765-1766, 1769-1771 & 1778

Transcribed by Reiley Kidd, MD

Colonial Roots
Millsboro, Delaware
2016

ISBN 978-1-68034-068-8

Printed February 2016

CONTENTS

INTRODUCTION v

HOW TO USE THESE LISTS vii

1765 Tithe Lists 1

1766 Tithe Lists 36

1769 Tithe Lists 72

1770 Tithe Lists, Part 1 96

1770 Tithe Lists, Part 2 108

1771 Tithe Lists 127

1772-1777 – NO Tithe Lists

1778 Tithe Lists 127

[this page intentionally blank]

TITHE LISTS OF AMELIA COUNTY, VIRGINIA, 1765-1766, 1769-1771 & 1778

SUMMARY

Prior to 1782, taxes (called 'poll taxes' or 'tithes') were taken each year by county tax commissioners in many if not all counties in the colony of Virginia. These commissioners were evidently appointed by the official state church of the Virginia colony, and the taxes ('tithes') collected went toward the care of the poor, the maintenance of the church, etc.

These annual tithe lists from Amelia County, Virginia, are among the earliest colonial records available for this county and for Nottoway County as well, since they contain the record of residents in the region that later became Nottoway County.

These records function much like a census, since every white male over the age of 16 (21 in some years) was supposed to be recorded. Moreover, (unlike the Personal Property Tax Lists in later years) these records list *every white male* over the age of 16 *in each household.* When the surname of other individuals in the household is the same as that of the taxpayer, these individuals are virtually always related in some way, and are usually the taxpayer's sons who have come of age. Thus these records represent an *annual* census of sorts, at least for the white males of Amelia and Nottoway counties. That they occurred annually, and include the names of other adult males in the household make them superior to the pre-1850 federal censuses, in the amount of information they can provide.

This document includes transcriptions of these Tithe Lists for the years **1765, 1766, 1769, 1770, 1771** (which is partial, missing all of Raleigh Parish) and **1778**. (No Tithables Lists exist for the years 1772-1777.)

INTRODUCTION

Amelia County was created from part of Prince George county in 1735. Until Nottoway County was formed in 1788, Amelia County consisted of two ecclesiastical parishes, Rawleigh (Raleigh) Parish and Nottoway Parish. In 1788, that portion of Amelia County which comprised Nottoway Parish became Nottoway County.

The Tithables Lists from Amelia County, Virginia, are among the earliest colonial records available for this county. While most other Virginia counties' Tax Lists start in 1782, Amelia County's Tithables Lists are available (for the most part) from 1736 forward.

Until the American Revolution (1775–1783), local governments in the colony collected most of their revenue by annually setting a tax rate for each male head of a household and for every white male laborer and every enslaved laborer over sixteen years of age. The parishes of the Church of England (the established state Church in Virginia until 1786) also levied poll taxes to pay ministers, to provide for upkeep of the churches, and to take care of the local poor and orphans. People on whom the tax was owed were called "tithables."

Every household or plantation was responsible for turning in a list of their "tithables" to the tax commissioner for their geographic district in the county. The commissioners then catalogued the tithables in their area, and turned their "Lists" each year in to the county government. Tithes were collected for each white male over the age of sixteen, and for all slaves over 16 years of age, whether male or female.[1] Some individuals, both free and slaves, were exempt, due to age or some other qualification (widows, soldiers, sailors, constables, "Patrolers," etc.). A person owning more than one plantation was taxed only once (apparently where they resided), and the tax lists for their other plantations did not include them among the tithes for those locations; in this instance, the tax commissioner typically added the term "List" or "Tithes" to that taxpayer's name, to indicate that the individual's personal tithe was not included.

With a few notable exceptions (see footnotes below) the Tithables Lists for Amelia County have never been published, and they remain unavailable to genealogists and other researchers, except via microfilm. Microfilms of these important records are available at the Library of Virginia, and from the main LDS Library in Salt Lake City, but are not available on-line, or in local or public libraries.

Below is a summary of the Amelia County Tithables Lists that are available for 1736-1853, and which of them have been indexed, published, or both.

MICROFILM	YEARS	INDEX?/COMMENTS
FHL US/CAN #1902616[2]	1736[3] through 1764	*Amelia Co., VA Tax Lists, 1736-1764: An Every-Name Index*, TLC Genealogy, 1993.
FHL US/CAN #1902616	1765 through 1771	1768 Tax Lists (Names only)[4] No other printed index or transcriptions, to my knowledge.
	1772 through 1777	NO RECORDS AVAILABLE; EITHER WERE LOST, OR NOT TAKEN.
FHL US/CAN #1902617[5]	1778 through 1782	No printed index or transcriptions.

[1] See this URL for more details: http://www.lva.virginia.gov/public/guides/rn17_tithables.htm .

[2] The author has a copy of this microfilm, obtained under the auspices of the Amelia County Historical Society.

[3] The 1736 Tithables List of Amelia County "below Deep Creek" was transcribed by Steve Light of Haslett, MI, and is available on the Amelia Co. web page, http://cousin-collector.com/index.php/amelia-county-virginia/122-tax-records/507-a-list-of-all-the-titheables-below-deep-creek-in-1736.html

[4] The names of Amelia Co. VA taxpayers for 1768 were abstracted by Stephen O. Southall, and published in Tyler's Quarterly Historical and Genealogical Magazine, vol. 53, pp. 54-69, 1952. Apparently Mr. Southall had the actual Poll Lists in his possession, and contributed them to the Quarterly, which published them. These lists do not include the details about the personal property owned by each taxpayer. The author has a photocopy of this article.

[5] Obtained from the LDS Library in Salt Lake City, reviewed and abstracted the 1778 Tax Lists in December 2011. This microfilm is now on permanent loan at the Bellevue, WA Family History Center.

FHL US/CAN #2024454[6]	1782 through 1813	1787 PPTL published by Netti Schreiber-Yantis, 1993.[7] 1790 and 1800 also available.[8]

Through the auspices of the Amelia County Historical Society, in 2008 I obtained the two microfilms above that covered the period 1736-1771 and 1782-1813 respectively. In addition, I obtained the other microfilm via my local Family History Center.
To date, I have transcribed the entire lists for 1765, 1766, 1769, 1770, 1771 (which is partial and incomplete), and 1778.
(Note that no tithe lists exist for the years 1772-1777.)

I decided to start with the 1765 Tithe Lists, since the earlier Tithe Lists have already been indexed (see above), and those indexes are available elsewhere. Unfortunately, the publisher of the main index is no longer in business, and finding a copy of that index may be difficult.

In the coming years, I hope to transcribe more of Amelia County tax lists, starting with the 1782 Personal Property Tax Lists (PPTLs). Unfortunately, starting with the 1783 PPTLs, some of the commissioners did not list the white male tithes (other than the person responsible for paying the tax) by name. The good news for those interested in Amelia (rather than Nottoway) County residents is that the commissioner for Raleigh Parish DID list by name all the white male tithes in the years **1782**, **1787** and **1788**. In 1788, the area designated as Nottoway Parish was carved out of Amelia County, becoming Nottoway County. The Amelia Co. PPTLs for **1789-1791** continued to list all white male tithes by name, a procedure that ended in 1792.

USING THESE TRANSCRIPTIONS OF THE AMELIA COUNTY TITHE LISTS

Each year's collection of tithe lists begins with a list of the names and initials of the commissioners who took each taxpayer's list of 'tithes.' **These are important, because they indicate in which part of the county that taxpayer resided.**

Next is an explanation of the column headings for that particular list, and any other comments pertinent to that particular year's lists.

Some provisos are true for ALL of these lists.

- First, there is no guarantee that any given list is complete. Individuals may have not turned in their list of tithables. Or a particular list may be damaged, contain faded ink, or be illegible, causing an individual to not appear in these transcriptions. Finally, there's no guarantee that the lists are complete. The most striking example of this is the 1771 Tithe List, which contains NO records of Raleigh Parish, the more populous parish of Amelia County at the time. Evidently those records have not survived (at least they have not been microfilmed, and are thus unavailable).

[6] The author has a copy of this microfilm, obtained under the auspices of the Amelia County Historical Society.

[7] *Individual 1787 Tax Lists for Virginia: Amelia County*, by Netti Schreiber-Yantis, available from BigTreeBooks.com, 1993.

[8] The 1790 and 1800 PPTLs have been indexed by Binns Genealogy, and may be viewed without charge online at this URL: http://freepages.misc.rootsweb.com/~vataxlists/Amelia/

- Second, a word about spelling: in this era, spelling was *phonetic*, and a surname or given name might be spelled differently *within a given record.* So the name FERGUSON appears as Farguson, Furgerson, etc. The astute user will look for *any and all* spelling variants of the names they are researching.
- Third, the Comment column is my own contrivance, where I recorded any concern or statement that I thought might help clarify a particular entry.

In these lists, the total tithe was the sum of the white male tithes and the tithable slaves (who are listed BY NAME in these records). In some instances, the sum of these two doesn't match the total tithe; in these instances, the taxpayer was presumably exempt, and thus was not included. Women household heads, for instance, were not taxable. In other cases, the taxpayer's tithe was collected elsewhere (at their main residence, in Amelia or another county); or it was paid by their employer, in cases of overseers and other who worked for someone else). In the latter instance, the Comments column will direct the user to the person who paid that person's tithe (e.g., "see ____").

I have made great efforts to capture the names and details on these records accurately. That said, I am bound to have made mistakes in this lengthy effort. I welcome any and all corrections, and other comments, in order to improve future editions of this information.

Reiley Kidd
5152 54th Avenue South
Seattle, WA 98118-2114
radcrk@comcast.net
October 14, 2015

Now, to the 1765 Amelia County Tithe Lists!

The 1765 AMELIA COUNTY TITHE LISTS

EXPLANATION OF COLUMN HEADINGS
NAME: the name of the person paying the Tithe
LIST: The initials of the person who compiled the tithe list on which the individual appears (an indication of the geographic area and the parish where these individuals lived.
OTHER WHITE MALE TITHES: The names of other men above the age of 16, whose tithe was paid by the taxpayer. When of the same surname, these were usually sons of the taxpayer. Otherwise, they were guests, overseers or other employees.
THE TAX "COMMISSIONERS" FOR 1765, AND THEIR AREA/PARISH

CW = Capt. Winn, Nottoway Parish
JB = John Booker, Raleigh Parish
RM = Robert Munford, Nottoway Parish
TT = Thomas Tabb, Raleigh Parish
WC = William Crawley, Raleigh Parish

COMMENTS

Land = individual taxed only for land, not for self; exempt for some reason.
List = individual named not taxed for self; exempt, or taxed personally elsewhere.
List? = number of individuals named is one more than number taxed; List implied but not stated.

TAXPAYER	LIST	OTHER FREE MALES	Slaves	Acres	COMMENTS
Adams, David	WC	-	-	-	see Adams, William
Adams, William	WC	Adams, David	4	335	
Allen, Daniel	WC	0	3	332	
Allen, Elizabeth	TT	Allen, David	0	100	"tithe"
Allgood, Edward	RM	0	0	0	
Anderson, Francis	TT	0	12	700	
Anderson, Francis Jr.	TT	0	5	650	
Anderson, Henry	JB	Anderson, West	30	2637	1 riding chair
Anderson, John	CW	0	0	0	
Anderson, John	TT	0	9	400	"Doct."?
Anderson, Mead	TT	-	-	-	see Anderson, Richard
Anderson, Pauling	TT	Townsend, John Caviner, Hugh	10	2221	
Anderson, Richard	TT	Anderson, Mead Foster, Robert	4	0	
Anderson, West	JB	-	-	-	see Anderson, Henry
Anderson, William	JB	Ellington, David	6	0	
Apling, John	RM	Apling, Thomas Mitchell, Wm.	5	643	
Apling, Thomas	RM	-	-	-	see Apling, John
Archer, John	JB	Johnson, Jeremiah	8	1200	1 riding chair
Archer, John	TT	-	-	-	see Archer, William
Archer, William	TT	Archer, John Mitchel, Evans	15	1315	

TAXPAYER	LIST	OTHER FREE MALES	Slaves	Acres	COMMENTS
Atkinson, John	TT	0	0	0	
Avery, Charles	WC	0	0	200	
Avery, George	JB	Avery, William	2	252	
Avery, John	WC	Smith, Nicholas	0	180	
Avery, William	JB	-	-	-	see Avery, George
Bagby, John	TT	0	2		
Bagby, Robert Jr.	TT	0	0	200	
Bagby, Robert Sr.	TT	0	0	200	
Bagley, James	RM	0	4	100	
Baker, Theo.	TT	-	-	-	see Crenshaw, Elkanah
Baldwin, John	JB	0	0	313	List of Land
Bales, Abner	CW	0	1	303	
Ball, Thos.	CW	-	2	260	
Ball, Thos. Jr.	CW	Tramell, Jno.	4	600	
Ballard, Thomas	TT	-	-	-	see Barnett, James
Balm, Thomas ?	JB	-	-	-	see Booker, Capt. Edmund
Barding, James	TT	-	-	-	see Williamson, Frances
Barnett, James	TT	Ballard, Thomas	3	200	List
Bass, Alexander	TT	-	-	-	see Bass, Christopher
Bass, Christopher	TT	Bass, Alexander	5	400	List
Bass, Edward	TT	0	9	697	1 riding chair
Bass, John	RM	0	3	330	
Bass, William Jr.	TT	-	-	-	see Bass, William Sr.
Bass, William Sr.	TT	Bass, William Jr.	8	400	List
Batte, Wm. Estate	CW	0	0	452	
Bayley, Micajer's land	RM	0	0	389	evidently only his land
Beadles, Augustiner	TT	-	-	-	see Munford, Thomas
Beasley, John P.	TT	-	-	-	see Tabb, Thomas
Beasley, Peter	WC	Harper, George	10	600	
Beasly, Ambose	RM	Beasly, Richd.	2	200	
Beasly, Richd.	RM	-	-	-	see Beasly, Ambose
Beckley, Humphrey	TT	-	-	-	see Tabb, Thomas
Beeves, James	WC	-	-	-	see Cuzens, Rossmond
Belcher, Edward	TT	0	0	0	
Belcher, John	TT	Belcher, John Jr.	0	50	
Belcher, John Jr.	TT	-	-	-	see Belcher, John
Bell, George	JB	-	-	-	see Booker, George O.
Bennit, Benjamin	WC	0	1	288	
Bentley, John	TT	Ware, William	1	0	List
Bentley, Samuel	RM	0	0	200	
Bently, John	JB	0	5	452	
Bently, Samuel	TT	0	8	700	
Berry, Peter	TT	-	-	-	see Ginkins, James
Berry, Thomas	WC	0	1	250	

TAXPAYER	LIST	OTHER FREE MALES	Slaves	Acres	COMMENTS
Beuford, Henry	CW	Beuford, Wm.	5	300	
Beuford, Henry	CW	-	-	-	see Jerby, Susanah
Beuford, James	CW	Beuford, Warren	5	363	
Beuford, Thomas	CW	0	2	100	
Beuford, Warren	CW	-	-	-	see Beuford, James
Beuford, Wm.	CW	-	-	-	see Beuford, Henry
Bevil, Archer	WC	-	-	-	see Bevil, James
Bevil, Carter	WC	-	-	-	see Vaden, Henry
Bevil, Daniel	JB	Bevil, Thomas	2	0	
Bevil, James	WC	Bevil, Robert Bevil, Archer	2	400	
Bevil, Joseph	WC	0	2	200	
Bevil, Robert	WC	-	-	-	see Bevil, James
Bevil, Thomas	JB	-	-	-	see Bevil, Daniel
Bevil, William	WC	0	1	200	
Bevill, Hezekiah	JB	-	-	-	see Bottom, Thomas Jr.
Bevill, Joell	JB	0	3	251	
Bevill, Robert	JB	0	0	0	"son of Daniel"
Bibb, William	JB	0	9	335	1 riding chair
Blanchet, Henry	TT	0	0	45	
Blanchet, Isaack	TT	0	0	30	
Bland, Col. Theodorick	RM	North, William North, Thos.	28	3612	List
Blankenship, John	JB	-	-	-	see Royall, Joseph
Blanton, Thomas	RM	0	0	0	
Boat____, Rachel	TT	R___, Parham Gree___, Robert	11	0	List; smudged
Bolling, Col. Alexander	CW	Jeffres, Thos. Ellis, Ellison Grinn, James	14	1672	List
Bolling, Col. Robert	WC	Cassells, William Neal, William	40	9224	
Bonny, Thomas	RM		1	2191	no tithes (why?)
Booker, Ann	JB	0	13	1025	List
Booker, Capt. Edmund	JB	Booker, Edmund Balm, Thomas ?	11	1074	1 riding chair
Booker, Edmund	JB	-	-	-	see Booker, Capt. Edmund
Booker, Edward	JB	0	3	200	
Booker, Edward	JB	Dunnivant, Hezekiah	6	0	
Booker, George	JB	0	0	0	
Booker, George	TT	0	8	973	1 riding chair
Booker, George Olney	JB	Bell, George	7	335	List
Booker, John	JB	0	4	150	
Booker, John	JB	0	15	1400	1 riding chair

TAXPAYER	LIST	OTHER FREE MALES	Slaves	Acres	COMMENTS
Booker, Mary	JB	Booker, William	7	218	List
Booker, Richard	TT	-	-	-	see Tabb, Thomas
Booker, William	JB	-	-	-	see Booker, Mary
Booth, George	WC	Booth, William Harris, William	4	500	
Booth, John	WC	Booth, Thomas	6	525	
Booth, Nathaniel	WC	0	2	336	
Booth, Thomas	WC	-	-	-	see Booth, John
Booth, Thomas Jr.	WC	Brinller, Jacob	1	382	
Booth, William	WC	0	2	352	
Booth, William	WC	-	-	-	see Booth, George
Borrum, Edward	JB	0	0	0	
Borrum, James	JB	-	-	-	Borrum, Richard
Borrum, Richard	JB	Borrum, James	1	475	
Borrum, Richard Jr.	JB	0	0	0	
Bott, Miles	JB	0	5	752	
Bott, William	JB	0	2	646	
Bottom, Thomas	JB	0	2	574	
Bottom, Thomas	RM	Pugh, Jno.	1	0	List
Bottom, Thomas Jr.	JB	Bevill, Hezekiah	5	400	
Boyd, George	CW	Burge, Wm.	3	0	
Boyd, Waller	CW	Buller, Wm.	6	450	List
Brackett, Thomas	TT	Brackett, Thomas Jr.?	5	918	
Brackett, Thomas Jr.?	TT	-	-	-	see Brackett, Thomas
Bradley, James	RM	-	-	-	see Short, Thomas
Bradley, James R.	JB	Cooper, Francis	11	953	List
Bradshaw, William	RM	0	0	0	
Bradshaw, William	TT	0	0	0	
Branch, Benjamin	JB	Roberts, Step(hen?)	5	200	List
Bregidine, Isaac	CW	Bregidine, Wm.	2	502	
Bregidine, Wm.	CW	-	-	-	see Bregidine, Isaac
Bridgforth, Benjamin	RM	Sneed, Jno.	5	800	
Brinller, Jacob	WC	-	-	-	see Booth, Thomas Jr.
Brintle, Wm.	RM	-	-	-	see Eppes, Francis
Brisbain, Edward	WC	-	-	-	see Greenhill, David
Broadnax, Stephen Edw.	WC	-	-	-	see Brookings, Vivion
Brookes, Thomas	JB	Brookes, William	2	550	
Brookes, Thomas Jr.	JB	0	0	0	
Brookes, William	JB	-	-	-	see Brookes, Thomas
Brookings, Vivion	WC	Broadnax, Stephen Edw. Kid, George	18	2217	1 riding chair
Brooks, John	JB	0	0	0	
Brown, Alexander	TT	0	3	200	

TAXPAYER	LIST	OTHER FREE MALES	Slaves	Acres	COMMENTS
Brown, John	TT	Sullivant, John	1	100	
Brown, Joseph	TT	-	-	-	see Gooch, John
Bruce, Alexander Jr.	RM	0	7	0	
Bruce, Alexander Sr.	RM	0	1	0	
Brumfield, Major	TT	0	0	200	
Brunshill, Rev. John	JB	0	3	400	
Buford, Warren	CW	0	1	0	List
Buller, Wm.	CW	-	-	-	see Boyd, Waller
Bullington, John	JB	Bullington, Robert Carter, Francis ??	0	100	name smudged
Bullington, Robert	JB	-	-	-	see Bullington, John
Burge, Thos.	CW	0	1	200	
Burge, Wm.	CW	0	0	300	
Burge, Wm.	CW	-	-	-	see Boyd, George
Burges, Joel	TT	-	-	-	see Marshal, William Jr.
Burton, Abraham	TT	0	2	400	
Burton, Charles	TT	-	-	-	see Cox, George (Henrico)
Burton, John	TT	Compton, Zachariah Hudson, John	11	482	1 riding chair
Burton, Peter	WC	Tucker, Hudson Cape, John	2	175	
Busley, John	CW	0	0	230	List?
Butler, William	TT	0	0	267	
Cabiness, George	RM	0	2	347	
Cabiness, Mat.	RM	-	-	-	see Watson, William
Callicott, James	JB	0	1	0	
Callicott, William	JB	0	2	1220	
Cape, John	WC				
Cardwell, Daniel	TT	-	-	-	see Tinsley, Isaack
Carter, Francis ??	JB	-	-	-	see Bullington, John
Caruthers, Dr. Joseph	RM	Thompson, Benjamin Sobisky, Charles	10	666	List; one (riding?) chair
Casey, Micaja	JB	-	-	-	see Hall, William
Cassells, William	WC	-	-	-	see Bolling, Col. Robert
Caudle, John	JB	0	0	200	
Cause, Richd.	CW	Nash, Thos.	0	240	
Caviner, Hugh	TT	-	-	-	see Anderson, Pauling
Chambers, Hugh	CW	0	3	195	
Chambers, Ruth	WC	Dodson, Edward Dodson, John	2	100	list
Chapman, John	TT	-	-	-	see Chapman, Samuel
Chapman, Samuel	TT	Chapman, John	3	400	
Chappell, John	CW	Hinton, Wood	6	443	
Chappell, John	WC	Chappell, Robert	4	450	

TAXPAYER	LIST	OTHER FREE MALES	Slaves	Acres	COMMENTS
Chappell, Robert	WC	-	-	-	see Chappell, John
Chapple, James	JB	0	7	710	
Cheatam, James	TT	Scott, George	3	550	
Cheatam, Leonard	TT	0	7	300	
Chisholm, John	CW	-	-	-	see Hoopper, Zachariah
Christian, Anthony	TT	Greenwood, Ladowick	8	560	
Chumley, John	JB	0	0	100	
Clandin?, Joshua	CW	-	-	-	see Pa__, Thos.
Clardy, Benjamin	WC	0	2	266	
Clardy, John	WC	0	0	60	
Clardy, John	WC	-	-	-	see Wilson, William
Clardy, John Sr.	WC	Clardy, Richard	0	100	
Clardy, Michael	WC	0	1	100	
Clardy, Richard	WC	-	-	-	see Clardy, John Sr.
Clark, George	RM	0	0	110	
Clark, Hed.?	RM	-	-	-	see Clark, Henry
Clark, Henry	RM	Clark, Hed.?	2	283	
Clark, John	RM	0	4	612	
Clark, Peter	RM	0	0	100	
Clark, Thomas	WC	0	1	0	
Clay, Caleb	WC	-	-	-	see Clay, Thomas
Clay, Charles	RM	0	1	132	
Clay, Charles	WC	Clay, Robert	1	150	
Clay, Jesse	WC	-	-	-	see Tucker, Robert
Clay, John	WC	Clay, John Oliver, Benjamin	6	400	
Clay, John	WC	-	-	-	see Clay, John
Clay, Robert	WC	-	-	-	see Clay, Charles
Clay, Thomas	WC	Clay, Caleb	0	150	
Clay, William	WC	-	-	-	see Crawley, William
Clayborn, Phillip W.	RM	Lipscomb, Ambrose	7	1272	List
Claybrook, Peter	TT	0	2	222	
Clayton, William	JB	-	-	-	see Thompson, Drury
Clement, Isham	TT	0	0	0	
Clements, John	TT	Tabb, Edward	8	300	1 riding chair
Clements, Obadiah	TT	-	-	-	see Clements, Simon
Clements, Simon	TT	Clements, Obadiah Clements, Zephaniah	2	234	
Clements, William	TT	Foster James Loving, James	4	725	
Clements, Zephaniah	TT	-	-	-	see Clements, Simon
Clemmons, William	WC	0	1	512	
Cloudas, George	TT	Gresham, Thomas	1	0	
Clough, Richard	JB	Jeter, William	8	654	
Cobbs, John Catling	JB	Haile, John	5	500	

TAXPAYER	LIST	OTHER FREE MALES	Slaves	Acres	COMMENTS
Cocke, Abraham	CW	Gunn, Thomas	4	0	
Cocke, Abraham's est.	CW	0	0	2648?	Estate (deceased?)
Cocke, James	TT	-	-	-	see Royall, John
Cocke, Mrs. Mary	CW	0	6	0	List?
Cocke, Stepnen	CW	0	0	0	
Cocks, John	CW	Hudgins, Thos.	10	903	List
Coleman, Abraham	WC	-	-	-	see Coleman, William
Coleman, Daniel Jr.	WC	0	1	297	
Coleman, Daniel Sr.	WC	Coleman, Jesse	3	472	
Coleman, Francis	WC	-	-	-	see Coleman, Joseph Sr.
Coleman, Hezekiah	WC	Tucker, Joseph	0	200	
Coleman, Jesse	WC	-	-	-	see Coleman, Daniel Sr.
Coleman, John	WC	-	-	-	see Coleman, Joseph Sr.
Coleman, John	WC	0	0	100	
Coleman, Joseph Jr.	WC	0	0	75	
Coleman, Joseph Sr.	WC	Coleman, John Coleman, Sutton Coleman, Francis	0	96	
Coleman, Peter	WC	Coleman, Peter	0	205	
Coleman, Peter	WC	-	-	-	see Coleman, Peter
Coleman, Sutton	WC	-	-	-	see Coleman, Joseph Sr.
Coleman, William	WC	Coleman, Abraham Huddleston, Robert	1	999	
Coley, David	WC	-	-	-	see Cuzens, George
Coley, David	WC	0	0	400	list
Combs, Frances	JB	0	1	150	
Combs, George	JB	0	2	300	
Compton, Zachariah	TT	-	-	-	see Burton, John
Conoly, Charles	RM	0	2	200	
Cook, James	TT	-	-	-	see Cook, Shem Sr.
Cook, John	TT	Cook, Joseph	3	1354	
Cook, Joseph	TT	-	-	-	see Cook, John
Cook, Shem Sr.	TT	Cook, James	3	200	
Cooper, Francis	JB	-	-	-	see Bradley, James R.
Cooper, Francis	JB	0	1	0	tithe
Cordle, John	WC	0	0	0	
Cordle, William	WC	0	0	0	
Cotten, James	JB	0	0	100	
Cove, Henry Jr.	TT	0	0	100	
Covington, William	RM	Hinton, Allen Covington, William	3	290	
Covington, William	RM	-	-	-	see Covington, William
Cowles, Thomas	WC	Weeks, Richard	6	984	
Cox, George (Henrico)	TT	Burton, Charles	10	964	List
Craddock, Richd.	CW	0	3	385	

TAXPAYER	LIST	OTHER FREE MALES	Slaves	Acres	COMMENTS
Cradock, Wm.	CW	0	3	654	
Crane, John	RM	0	0	50	
Crawley, William	WC	Morgan, John Clay, William Liggon, John	31	3981	1 riding chair
Creel, Absolom	WC	0	0	0	
Crenshaw, Bartlett	CW	-	-	-	see Crenshaw, James
Crenshaw, Benjamin	TT	-	-	-	see Murray, James
Crenshaw, Cornelius	CW	-	-	-	see Crenshaw, James
Crenshaw, Elkanah	TT	Baker, Theo.	3	400	
Crenshaw, James	CW	Crenshaw, Cornelius Crenshaw, Bartlett	3	400	
Crenshaw, Robert	CW	0	2	200	
Crenshaw, William	RM	0	2	478	
Crenshaw, Wm.	CW	0	7	800	
Crenshaw, Wm. Jr.	CW	0	0	200	
Crindle?, Parrot	TT	0	0	0	
Crittendon, Henry	JB	Crittendon, William	1	74	
Crittendon, William	JB	-	-	-	see Crittendon, Henry
Cross, Jno.	CW	-	-	-	see Cross, Wm.
Cross, Richd.	CW	-	-	-	see Cross, Wm.
Cross, Wm.	CW	Cross, Jno. Cross, Richd.	9	226	
Crowder, Abraham	WC	0	0	488	
Crowder, John	WC	0	0	300	
Crowder, Joseph	WC	0	2	200	
Crowder, Nathaniel	WC	-	-	-	see Kennon, Robert
Cryer, William	RM	Frank, Jno.	4	700	
Cumpton, Ambrose	TT	-	-	-	see Ford, Christopher
Cumpton, Caleb	TT	-	-	-	see Cumpton, John Jr.
Cumpton, John	JB	-	-	-	see Eustice, Moses
Cumpton, John Jr.	TT	Cumpton, Caleb Cumpton, Meridith	3	600	
Cumpton, John Sr.	TT	0	1	100	
Cumpton, Meridith	TT	-	-	-	see Cumpton, John Jr.
Cumpton, Richard	TT	-	-	-	see Scott, John
Cuzens, George	WC	Coley, David	4	800	list
Cuzens, John	WC	0	3	0	
Cuzens, Peter	WC	-	-	-	see Cuzens, Robert Sr.
Cuzens, Robert	WC	-	-	-	see Cuzens, Robert Sr.
Cuzens, Robert Sr.	WC	Cuzens, Robert Cuzens, Peter R____, Thomas	6	1043	
Cuzens, Rossmond	WC	Beeves, James Cuzens, William	3	600	list

TAXPAYER	LIST	OTHER FREE MALES	Slaves	Acres	COMMENTS
Cuzens, Thomas	WC	0	0	0	
Cuzens, William	WC	0	5	843	
Cuzens, William	WC	-	-	-	see Cuzens, Rossmond
Dalby, John	RM	-	-	-	see Dalby, Nightingale
Dalby, Nightingale	RM	Dalby, John	0	673	List
Daley, Josiah	JB	0	0	0	
Davis, Gresset	TT	-	-	-	see Tabb, Thomas
Davis, Jacob	CW	Davis, Wm. Hawkins, John	3	240	
Davis, James	CW	0	0	0	
Davis, Joseph	CW	-	-	-	see Lankaster?, John
Davis, Robert	CW	0	0	200	
Davis, Samuel	TT	-	-	-	see Munford, Thomas
Davis, Thomas	TT	Jones, David	0	98	
Davis, Wm.	CW	-	-	-	see Davis, Jacob
Deaton, Jabez	JB	-	-	-	see Deaton, John
Deaton, James	JB	-	-	-	see Gibbs, William
Deaton, John	JB	Deaton, Jabez Deaton, Levy	2	170	
Deaton, Levy	JB	-	-	-	see Deaton, John
Deaton, William	JB	0	0	0	
Dennis, Henry	RM	0	4	540	
Dennis, Richard Jr.	RM	0	3	0	
Dennis, Richard Sr.	WC	0	9	750	
Dixon, Reubin	RM	0	0	0	
Dixon, Wm.	RM	-	-	-	see Watson, William
Dodson, Edward	WC	-	-	-	see Chambers, Ruth
Dodson, John	WC	-	-	-	see Chambers, Ruth
Doggett, Challin Jr.	CW	-	-	-	see Hoopper, Zachariah
Draper, James	RM	0	0	149	
Drinkard, John	JB	0	2	200	
Drinkwater, John	JB	Drinkwater, Josiah	0	200	
Drinkwater, Josiah	JB	-	-	-	see Drinkwater, John
Dublin, Harry	RM	-	-	-	see Pryor, John
Dudley, Ambrose	WC	0	0	178	
Dudley, Edward	WC	Dudley, James	7	458	
Dudley, James	WC	-	-	-	see Dudley, Edward
Dudley, Marlow	TT	0	0	900	"Estate of"
Dudley, Robert	WC	0	0	0	
Dunnavant, Hodge	TT	Dunnavant, Thomas	2	250	
Dunnavant, Norrvil	TT	-	-	-	see Dunnavant, Phillip
Dunnavant, Phillip	TT	Dunnavant, Shadrack Dunnavant, Norrvil	0	250	
Dunnavant, Shadrack	TT	-	-	-	see Dunnavant, Phillip
Dunnavant, Thomas	TT	-	-	-	see Dunnavant, Hodge

TAXPAYER	LIST	OTHER FREE MALES	Slaves	Acres	COMMENTS
Dunnavant, William	TT	0	3	200	
Dunnavant, William	TT	-	-	-	see Moulson, William
Dunnivant, Hezekiah	JB	-	-	-	see Booker, Edward
Dupee, Bartholomew	RM	0	3	600	
Dupee, John	RM	0	3	197	
Dupee, John James	RM	0	0	400	no tithe – List?
Dyson, Benjamin	WC	Perkinson, Seth	5	156	list
Dyson, Benjamin	WC	-	-	-	see Gilliam, John
Eastice, Moses Sr.	TT	Land, Epharaim	0	222	
Eastice, William	TT	0	0	0	
Easton, William	TT	0	0	0	
Eccles, Robert	RM	0	0	330	
Eckels, James	RM	0	0	322	no tithe (List?)
Eckles, Edward	RM	0	0	320	
Eckles, Thos.	RM	0	0	320	
Edmonson, Benjamin	RM	-	-	-	see Edmonson, Upton
Edmonson, Upton	RM	Edmonson, Benjamin St. John, Wm Vaughn, Zacharias	6	784	
Eggles(ton?), Joseph	TT	0	16	1200	1 riding chair; smudged
Eggleston, John	TT	-	-	-	see Eggleston, Richard
Eggleston, Richard	TT	Eggleston, John	8	800	List; ink blot obscures
Elington, David	RM	Elington, Josiah	4	1883	
Elington, Jeremiah	RM	0	3	0	
Ellington, David	JB	-	-	-	see Anderson, William
Ellington, John	JB	Ellington, William	7	1138	
Ellington, John	WC	-	-	-	see Ellington, William
Ellington, John Jr.	JB	-	-	-	see Marshall, Robert
Ellington, William	JB	-	-	-	see Ellington, John
Ellington, William	WC	Ellington, John	0	0	
Elliot, John	CW	0	3	285	
Ellis, Ambrose	CW	-	-	-	see Ellis, Thos.
Ellis, Capt. Richd.	CW	0	18	1951	
Ellis, Ellison	CW	-	-	-	see Bolling, Col. Alexander
Ellis, Ha___	CW	-	-	-	see Ellis, Thos.
Ellis, Richd.	CW	-	-	-	see Ellis, Thos.
Ellis, Thomas	TT	0	1	108	
Ellis, Thos.	CW	Ellis, Richd. Ellis, Ambrose Ellis, Ha___	2	273	
Elmore, Abija	RM	0	0	166	
Elmore, Archelus	CW	0	0	167	
Elmore, Cecelia	CW	0	2	166	List
Eppes, Francis	RM	Shelly, Jno.	14	1697	1 pr. chair wheels

TAXPAYER	LIST	OTHER FREE MALES	Slaves	Acres	COMMENTS
		Brintle, Wm.			
Eppes, Tabitha	WC	Moor, Eleazer	4	750	list
Erskine, Alexr.	CW	Shelton, Jno.	7	940	
Eustice, Moses	JB	Cumpton, John	0	0	
Evans, Evan	WC	0	0	200	list of land in Amelia & Lunenberg
Evans, Richard	WC	0	0	239	list
Evans, Robert	CW	Shelton?, Josiah	2	161	List
Evans, Wm.	CW	Finnie, Elijah	5	200	
Fannin, Achals	RM	0	0	140	
Fannin, Briant	RM	0	0	140	
Fannin, Elizabeth	RM	0	0	154	no tithables
Fannin, Jehu	RM	0	0	0	
Fannin, Laughlin	RM	0	0	0	
Farley, George	JB	0	4	268	
Farley, Jeremiah	WC	-	-	-	see Farley, Peter
Farley, John	JB	0	0	240	
Farley, John James	TT	-	-	-	see Farrar, Peter
Farley, Joseph	WC	Joiner, Daniel	6	689	
Farley, Matthew	WC	-	-	-	see Thompson, William
Farley, Peter	TT	-	-	-	see Farley, William Jr.
Farley, Peter	WC	Farley, Peter Farley, Jeremiah	1	250	
Farley, Peter	WC	-	-	-	see Farley, Peter
Farley, Stephen	JB	0	0	0	
Farley, Stewart	JB	0	0	250	
Farley, William Jr.	TT	Farley, Peter	0	100	
Farley, William Sr.	JB	0	4	240	
Farrar, Peter	TT	Farley, John James	14	2980	
Featherston, Lewis	CW	-	-	-	see Featherston, Wm.
Featherston, Wm.	CW	Featherston, Wm. Greg Featherston, Lewis	4	400	
Featherston, Wm. Greg	CW	-	-	-	see Featherston, Wm.
Ferguson, Daniel	TT	0	0	0	
Ferguson, Edward	RM	0	0	0	
Ferguson, James Jr.	TT	0	0	0	
Ferguson, John	JB	0	8	500	
Ferguson, Richard	JB	Jackson, Thomas	0	0	
Ferguson, Robert Jr.	TT	0	0	0	
Ferguson, Robert Sr.	TT	Foster, James	5	300	
Ferguson, Robert's land	RM	0	0	300	no tithables
Field, Robert	TT	0	1	0	
Finnie, Elijah	CW	-	-	-	see Evans, Wm.

TAXPAYER	LIST	OTHER FREE MALES	Slaves	Acres	COMMENTS
Fitzgerrald, Wm.	CW	Thomas, Henry Willis, Wm.	15	1998	
Foord, Albery	CW	0	0	100	
Foord, Frederick	CW	Foord, John	1	300	
Foord, John	CW	-	-	-	see Foord, Frederick
Ford, Abraham	RM	0	0	200	
Ford, Christopher	TT	Cumpton, Ambrose Geers, Thomas	7	461	
Ford, Culverine	TT	0	3	200	
Ford, George	RM	Ford, Richd.	0	200	
Ford, Hezekiah est. of	JB	0	0	300	
Ford, John	JB	0	4	402	
Ford, John Jr.	TT	Ford, William	0	832	
Ford, Mary	TT	Geers, Robt.	2	0	List
Ford, Natha.	CW	0	3	480	
Ford, Reubin	JB	0	0	300	
Ford, Richd.	RM	-	-	-	see Ford, George
Ford, William	TT	-	-	-	see Ford, John Jr.
Ford, William's land	RM	0	0	142	no tithables
Forrest, Abraham	RM	Forrest, John Forrest, Abraham Jr.	2	200	
Forrest, Abraham Jr.	RM	-	-	-	see Forrest, Abraham
Forrest, John	CW	-	-	-	see Hurt, Moses
Forrest, John	RM	-	-	-	see Forrest, Abraham
Forrest, Richard	RM	0	3	480	
Foster James	TT	-	-	-	see Clements, William
Foster, Anthony	TT	-	-	-	see Foster, George
Foster, George	TT	Foster, George Pollard Foster, Anthony	0	147	title "S.C."
Foster, George Pollard	TT	-	-	-	see Foster, George
Foster, James	JB	-	-	-	see Foster, William
Foster, James	TT	-	-	-	see Jones, Robert
Foster, James	TT	-	-	-	see Ferguson, Robert Sr.
Foster, John	CW	0	0	50	
Foster, John	JB	-	-	-	see Foster, William
Foster, John	TT	-	-	-	see Foster, Thomas
Foster, John	TT	-	-	-	see Foster, William
Foster, Moses	TT	-	-	-	see Foster, Thomas
Foster, Richard	WC	-	-	-	see Jones, Wood
Foster, Robert	TT	-	-	-	see Anderson, Richard
Foster, Thomas	TT	Foster, John Foster, Moses	4	600	title "S.C."
Foster, William	JB	Foster, James Foster, John	5	797	
Foster, William	TT	0	0	50	"son of George"!

TAXPAYER	LIST	OTHER FREE MALES	Slaves	Acres	COMMENTS
Foster, William	TT	Foster, John	0	100	"S.C."
Frank, Jno.	RM	-	-	-	see Cryer, William
Frankling, Ben	JB	-	-	-	see Watkins, James
Freeman, James	TT	0	0	0	
Freeman, M____	JB	-	-	-	see Thompson, William
Fulks, Gabriel	RM	0	8	775	
Gailes, James	JB	-	-	-	see Harding, Erasmus
Gatlings, Philip	RM	0	0	0	
Geers, Robt.	TT	-	-	-	see Ford, Mary
Geers, Thomas	TT	-	-	-	see Ford, Christopher
Gibbs, Mary	JB	Gibbs, William	4	200	List
Gibbs, Matthew	JB	Webster, William	1	0	List
Gibbs, William	JB	-	-	-	see Gibbs, Mary
Gibbs, William	JB	Deaton, James	3	116	list
Giles, William	TT	0	9	976	1 riding chair
Gilliam, John	WC	Dyson, Benjamin	14	1037	list
Gilliam, John Sr.	RM	0	4	0	List?
Ginkins, James	TT	Berry, Peter	4	420	
Glasby, William	TT	0	0	0	
Gooch, John	TT	Gooch, Rowland Gooch, William Mason, Charles Brown, Joseph	0	0	
Gooch, Joseph	JB	0	1	223	
Gooch, Rowland	TT	-	-	-	see Gooch, John
Gooch, William	TT	-	-	-	see Gooch, John
Grant, Gregory	TT	-	-	-	see Murray, James
Grant, William	WC	-	-	-	see Hardaway, Seth
Gray, Henry	TT	-	-	-	see Hudson, Christopher
Gray, John	WC	Spain, William	4	100	
Gree___, Robert	TT	-	-	-	see Boat____, Rachel
Green, Abraham	WC	Green, Abraham Wills, William	18	1750	
Green, Abraham	WC	-	-	-	see Green, Abraham
Green, Henry	RM	0	4	300	
Green, John	TT	-	-	-	see Green, Thomas
Green, John	WC	-	-	-	see Green, Thomas
Green, Martin	WC	0	0	390	list
Green, Thomas	TT	Green, John Green, Thomas Jr.	0	150	title "S.C."
Green, Thomas	WC	Green, John	1	268	
Green, Thomas Jr.	TT	-	-	-	see Green, Thomas
Greenhill, David	RM	0	2	0	List?
Greenhill, David	WC	Greenhihll, Paschall	23	0	1 pr chair wheels

TAXPAYER	LIST	OTHER FREE MALES	Slaves	Acres	COMMENTS
		Jonray, John Mackey, John Brisbain, Edward Wilkinson, Thomas			List
Greenhill, Paschall	WC	-	-	-	see Greenhill, David
Greenwood, Ladowick	TT	-	-	-	see Christian, Anthony
Greenwood, William	TT	-	-	-	see Tabb, Thomas
Gresham, John	RM	0	0	0	
Gresham, Thomas	TT	-	-	-	see Cloudas, George
Griffin, Richd.	CW	0	0	0	
Grigg, James	RM	0	2	50	
Grigg, Josiah	RM	0	1	136	
Grigg, Peter	CW	0	1	0	
Grigg, Peter	RM	0	1	0	
Griggory, Joseph	WC	-	-	-	see Wills, Elias
Grinn, James	CW	-	-	-	see Bolling, Col. Alexander
Gunn, Thomas	CW	-	-	-	see Cocke, Abraham
Gunn, Thos.	CW	Gunn, Thos. Walker, Thos.	2	150	
Gunn, Thos.	CW	-	-	-	see Gunn, Thos.
Haile, John	JB	-	-	-	see Cobbs, John Catling
Hall, Ambrose	WC	0	0	0	
Hall, Henry Jr.	WC	0	0	0	
Hall, Henry Sr.	WC	Hall, Leonard	0	0	
Hall, John	RM	0	1	200	
Hall, John Jr.	RM	Quisenberry, Nicholas Hall, William	9	646	1 pair chair wheels
Hall, Leonard	WC	-	-	-	see Hall, Henry Sr.
Hall, Robert	WC	Nervart, John	0	700	1 riding chair
Hall, Thomas	JB	-	-	-	see Hall, William
Hall, William	JB	Casey, Micaja Hall, Thomas	8	460	
Hall, William	RM	-	-	-	see Hall, John Jr.
Hall, William	WC	0	0	190	
Hamlet, Obediah	RM	-	-	-	see Muse, George
Hamlin, Charles	WC	Hamlin, John	12	366	
Hamlin, Henry	TT	-	-	-	see Powell, Obedience
Hamlin, John	WC	-	-	-	see Hamlin, Charles
Hamlin, Stephen	WC	Roach, William	6	0	list
Hamlin, William	RM	0	1	275	
Hamm, George	TT	0	1	150	
Hamm, Robert	TT	0	0	125	
Hamm, Thomas	TT	-	-	-	see Tabb, Thomas
Hamm, William	TT	0	0	125	

TAXPAYER	LIST	OTHER FREE MALES	Slaves	Acres	COMMENTS
Hammock, John	RM	0	0	100	
Hammond, Joshua	RM	-	-	-	see Hammond, Lewis
Hammond, Lewis	RM	Hammond, Joshua	1	200	
Hancock, Daniel	TT	0	0	0	
Hancock, George	TT	0	9	220	
Hanks, James	RM	0	0	100	
Hanks, James	WC	0	0	0	
Hanks, Richd.	RM	0	0	243	
Hardaway, Col. __	CW	Walker, Henry	4	0	List
Hardaway, Daniel	WC	-	-	-	see Hardaway, Seth
Hardaway, James	CW	Moon, Wm.	3	300	
Hardaway, Joseph	WC	Young, Stephen	3	290	list
Hardaway, Seth	WC	Hardaway, Daniel Grant, William	19	1538	
Harding, Erasmus	JB	Gailes, James	3	150	List
Hardy, Covington	CW	-	-	-	see Hardy, John
Hardy, John	CW	Hardy, Covington	1	200	
Hargue, Joseph	TT	-	-	-	see Wood, William
Harper, George	WC	-	-	-	see Beasley, Peter
Harper, Joseph Jr.	RM	Smith, Mathew	1	200	List
Harris, William	TT	-	-	-	see Vasser, Abraham
Harris, William	WC	-	-	-	see Booth, George
Harrison, W. Nathaniel	JB	Lightfoot, Phillip	12	1800	List
Hart, William	JB	Newbell, William	2	0	
Harthway, Frances	CW	0	1	0	
Haskins, Christopher	RM	Willis, Reubin	5	460	
Hastens, John	WC	Tolty, Thomas	0	300	
Hastens, William	WC	0	0	200	
Hatchett, Archibald	JB	-	-	-	see Hatchett, William
Hatchett, John	JB	Roberts, Thomas	2	50	
Hatchett, William	JB	Hatchett, Archibald	3	150	
Hawkins, David	WC	0	1	200	
Hawkins, John	CW	-	-	-	see Davis, Jacob
Hawkins, Zacharias	RM	-	-	-	see Pincham, Samuel
Hawks, Abraham	WC	Hawks, William	0	284	HANKS?
Hawks, George	WC	-	-	-	see Hawks, Joshua
Hawks, Joshua	WC	Hawks, Richard Hawks, George	4	536	HANKS?
Hawks, Richard	WC	-	-	-	see Hawks, Joshua
Hawks, William	WC	-	-	-	see Hawks, Abraham
Hayan?, Wm.	RM	-	-	-	see Haymes, William
Hayes, Richard	JB	0	5	500	
Haymes, Edmond	RM	0	0	90	
Haymes, John	RM	0	2	257	
Haymes, William	RM	Hayan?, Wm.	0	150	

TAXPAYER	LIST	OTHER FREE MALES	Slaves	Acres	COMMENTS
Haymes, Wm. Jr.	RM	0	0	296	
Haynes, Anthony's est.	RM	Baker, Charles	6	329	estate – deceased?
Henderson, James	JB	Pride, Rowlie	3	0	
Hendrich, John	JB	Hendrich, John Jr.	1	0	
Hendrich, John Jr.	JB	-	-	-	see Hendrich, John
Hendrich, Obediah	JB	0	0	504	
Hendrick, Benjamin Jr.	TT	0	1	200	
Hendrick, Benjamin Sr.	TT	Hendrick, Obadiah	8	500	
Hendrick, Hanser	TT	0	6	0	
Hendrick, James	TT	0	0	200	
Hendrick, John	TT	0	0	200	
Hendrick, Obadiah	TT	-	-	-	see Hendrick, Benjamin Sr.
Hendrick, Natha.	CW	0	0	200	
Henson, Nimrod	CW	0	0	0	
Herman, William	JB	0	0	0	
Hightower, Charnal	RM	-	-	-	see Hightower, Joshua Sr.
Hightower, Eppafee	RM	-	-	-	see Hightower, John
Hightower, George	RM	0	2	250	
Hightower, John	RM	Hightower, Eppafee	6	300	
Hightower, John Jr.	RM	0	5	0	
Hightower, Joseph	RM	Hightower, Lavender	6	0	
Hightower, Joshua	RM	Winter, Henry Bailey, John	3	450	
Hightower, Joshua Sr.	RM	Hightower, Charnal	4	200	
Hightower, Lavender	RM	-	-	-	see Hightower, Joseph
Hightower, Richard	RM	0	3	250	
Hightower, Thos.	RM	0	2	100	
Hightower, William	WC	0	0	489	list of land
Hill, George	RM	0	0	0	
Hill, Joell	TT	-	-	-	see Hill, John Sr.
Hill, John Jr.	TT	0	0	0	
Hill, John Sr.	TT	Hill, Joell	1	375	
Hill, Moses	TT	0	0	0	
Hill, Wm.	CW	-	-	-	see Lewis, Charles
Hillsman, Matthew	TT	0	0	200	
Hillsman, William	TT	0	1	100	
Hinton, Allen	RM	-	-	-	see Covington, William
Hinton, Christopher	WC	-	-	-	see Jones, Lewelling
Hinton, Wood	CW	-	-	-	see Chappell, John
Holland, Joseph	CW	0	0	0	
Holland, Phi__	CW	Shelton, Lewis	1	200	List; Phebe??
Holt, David	RM	-	-	-	see Holt, Richd.
Holt, David	WC	Young, Ridley	6	200	list

TAXPAYER	LIST	OTHER FREE MALES	Slaves	Acres	COMMENTS
Holt, Debnal	RM	Harris, Skip	3	200	List?
Holt, Richd.	RM	Holt, David	0	150	
Holt, Thomas	JB	-	-	-	see Worsham, Thomas
Hood, Abraham	WC	0	0	240	
Hood, John	WC	0	4	372	
Hood, Nathaniel	RM	0	0	100	
Hood, Robert	WC	0	0	x	land erased?
Hood, Thomas	RM	0	0	100	
Hood, Tucker	WC	-	-	-	see Hood, William
Hood, William	WC	Hood, Tucker	o	75	
Hoopper, Zachariah	CW	Doggett, Challin Jr. Chisholm, John Irby, Wm.	2	0	List?
Horolate, William?	JB	0	2	148	name illegible
Hoskins, John	CW	0	1	108	
House, Thos	CW	-	-	-	see Pa__, John
Howell, Stephen	RM	0	0	100	
Hubbard, John	TT	0	0	186	
Hubbard, Joseph	TT	0	1	140	
Huddleston, Robert	WC	-	-	-	see Coleman, William
Huddleston, Thomas	WC	-	-	-	see Morgan, John
Hudgins, Thos.	CW	-	-	-	see Cocks, John
Hudson, Christopher	TT	Gray, Henry	16	0	1 riding chair
Hudson, Hall	RM	Hudson, Obediah	2	530	
Hudson, John	RM	0	0	200	
Hudson, John	TT	-	-	-	see Burton, John
Hudson, John	WC	-	-	-	see Tucker, John Sr.
Hudson, Joshua	RM	0	0	0	
Hudson, Nicholas	JB	Hudson, William	8	928	
Hudson, Obediah	RM	-	-	-	see Hudson, Hall
Hudson, Peter	RM	0	1	100	
Hudson, Ward	RM	0	3	125	
Hudson, William	JB	-	-	-	see Hudson, Nicholas
Hughes, Jack	RM	0	1	200	
Hughes, John	TT	Jones, William	4	200	List
Hulme, John	RM	-	-	-	see Sherwin, Samuel
Hundly, Anthony	RM	-	-	-	see Jones, Col. Wood
Hurt, Abraham	TT	0	0	0	
Hurt, James	RM	0	0	0	
Hurt, Moses	CW	Forrest, John	7	300	
Hurt, Moses Jr.	CW	0	0	161	
Hurt, William	TT	Smith, James	4	463	
Hutchason, Charles	TT	-	-	-	see Tabb, Thomas
Hutchason, Drury	TT	-	-	-	see Hutchason, William
Hutchason, William	TT	Hutchason, Drury	0	100	

TAXPAYER	LIST	OTHER FREE MALES	Slaves	Acres	COMMENTS
Irby, ___	CW				see Jrby, Jerby
Irby, Wm.	CW	-	-	-	see Hoopper, Zachariah
Jackson, Arther (sic)	RM	-	-	-	see Jackson, John
Jackson, Charles	RM	0	0	600	
Jackson, Daniel	RM	-	-	-	see Jackson, William
Jackson, Danl.	RM	-	-	-	see Jackson, Edward
Jackson, Edward	RM	Jackson, Danl.	2	384	
Jackson, Frances	JB	Jackson, Rowlan Jackson, Josiah	1	160	
Jackson, Francis	JB	0	3	200	
Jackson, Jas.	RM	-	-	-	see Jackson, Thomas
Jackson, Jno.	RM	-	-	-	see Jackson, Thomas
Jackson, Joell	JB	Roberts, John	3	250	
Jackson, John	RM	Jackson, Arther (sic)	2	590	
Jackson, John	RM	0	0	0	
Jackson, Joseph	TT	0	0	200	
Jackson, Josiah	JB	-	-	-	see Jackson, Frances
Jackson, Matthew	JB	Jackson, Matthew Jr.	2	200	
Jackson, Matthew Jr.	JB	-	-	-	see Jackson, Matthew Sr.
Jackson, Rowlan	JB	-	-	-	see Jackson, Frances
Jackson, Thomas	JB	-	-	-	see Ferguson, Richard
Jackson, Thomas	RM	Jackson, Jno.	3	600	
Jackson, Thomas	RM	Jackson, Jas.	0	200	
Jackson, William	JB	0	0	0	
Jackson, William	RM	Jackson, Wm. Jr. Jackson, Daniel	3	1131	
Jackson, William	TT	0	2	354	
Jackson, Wm. Jr.	RM	-	-	-	see Jackson, William
James, Thomas	TT	0	2	200	
Jeffres, Thos.	CW	-	-	-	see Bolling, Col. Alexander
Jeffries, Thomas	CW	Moon, Robert	6	449	List
Jenkins, James	TT	-	-	-	see Ginkins, James
Jennings, James	RM	0	1	0	
Jennings, Wm.	CW	0	4	300	
Jerby, Susanah	CW	Beuford, Henry	5	565	List; IRBY intended?
Jers__, Thos.	CW	0	3	404	
Jessey, John	TT	-	-	-	see Kennon, Col. William
Jeter, Hary (sic)	CW	-	-	-	see Jeter, Oliver
Jeter, Oliver	CW	Jeter, Hary (sic) Jeter, Saml.	0	0	
Jeter, Saml.	CW	-	-	-	see Jeter, Oliver
Jeter, William	JB	-	-	-	see Clough, Richard

TAXPAYER	LIST	OTHER FREE MALES	Slaves	Acres	COMMENTS
Johns, John	RM	Johns, John Jr.	2	300	
Johns, John Jr.	RM	-	-	-	see Johns, John
Johnson, Ashly	RM	0	1	125	
Johnson, Charles	RM	0	0	100	
Johnson, James	JB	-	-	-	see Worsham, John
Johnson, James	TT	-	-	-	see Johnson, Richard
Johnson, Jeremiah	JB	-	-	-	see Archer, John
Johnson, Jessee	RM	0	1	125	
Johnson, John	CW	-	-	-	see Osborne, William
Johnson, John	RM	0	4	125	
Johnson, John	WC	0	0	0	
Johnson, John Jr.	RM	0	0	125	
Johnson, Richard	TT	Johnson, James	0	0	
Johnson, William	RM	0	0	0	
Johnson, William	TT	0	2	300	
Johnston, Andrew	CW	0	0	435	
Johnston, James	CW	0	1	0	
Joiner, Daniel	WC	-	-	-	see Farley, Joseph
Jones, Adam	CW	Jones, Ben	4	200	List
Jones, Agnes	WC	0	7	1195	list
Jones, Ben	CW	-	-	-	see Jones, Adam
Jones, Branch	WC	-	-	-	see Jones, Peter Sr.
Jones, Col. Wood	RM	Hundly, Anthony	7	0	List?
Jones, Daniel	WC	Jones, Daniel Jr. Vaughn, Cradock	10	1341	
Jones, Daniel Jr.	WC	-	-	-	see Jones, Daniel
Jones, David	TT	-	-	-	see Davis, Thomas
Jones, Dorothy	WC	0	10	0	list
Jones, Henry	RM	0	2	0	
Jones, Henry	WC	0	5	1303	list
Jones, John	WC	0	4	1000	
Jones, John Jr.	WC	0	1	0	
Jones, Lewelling	WC	Hinton, Christopher	7	1800	
Jones, Maj. Peter's estate	WC	Jones, Richard	5	1316	
Jones, Maj. Richard	RM	Jones, Richard Jr. Wilson, Richard	17	1791	List?
Jones, Maj. Richard	WC	Murray, Leonard	6	0	list
Jones, Nelson	CW	0	9	0	1 Chair
Jones, Peter	WC	Verser, Richard	3	1000	
Jones, Peter Sr.	RM	Lewis, David	9	0	List?
Jones, Peter Sr.	WC	Jones, Branch Peter Jones	6	2210	
Jones, Peter's sweathouse	WC	0	6	748	

TAXPAYER	LIST	OTHER FREE MALES	Slaves	Acres	COMMENTS
Jones, Richard	TT	Jolly, Dudley	3	200	title "S.C."
Jones, Richard	TT	0	0	195	"Overseer"; no tithe
Jones, Richard	TT	-	-	-	see Tabb, Thomas
Jones, Richard	WC	-	-	-	see Jones, Maj. Peter's estate
Jones, Richard Jr.	RM	-	-	-	see Jones, Maj. Richard
Jones, Robert	TT	Foster, James	5	400	
Jones, Sarah	WC	0	6	0	list
Jones, Thomas	RM	0	3	300	
Jones, Thomas	WC	Mathie_, Peter	7	572	"West Creek"
Jones, Thomas F.	TT	0	0	0	
Jones, Thomas Nott.	RM	0	4	200	Nott. = of Nottoway Co.?
Jones, Thomas Petersburg	WC	0	0	510	
Jones, Uriah	TT	-	-	-	see Tabb, Thomas
Jones, William	RM	0	3	393	
Jones, William	RM	0	0	0	
Jones, William	TT	-	-	-	see Hughes, John
Jones, William	WC	0	0	0	
Jones, Wood	WC	Foster, Richard	9	914	
Jonray, John	WC	-	-	-	see Greenhill, David
Jordan, ___ estate	CW	Phillips, Joseph	9	1510	List?
Jordan, Absolam	TT	-	-	-	see Jordan, Jonas
Jordan, Edward	CW	0	0	400	List?
Jordan, Jonas	TT	Jordan, Absolam	0	400?	smudged
Jordan, Wm.	CW	Jordan, Wm. Jr. Stout?, Hosea	7	360	
Jordan, Wm. Jr.	CW	-	-	-	see Jordan, Wm.
Jrby, Charles	CW	0	6	400	IRBY intended?
Kealles, Curtis	WC	Kealles, John	0	400	crossed out
Kealles, John	WC	-	-	-	see Kealles, Curtis
Kennon, Col. William	TT	Jessey, John	9	1000	His "Estate List"
Kennon, Robert	WC	Crowder, Nathaniel	9	0	list
Kid, George	WC	-	-	-	see Brookings, Vivion
Lamkin, James	CW	0	0	0	
Land, Epharaim	TT	-	-	-	see Eastice, Moses Sr.
Lander, Ballis	WC	-	-	-	see Tucker, George
Lane, John	JB	0	0	0	
Lane, William	JB	0	0	0	
Lankaster?, John	CW	Davis, Joseph	0	0	
Lea, William	WC	0	0	0	
Leaveston?, Alexander	RM	-	-	-	see Williams, Thomas
Lee, Joseph	CW	-	-	-	see Lee, William
Lee, William	CW	Lee, Joseph	5	662	

TAXPAYER	LIST	OTHER FREE MALES	Slaves	Acres	COMMENTS
Leiht, Arthur	CW	0	5	639	
Leonard, Joseph	RM	0	0	0	
Lester, Jeremiah	WC	0	0	100	
Lewis, Charles	CW	Hill, Wm.	2	400	
Lewis, Francis	CW	-	-	-	see Lewis, George
Lewis, George	CW	Lewis, Francis	3	400	
Lewis, Griffin	CW	Suggitt?, Edgecomb	3	2257	
Lewis, John	RM	Ward, Wiley	3	220	X
Lewis, John	RM	0	0	0	X
Liggon, John	WC	-	-	-	see Crawley, William
Lightfoot, Phillip	JB	-	-	-	see Harrison, W. Nathaniel
Ligon, Robert	JB	-	-	-	see Ligon, William Sr.
Ligon, Thomas	JB	0	4	0	
Ligon, William Jr.	JB	-	-	-	see Ligon, William Sr.
Ligon, William Sr.	JB	Ligon, William Jr. Ligon, Robert	10	1108	
Lipscom, Thomas	WC	-	-	-	see Southerland, Fendall
Lipscomb, Ambrose	CW	0	0	404	List?
Lister, Thomas	CW	0	0	50	
Loafman, John	WC	-	-	-	see Walthall, William
Locket, James	RM	Roberts, Armstead	2	200	X
Lockett, Abram	TT	-	-	-	see Lockett, Benjamin
Lockett, Benjamin	TT	Lockett, Abram	3	239	
Lockett, Stephen	JB	-	-	-	see Oglesby, John
Lockett, Thomas	TT	0	0	100	
Long, George	CW	0	1	370	
Lorton, John	TT	-	-	-	see Lorton, Thomas
Lorton, Thomas	TT	Lorton, John Walden, John	4	400	
Lovesy, Bolling	RM	-	-	-	see Lovesy, Richard
Lovesy, Richard	RM	Lovesy, Bolling	1	150	X
Loving, David	CW	0	0	100	
Loving, James	TT	-	-	-	see Clements, William
Loving, John	TT	0	0	0	
Loving, Moses	TT	0	0	150	
Loving, William	TT	0	0	100	
Loving, Wm.	CW	0	0	100	List
Loyde, John	WC	-	-	-	see Wills, Laurence
Lumkin, Diderson	RM	0	1	0	X
Mackey, John	WC	-	-	-	see Greenhill, David
Major, Bathsheba	TT	Major, Phillip	3	150	List
Major, Phillip	TT	-	-	-	see Major, Bathsheba
Malone, David	WC	0	0	0	
Manire, William	RM	Manire, Wm. Jr.	1	100	X

TAXPAYER	LIST	OTHER FREE MALES	Slaves	Acres	COMMENTS
Manire, Wm. Jr.	RM	-	-	-	see Manire, Wm.
Mann, Cain	JB	-	-	-	see Tatum, Josiah
Mann, Charles	TT	0	1	0	
Mann, Elizabeth	WC	Mann, Joel	2	200	list
Mann, Field	JB	-	-	-	see Mann, Robert
Mann, Joel	WC	-	-	-	see Mann, Elizabeth
Mann, Robert	JB	Mann, Field	1	150	
Mann, Samuel Jr.	TT	0	0	0	
Marshal, William Jr.	TT	Burges, Joel	4	400	
Marshall, Robert	JB	Ellington, John Jr.	11	796	
Marshall, William	TT	0	0	399	"Cumb[erlan]d"
Marshall, William Jr.	JB	0	3	400	
Martin, Thomas	TT	0	0	0	
Mason, Charles	TT	-	-	-	see Gooch, John
Mathie_, Peter	WC	-	-	-	see Jones, Thomas
May, Jas.	RM	-	-	-	see May, John; X
May, John	RM	May, Jas.	3	224	X
May, John	RM	-	-	-	see May, William
May, William	RM	May, John	4	945	X
May, William Jr.	RM	0	0	0	X
Mayes, Daniel	JB	-	-	-	see Mayes, Gardner
Mayes, Gardner	JB	Mayes, Daniel	3	100	
Maynard, Edward	CW	0	0	200	
McCann, Owen	RM	0	0	0	X
McKenny, Tra__	RM	0	0	125	X; name illegible
Meadow, Henry	TT	0	0	100	
Meadow, James	TT	-	-	-	see Wright, Thomas Sr.
Meadow, Jeremiah	TT	-	-	-	see Wright, Thomas Sr.
Meadow, Joell	TT	Meadows, Joell Jr.	0	225	
Meadow, Joell Jr.	TT	-	-	-	see Meadow, Joell
Meadow?, Benjamin	TT	-	-	-	see Wright, John
Meadows, Jehu	TT	-	-	-	see Robertson, George
Merrimoon, David	WC	0	0	0	
Merrimoon, Peter	WC	0	0	0	
Milner, John	CW	Milner, Richd. Milner, John Milner, Wm.	0	285	
Milner, John	CW	-	-	-	see Milner, John
Milner, Richd.	CW	-	-	-	see Milner, John
Milner, Wm.	CW	-	-	-	see Milner, John
Minear, John	RM	0	0	100	X
Minor, James	TT	0	0	0	
Mitchel, Evans	TT	-	-	-	see Archer, William
Mitchel, James	RM	0	3	500	X
Mitchel, John	RM	0	1	224	X

TAXPAYER	LIST	OTHER FREE MALES	Slaves	Acres	COMMENTS
Mitchell, Wm.	RM	-	-	-	see Apling, John
Moon, Robert	CW	-	-	-	see Jeffries, Thomas
Moon, Wm.	CW	-	-	-	see Hardaway, James
Moor, Eleazer	WC	-	-	-	see Eppes, Tabitha
Moor, George	RM	0	0	75	X
Moor, John	RM	0	0	100	X
Moor, Mark?	RM	0	0	0	X
Moor, Mary	RM	Moor, Wm.	0	100	X
Moor, Wm.	RM	-	-	-	see Moor, Mary
Moore, David	CW	0	1	200	
Moore, David	CW	-	-	-	see Walker, Thos.
Moors, Thomas	WC	0	0	0	
Morgan, Jacob	RM	Morgan, Jacob Phillip Whitworth, William	18	905	X
Morgan, Jacob Phillip	RM	-	-	-	see Morgan, Jacob
Morgan, John	WC	-	-	-	see Crawley, William
Morgan, John	WC	Huddleston, Thomas	2	250	list
Morgan, Samuel Sr.	JB	Morgan, William	4	688	
Morgan, William	JB	-	-	-	see Morgan, Samuel Sr
Morgin, John	RM	0	0	45	X
Morgin, Thomas	RM	0	0	100	X
Morris, Isaac	TT	-	-	-	see Wales, John
Morriss, Robert	WC	-	-	-	see Morriss, Thomas
Morriss, Thomas	WC	Morriss, Robert	1	350	
Morton?, John	RM	-	-	-	see Poythress, Capt. Peter
Motley, Abraham	CW	0	1	362	
Moulson, William	TT	Dunnavant, William	15	1070	1 riding chair
Munford, Robert	RM	Yarborough, Henry	15	1640	X; 1 pr. chair wheels
Munford, Thomas	TT	Davis, Samuel Beadles, Augustiner	11	1379	1 riding chair
Munford, Thomas B.	RM	Munford, William Nunnely, John	8	743	X; 1 pr. chair wheels
Munford, William	RM	-	-	-	see Munford, Thomas B.
Murray, James	TT	Grant, Gregory Crenshaw, Benjamin	19	4832	List
Murray, Leonard	WC	-	-	-	see Jones, Maj. Richard
Muse, George	RM	Hamlet, Obediah	5	300	List; X
Nash, Thos.	CW	-	-	-	see Cause, Richd.
Navierr, James	CW	-	-	-	see Wilkinson?, Rev. Wm.
Neal, David	JB	0	5	400	
Neal, Joel	WC	-	-	-	see Neal, William
Neal, John	JB	0	0	250	“estate of, dec’d”

TAXPAYER	LIST	OTHER FREE MALES	Slaves	Acres	COMMENTS
Neal, John	WC	0	0	299	
Neal, Roger	JB	0	1	0	
Neal, Stephen	JB	0	2	0	
Neal, William	WC	-	-	-	see Bolling, Col. Robert
Neal, William	WC	Neal, Joel	5	351	
Nelson, Henry	RM	0	0	0	
Nervart, John	WC	-	-	-	see Hall, Robert
Nevills, John	TT	-	-	-	see Royall, John
Newbell, William	JB	-	-	-	see Hart, William
Newman, Richard	WC	0	2	283	list
Nicholas, Zachariah	JB	0	0	0	
Nobles, Joseph	RM	0	0	200	
North, Thos.	RM	-	-	-	see Bland, Col. Theodorick
North, William	RM	-	-	-	see Bland, Col. Theodorick
Nunn?, Giles	CW	0	1	75	
Nunn?, John	CW	0	0	121	
Nunnely, John	RM	-	-	-	see Munford, Thomas B.
O'Neal, Tyre	RM	0	0	0	X
Oglesby, John	JB	Lockett, Stephen	6	611	
Olds, John	WC	0	6	885	
Oliver, Benjamin	WC	-	-	-	see Clay, John
Oliver, Isaack	RM	-	-	-	see Oliver, James
Oliver, James	RM	Oliver, Isaack	10	1000	X
Orsin?, Nathaniel	CW	-	-	-	see Robertson, Nathaniel
Osborne, Joseph	JB	0	7	850	
Osborne, Thos.	CW	0	2	0	List
Osborne, William	CW	Johnson, John	5	0	List
Osborne, William	JB	Osborne, William Jr.	10	1170	
Osborne, William Jr.	JB	-	-	-	see Osborne, William
Overstreet, James	CW	Overstreet, Thos.	0	0	
Overstreet, Thos.	CW	-	-	-	see Overstreet, James
Owley, Thomas ?	JB	-	-	-	see Owley, Thomas ?
Pa__, John	CW	House, Thos.	0	300	name smudged
Pa__, Thos.	CW	Clandin?, Joshua	1	497	name smudged
Palmore, Reubin	JB	0	2	241	
Pardue, Joseph	WC	0	0	200	
Pardue, William	WC	0	0	200	
Parham, Gower	WC	Parham, James	3	250	
Parham, James	WC	-	-	-	see Parham, Gower
Parham, William	WC	0	2	206	
Parrott, John	JB	-	-	-	see Tigard, John ?

TAXPAYER	LIST	OTHER FREE MALES	Slaves	Acres	COMMENTS
Parry, Thomas	CW	0	0	100	
Patterson, John	WC	0	0	400	
Patterson, Joseph	WC	0	1	200	
Paynes, Thos.	CW	0	3	334	
Peachey, Thos. Griffin	RM	Eldridge, Rolfe Spain, David	8	1720	
Perkinson, Constable Seth	WC	Perkinson, Jeremiah	1	300	
Perkinson, Jeremiah	WC	-	-	-	see Perkinson, Constable
Perkinson, Matthew	JB	0	0	231	list of land
Perkinson, Ralph	JB	0	1	127	
Perkinson, Seth	WC	-	-	-	see Dyson, Benjamin
Peter Jones	WC	-	-	-	see Jones, Peter Sr.
Phillips, Richard	TT	0	2	150	
Phillips, Thos.	CW	0	0	800	
Pincham, Peter	RM	0	4	500	X
Pincham, Samuel	JB		2	816	
Pincham, Samuel	RM	Hawkins, Zacharias	3	0	List; X
Pinnock, John	JB	0	0	512	
Pitchford, Daniel	WC	-	-	-	see Swinney, Abraham
Pollard, Henry	TT	0	2	0	smudged
Pollard, Joseph	TT	0	1	148	
Pollard, Thomas	TT	0	2	150	
Ponton, William	TT	-	-	-	see Williamson, Frances
Pope, William	RM	-	-	-	see Smith, Abraham
Powel, John	WC	0	1	200	
Powel, Robert	WC	0	1	200	
Powell, Mary	WC	0	4	0	list
Powell, Obedience	TT	Hamlin, Henry	4	?	List; smudged
Powells, Simon	WC	West, John	0	152	
Poyner, John	WC	Smith, Adam	0	200	
Poythress, Capt. Peter	RM	Morton?, John	7	578	List; X
Pride, Francis	JB	-	-	-	see Pride, John Sr.
Pride, John Sr.	JB	Pride, Francis	5	400	
Pride, Rowlie	JB	-	-	-	see Henderson, James
Pringle, Richard	TT	-	-	-	see Tabb, Thomas
Pryor, John	RM	Ward, Richard Dublin, Harry	4	250	X; 1 (riding?) Chair
Pryor, John	WC	-	-	-	see Pryor, Samuel
Pryor, Samuel	WC	Pryor, John	7	1000	list
Puckett, James	TT	-	-	-	see Puckett, Richard
Puckett, Richard	TT	Puckett, Thomas Puckett, James	2	100	
Puckett, Thomas	TT	-	-	-	see Puckett, Richard

TAXPAYER	LIST	OTHER FREE MALES	Slaves	Acres	COMMENTS
Pugh, Jno.	RM	-	-	-	see Bottom, Thomas's list
Quales, Richard	RM	-	-	100	X
Quesinbury, Nicholas	CW	0	0	0	
Quinn, Wm.	CW	0	0	0	
Quisenberry, Nicholas	RM	-	-	-	see Hall, John Jr.
R___, Parham	TT	-	-	-	see Boat____, Rachel
R____, Thomas	WC	-	-	-	see Cuzens, Robert Sr.
Ragsdale, George	JB	0	2	100	
Randolph, Henry	JB	0	23	1054	1 riding chair
Ray, John Jr.	RM	0	0	0	
Ray, William	TT	0	0	0	
Reams, Frederick	JB	-	-	-	see Reams, Thomas
Reams, Thomas	JB	Reams, Frederick	1	150	
Redford, Andrew	RM	Shelton, Ralph	6	200	X
Roach, William	WC	-	-	-	see Hamlin, Stephen
Roberts, Armstead	RM	-	-	-	see Locket, James
Roberts, Francis	JB	Roberts, John	1	0	
Roberts, John	JB	-	-	-	see Jackson, Joell
Roberts, John	JB	-	-	-	see Roberts, Francis
Roberts, Sarah	TT	Wiltshire, Henry	2	200	List
Roberts, Step(hen?)	JB	-	-	-	see Branch, Benjamin
Roberts, Thomas	JB	-	-	-	see Hatchett, John
Roberts, William	JB	0	0	0	
Robertson, George	TT	Meadows, Jehu	3	558	List
Robertson, George	TT	0	0	0	
Robertson, Henry	CW	0	5	900	
Robertson, James*	TT	Stewart, William	12	1161?	* = "estate list"; deceased?
Robertson, John	TT	Sears, Thomas	9	1599	List
Robertson, Nathaniel	CW	Robertson, Richard Orsin?, Nathaniel	5	1061	"Constable"
Robertson, Richard	CW	-	-	-	see Robertson, Nathaniel
Robinson, Robert	TT	Sanders, Daniel	0	0	
Rowlett, George	JB	0	0	116.5	
Royall, John	TT	Cocke, James Nevills, John Young, Peter	10	960	1 Riding Chair
Royall, Joseph	JB	Blankenship, John	4	400	list
Rucker, Elisha	TT	-	-	-	see Rucker, William Sr.
Rucker, Gideon	TT	0	0	0	
Rucker, Joshua	TT	0	0	0	
Rucker, William Jr.	TT	0	0	0	
Rucker, William Sr.	TT	Rucker, Elisha	4	250	

TAXPAYER	LIST	OTHER FREE MALES	Slaves	Acres	COMMENTS
Sallard, Charles	RM	0	11	1000	X
Sammons, Thomas	WC	0	0	0	
Sanders, Daniel	TT	-	-	-	see Robinson, Robert
Scarriot, John	RM	0	0	0	X
Scott, George	TT	-	-	-	see Cheatam, James
Scott, John	TT	Cumpton, Richard	8	1400	
Scott, John	TT	0	0	96	"& Company"
Scott, Roger	JB	Truley, Peter	1	95.5	crossed out
Scruggs, John	TT	-	-	-	see Swan, Thompson
Seah, Josiah	TT	-	-	-	see Seay, James Sr.
Searman, John Jr.	RM	0	0	50	X
Sears, Thomas	TT	-	-	-	see Robertson, John
Seay, Gideon	TT	-	-	-	see Seay, Jesse
Seay, Jacob	TT	0	6	560	
Seay, James	CW	0	0	150	
Seay, James Sr.	TT	Seay, Josiah	2	193	
Seay, Jesse	TT	Seay, Gideon	3	196	
Seay, Moses	TT	0	1	200	
Shannon, William dec'd	JB	0	0	200	
Shelly, Jno.	RM	-	-	-	see Eppes, Francis
Shelton, Ben	CW	0	0	100	
Shelton, Crespin	CW	Shelton, Gabriel	3	362	
Shelton, Gabriel	CW	-	-	-	see Shelton, Crespin
Shelton, Gabriel	CW	0	2	0	List
Shelton, James	CW	0	1	119	Constable
Shelton, Jno.	CW	-	-	-	see Erskine, Alexr.
Shelton, John	CW	0	1	169	
Shelton, Lewis	CW	-	-	-	see Holland, Phi__
Shelton, Ralph	RM	-	-	-	see Redford, Andrew
Shelton?, Josiah	CW	-	-	-	see Evans, Robert
Sherwin, Samuel	RM	Hulme, John	7	530	List; X
Sherwin, Samuel	TT	-	-	-	see Tabb, Thomas
Short, Thomas	RM	Bradley, James	12	600	X
Shurt?, John	RM	0	0	0	X
Simmons, Benjamin	RM	Simmons, Thos.	2	183	X
Simmons, Thos.	RM	-	-	-	see Simmons, Benjamin
Smith, Abraham	RM	Pope, William	4	444	List; X
Smith, Adam	WC	-	-	-	see Poyner, John
Smith, George	JB	Smith, John	6	224	
Smith, George	RM	0	1	0	X
Smith, Isaac	CW	-	-	-	see Smith, Saml.
Smith, James	TT	-	-	-	see Hurt, William
Smith, John	JB	-	-	-	see Smith, George
Smith, John	WC	-	-	-	see Walthall, William
Smith, Nicholas	WC	-	-	-	see Avery, John

TAXPAYER	LIST	OTHER FREE MALES	Slaves	Acres	COMMENTS
Smith, Saml.	CW	Smith, Isaac Standley, Thomas	7	800	
Sneed, Jas.	RM	-	-	-	see Stokes, Robert
Sneed, Jno.	RM	-	-	-	see Bridgforth, Benjamin
Sneed, Zachariah	CW	0	0	0	
Sneed?, Wm.	CW	Thompson, Miles?	3	25	List?
Snellins, Alexander	RM	-	-	-	see Trab___, John
Sobisky, Charles	RM	-	-	-	see Caruthers, Dr. Joseph
Southall, James	TT	-	-	-	see Southall, William
Southall, James	WC	0	1	100	
Southall, William	TT	Southall, James	0	255	
Southerland, Fendall	WC	Lipscom, Thomas	11	1447	list
Sowell, Thomas	RM	0	1	200	X
Spain, Francis	WC	0	0	50	
Spain, Frederick	WC	0	1	100	
Spain, John	WC	0	0	0	
Spain, William	WC	-	-	-	see Gray, John
St. John, Wm	RM	-	-	-	see Edmonson, Upton
Stamper, Powel	CW	Webster, Charles	0	0	
Standfield, Robert	JB	0	0	0	
Standley, James	RM	0	0	75	X
Standley, Jas.	RM	-	-	-	see Standley, William
Standley, Thomas	CW	-	-	-	see Smith, Saml.
Standley, William	RM	Standley, Jas.	2	75	X
Starnes, Ann	TT	0	50	370	List
Stearman, William	JB	0	0	0	
Stell, George	CW	0	0	189	
Stern, John	TT	0	0	0	
Stewart, Charles	RM	0	0	192	X
Stewart, John Sr.	RM	0	1	150	X
Stewart, Littleberry	RM	0	0	0	X
Stewart, William	TT	-	-	-	see Robertson, James*
Stoe, Joel	RM	-	-	-	see Stoe, William
Stoe, William	RM	Stoe, Joel	0	120	X
Stoker, Mathew	RM	0	0	200	X
Stokes, Robert	RM	Sneed, Jas.	2	300	X; List?
Stokes, Robert Jr.	RM	0	0	0	X
Stone, Phillip	RM	0	0	403	X
Stout?, Hosea	CW	-	-	-	see Jordan, Wm.
Stubblefield, Joel	TT	0	0	0	
Sturdivant, James	WC	0	2	200	"son of Daniel"
Sturdivant, James	WC	0	7	480	
Suggitt?, Edgecomb	CW	-	-	-	see Lewis, Griffin

TAXPAYER	LIST	OTHER FREE MALES	Slaves	Acres	COMMENTS
Sullivant, John	TT	-	-	-	see Brown, John
Swan, Thompson	TT	Scruggs, John	4	300	List
Swinney, Abraham	WC	Pitchford, Daniel	4	200	
Tabb, Edward	TT	-	-	-	see Clements, John
Tabb, Thomas	TT	Sherwin, Samuel Davis, Gresset Sringle, Richard Booker, Richard Y. Hamm, Thomas Hutchason, Charles Jones, Richard Jones, Uriah Greenwood, William Beasley, John P. Truman, Gideon Beckley, Humphrey	87	6484	
Talley, David	WC	-	-	-	see Talley, William Jr.
Talley, Jesse	WC	-	-	-	see Talley, Lodowick
Talley, Lodowick	WC	Talley, Jesse	0	200	
Talley, Richard Jr.	WC	0	1	70	
Talley, Richard Sr.	WC	0	0	0	
Talley, Tucker	WC	0	1	200	
Talley, William Jr.	WC	0	0	0	
Talley, William Jr.	WC	Talley, David	3	168	
Tanner, Ann	JB	0	5	0	List
Tanner, Branch	JB	0	9	327	1 riding chair
Tanner, Edward	WC	Tanner, Jeremiah Tanner, Robert	0	300	
Tanner, Jeremiah	WC	-	-	-	see Tanner, Edward
Tanner, Joseph	TT	0	1	230	
Tanner, Lodowick	JB	0	9	572	1 riding chair
Tanner, Robert	WC	-	-	-	see Tanner, Edward
Tatum, Josiah	JB	Mann, Cain	5	390	crossed out
Taylor, Henry	RM	-	-	-	see Taylor, Robert
Taylor, Joseph	TT	0	0	0	
Taylor, Robert	RM	Taylor, Wm. Taylor, Robt Jr. Taylor, Henry	1	200	X
Taylor, Robt Jr.	RM	-	-	-	see Taylor, Robert
Taylor, Wm.	RM	-	-	-	see Taylor, Robert
Thomas, Henry	CW	-	-	-	see Fitzgerrald, Wm.
Thomas, Samuel	CW	0	4	775	
Thomas, William Jr.	RM	-	-	-	see Thomas, William Sr.
Thomas, William Sr.	RM	Thomas, William Jr.	0	200	X
Thompson, Benjamin	RM	-	-	-	see Caruthers, Dr.

TAXPAYER	LIST	OTHER FREE MALES	Slaves	Acres	COMMENTS
					Joseph
Thompson, Drury	JB	Clayton, William	10	500	
Thompson, Hermon	TT	0	1	0	List
Thompson, James	TT	0	0	0	
Thompson, Miles?	CW	-	-	-	see Sneed?, Wm.
Thompson, Peter	JB	0	6	400	
Thompson, Roger	TT	0	3	0	
Thompson, William	JB	Freeman, M____	0	0	freed slave?
Thompson, William	WC	Farley, Matthew	10	300	
Thorp, Charles	JB	-	-	-	see Thorp, William
Thorp, John	JB	0	2	50	
Thorp, William	JB	Thorp, Charles	0	150	
Tigard, John ?	JB	Parrott, John	6	200	List
Tinsley, David	TT	-	-	-	see Tinsley, Thomas
Tinsley, Isaack	TT	Cardwell, Daniel	4	200	
Tinsley, Thomas	TT	Tinsley, David	0	0	
Tolty, Thomas	WC	-	-	-	see Hastens, John
Toney, Charles	WC	0	0	0	
Townes, James	JB	0	4	545	
Townes, John	JB	0	2	674	List
Townes?, William	TT	0	4	150	
Townsend, John	TT	-	-	-	see Anderson, Pauling
Trab___, John	RM	Snellins, Alexander	3	200	X; List?
Tramell, Jno.	CW	-	-	-	see Ball, Thos. Jr.
Truley, Peter	JB	-	-	-	see Scott, Roger
Truman, Gideon	TT	-	-	-	see Tabb, Thomas
Tucker, Absalom	WC	-	-	-	see Tucker, Francis Sr.
Tucker, Daniel	WC	-	-	-	see Tucker, Robert Sr.
Tucker, Daniel	WC	-	-	-	see Tucker, William Sr.
Tucker, Daniel Sr.	WC	0	2	75	
Tucker, David	WC	0	0	0	
Tucker, Francis Jr.	WC	Walker, Vinson Vaughan, Samuel	0	75	
Tucker, Francis Sr.	WC	Tucker, Absalom	1	376	
Tucker, George	WC	Tucker, Henry Tucker, George Lander, Ballis	0	0	
Tucker, George	WC	-	-	-	see Tucker, George
Tucker, Godphrey	WC	-	-	-	see Tucker, Robert Sr.
Tucker, Henry	WC	0	0	0	
Tucker, Henry	WC	-	-	-	see Tucker, George
Tucker, Hudson	WC				
Tucker, James	WC	0	4	397	
Tucker, John	RM	0	0	0	X
Tucker, John	WC	-	-	-	see Tucker, William Sr.

TAXPAYER	LIST	OTHER FREE MALES	Slaves	Acres	COMMENTS
Tucker, John	WC	0	1	200	"William's son"
Tucker, John Sr.	WC	Hudson, John	1	566	
Tucker, Joseph	WC	-	-	-	see Coleman, Hezekiah
Tucker, Joseph	WC	0	1	190	
Tucker, Matthew Jr.	WC	0	0	116	
Tucker, Matthew Sr.	WC	0	0	100	
Tucker, Robert "blacksmith"	WC	Clay, Jesse	0	0	
Tucker, Robert Sr.	WC	Tucker, Daniel Tucker, Godphrey	4	811	
Tucker, Thomas	WC	0	0	0	
Tucker, William	RM	0	1	333	X
Tucker, William	RM	0	4	137	X
Tucker, William	WC	0	0	0	"son of Jno."
Tucker, William	WC	-	-	-	see Tucker, William Sr.
Tucker, William Jr.	WC	0	0	400	
Tucker, William Sr.	WC	Tucker, William Tucker, Daniel Tucker, John	2	644	
Turner, Wm.	CW	0	1	0	
Vaden, Henry	WC	Bevil, Carter	1	0	
Varser, Jonas	RM	Varser, William	0	124	X
Varser, William	RM	-	-	-	see Varser, Jonas
Vassar, Jesse	JB	-	-	-	see Vassar, Mary
Vassar, Mary	JB	Vassar, William Vassar, Jesse	2	362	list
Vassar, William	JB	-	-	-	see Vassar, Mary
Vasser, Abraham	TT	Harris, William	0	300	
Vaughan, Samuel	WC	-	-	-	see Tucker, Francis Jr.
Vaughn, Cradock	WC	-	-	-	see Jones, Daniel
Vaughn, David	RM	-	-	-	see Vaughn, Isham
Vaughn, Isham	RM	Vaughn, David	0	0	X
Vaughn, Jane	JB	Worsham, George	2	652	
Vaughn, Jesse	JB	-	-	-	see Vaughn, Lewis
Vaughn, John	JB	0	0	0	
Vaughn, Lewis	JB	Vaughn, Jesse	3	350	
Vaughn, Nicholas	JB	0	0	0	
Vaughn, Robert Sr.	TT	0	1	500	
Vaughn, Samuel	RM	Vaughn, Silvester Vaughn, Stephen	0	353	
Vaughn, Samuel Jr.	RM	0	0	0	X
Vaughn, Silvester	RM	-	-	-	see Vaughn, Samuel
Vaughn, Stephen	RM	-	-	-	see Vaughn, Samuel
Vaughn, Zacharias	RM	-	-	-	see Edmonson, Upton
Verser, Richard	WC	-	-	-	see Jones, Peter

TAXPAYER	LIST	OTHER FREE MALES	Slaves	Acres	COMMENTS
Vowall, William	WC	0	0	190	
Walden, John	TT	-	-	-	see Lorton, Thomas
Waldrop, Michael	WC	0	0	0	"son of Joseph"
Wales, John	TT	Morris, Isaac	9	964	List
Walker, Alexander	TT	0	3	0	
Walker, Charles	TT	0	0	0	
Walker, Edmund	JB	Walker, Edmund Jr. Owley, Thomas ?	14	200	
Walker, Edmund Jr.	JB	-	-	-	see Walker, Edmund
Walker, Henry	CW	-	-	-	see Hardaway, Col. __
Walker, Thomas	RM	-	-	-	see Williams, Thomas
Walker, Thos.	CW	-	-	-	see Gunn, Thos.
Walker, Thos.	CW	Moore, David	6	560	
Walker, Vinson	WC	-	-	-	see Tucker, Francis Jr.
Walker, William	JB	0	3	0	
Waller, Major	CW	0	3	306	
Walthall, Ben	JB	-	-	-	see Willson, Thomas B.
Walthall, Chris Jr.	JB	-	-	-	see Walthall, Christopher
Walthall, Christopher	JB	Walthall, Chris Jr.	6	500	
Walthall, Daniel	TT	-	-	-	see Walthall, Thomas
Walthall, Henry	JB	0	6	400	
Walthall, Richard	WC	-	-	-	see Walthall, William
Walthall, Thomas	TT	Walthall, Daniel	12	803	
Walthall, William	WC	Walthall, Richard Smith, John Loafman, John	8	677	
Walthall, William Jr.	JB	0	3	388	
Ward, Benjamin	TT	0	11	980	1 riding chair
Ward, Richard	RM	-	-	-	see Pryor, John
Ward, Roland	TT	0	8	992	
Ward, Wiley	RM	-	-	-	see Lewis, John
Ware, William	TT	-	-	-	see Bentley, John
Waters, William	TT	-	-	-	see Wiley, William
Watkins, James	JB	Frankling, Ben	3	300	list
Watson, Luke	TT	0	0	0	
Watson, William	RM	Dixon, Wm. Cabiness, Mat.	15	8930	List?
Webb, John	CW	0	0	105	
Webster, Anthony	JB	-	-	-	see Webster, Peter
Webster, Charles	CW	-	-	-	see Stamper, Powel
Webster, John	JB	0	0	0	
Webster, Peter	JB	Webster, Anthony	3	780	
Webster, Peter Jr.	JB	0	1	0	
Webster, Thomas	JB	Webster, Thomas Jr.	2	450	

TAXPAYER	LIST	OTHER FREE MALES	Slaves	Acres	COMMENTS
Webster, Thomas Jr.	JB	-	-	-	see Webster, Thomas
Webster, William	JB	-	-	-	see Gibbs, Matthew
Weeks, Emanuel	WC	-	-	-	see Wills, Willis
Weeks, Richard	WC	-	-	-	see Cowles, Thomas
West, John	WC	-	-	-	see Powells, Simon
Westbrook, Charles	RM	Westbrook, Henry	1	0	X
Westbrook, Henry	RM	-	-	-	see Westbrook, Charles
Westbrook, James	RM	0	0	50	X
Westbrook, Thomas	RM	0	0	150	X
White, George C.	JB	0	7	360	
White, Joseph	CW	0	1	200	
Whitlock, Achilles	TT	0	1	0	
Whitworth, Abraham	TT	0	3	300	
Whitworth, John	TT	-	-	-	see Whitworth, Thomas
Whitworth, Samuel	TT	0	2	106	
Whitworth, Thomas	TT	Whitworth, John	0	502	
Whitworth, William	RM	-	-	-	see Morgan, Jacob
Wiley, William	TT	Waters, William	7	318	
Wilkinson, Edward	TT	Wilkinson, Martin	6	553	List
Wilkinson, Joseph	JB	0	6	300	
Wilkinson, Martin	TT	-	-	-	see Wilkinson, Edward
Wilkinson, Thomas	WC	-	-	-	see Greenhill, David
Wilkinson, Wm	JB	"orphans of"	0	200	written on margin of p.4
Wilkinson?, Rev. Wm.	CW	Navierr, James	10	250	Chair; List
Wilks, John	RM	0	2	0	X
Williams, Billington	RM	0	0	270	X
Williams, Charles	RM	0	1	253	X
Williams, Reubin	CW	0	0	239	
Williams, Thomas	RM	Williams, Wm.	3	400	X
Williams, Thomas	RM	Leaveston?, Alexander Walker, Thomas	19	903	a Chair
Williams, Wm.	RM	-	-	-	see Williams, Thomas
Williamson, Frances	TT	Ponton, William Barding, James	8	536	List
Williamson, Jacob	TT	0	5	300	
Williamson, John	RM	0	0	220	X
Willis, Reubin	RM	-	-	-	see Haskins, Christopher
Willis, Wm.	CW	-	-	-	see Fitzgerrald, Wm.
Wills, Abraham	RM	Wills, Mat. Wills, Frederick Wills, Burwell	1	100	X
Wills, Burwell	RM	-	-	-	see Wills, Abraham
Wills, Elias	WC	Griggory, Joseph	3	531	list
Wills, Frederick	RM	-	-	-	see Wills, Abraham

TAXPAYER	LIST	OTHER FREE MALES	Slaves	Acres	COMMENTS
Wills, Laurence	WC	Loyde, John	6	588	1 pr chair wheels
Wills, Mat.	RM	-	-	-	see Wills, Abraham
Wills, William	WC	-	-	-	see Green, Abraham
Wills, Willis	WC	Weeks, Emanuel	3	509	list
Willson, Thomas B.	JB	Walthall, Ben	7	900	1 riding chair
Wilson, Capt. Daniel	JB	0	6	689	
Wilson, Charles	WC	-	-	-	see Wilson, John Sr.
Wilson, Daniel Jr.	JB	0	4	0	
Wilson, George	JB	0	0	266	
Wilson, John Jr.	WC	0	1	407	
Wilson, John Sr.	JB	0	4	0	
Wilson, John Sr.	WC	Wilson, Charles	7	300	
Wilson, Richard	RM	-	-	-	see Jones, Maj. Richard
Wilson, William	WC	Clardy, John	2	580	list
Wilson, Wm.	CW	0	4	100	
Wiltshire, Henry	TT	-	-	-	see Roberts, Sarah
Wingo, James	TT	Wingo, John	0	104	
Wingo, John	TT	0	0	200	
Wingo, John	TT	-	-	-	see Wingo, James
Wingo, Sarah	TT	0	0	140	
Wingo, Thomas Sr.	TT	0	0	60	
Winn, John	CW	0	14	740	
Wood, James	TT	0	2	200	
Wood, William	CW	0	0	0	
Wood, William	TT	Hargue, Joseph	5	400	
Wood, William	TT	0	0	0	"Carpenter"
Worsham, Daniel	JB	0	6	819	
Worsham, Drury	JB	0	1	150	
Worsham, George	JB	-	-	-	see Vaughn, Jane
Worsham, George	JB	Worsham, John Worsham, Joshua	6	200	
Worsham, Henry	TT	0	2	150	List?
Worsham, John	JB	Johnson, James	4	900	list
Worsham, John	JB	-	-	-	see Worsham, George
Worsham, Joshua	JB	-	-	-	see Worsham, George
Worsham, Thomas	JB	Holt, Thomas	3	646	List
Worsham, William	JB	0	2	100	
Wright, John	TT	Meadow?, Benjamin	4	530	
Wright, Thomas Sr.	TT	Meadow, James Meadow, Jeremiah	9	150	
Wright, Thomas, Jr.	TT	0	0	100	
Wynne, John	RM	0	1	0	
Yarborough, Henry	RM	-	-	-	see Munford, Robert
Yarbrough, Jordan	CW	-	-	-	see Yarbrough, Thos
Yarbrough, Samuel	CW	0	0	372	List?

TAXPAYER	LIST	OTHER FREE MALES	Slaves	Acres	COMMENTS
Yarbrough, Thos.	CW	Yarbrough, Jordan	4	600	
Young, Ellison	WC	-	-	-	see Young, Samuel
Young, Peter	TT	-	-	-	see Royall, John
Young, Ridley	WC	-	-	-	see Holt, David
Young, Samuel	WC	Young, Samuel Young, Ellison	1	77	
Young, Samuel	WC	-	-	-	see Young, Samuel
Young, Stephen	WC	-	-	-	see Hardaway, Joseph
Zackrey, David	CW	Zackrey, David	2	400	

The 1766 TITHE LISTS FOR AMELIA COUNTY, VIRGINIA

Users are referred to the INTRODUCTION to these tithe lists for an explanation of the lists, terms used, and methodology of creating these indexes from the microfilmed records.

EXPLANATION OF COLUMN HEADINGS

NAME: the name of the person paying the Tithe

LIST: The initials of the person who compiled the tithe list on which the individual appears (an indication of the geographic area and the parish where these individuals lived.

THE TAX "COMMISSIONERS" FOR 1766, AND THEIR AREA/PARISH

AE = Alexander Erskine of Nottoway Parish, "lower part"
JB = John Booker, of Raleigh (Raleigh) Parish
JW = John Winn, of Nottoway Parish
RM = Robert Munford of Nottoway Parish
TT = Thomas Tabb of Rawleigh Parish

Both John Winn and John Booker evidently produced TWO lists. In John Winn's case, both lists have some names in common, but each list contains names of individuals not found on the other. I've designated those that appear ONLY on the second list as JW2. Winn's handwriting is very difficult to read on the second list, and it may have been a draft or working list.

I have transcribed John Booker's lists in full; there may be duplicate listings as a result.

Thomas Tabb's list is blurred across the top of each page, and some names were obviously present, but obscured and therefore unreadable. So if your ancestor's name was on this list in 1765 and/or 1767 but isn't found in this transcription, that may be the explanation.

OTHER WHITE MALE TITHES: The names of other men above the age of 16, whose tithe was paid by the taxpayer. When of the same surname, these were usually sons of the taxpayer. Otherwise, they were guests, overseers or other employees.

COMMENTS

Land = individual taxed only for land, not for self; exempt for some reason.
List = individual named not taxed for self; exempt, or taxed personally elsewhere.
List? = number of individuals named is one more than number taxed; List implied but not stated.

NAME	LIST	Other white male tithes	Slaves	Acres	COMMENTS
Adams, Charles	JW	-	-	-	see Tabb, Col. Thos.
Adkins, John	TT	0	1	0	
Admerson?, John	JW2	-	-	-	See Jeffries, Thomas
Allen, Daniel	JB	0	3	392	"Patroler"
Allen, Elizabeth	TT	0	0	100	
Allen, John	AE	0	1	0	
Allen, Samuel	TT	-	-	-	See Cox, Henry Jr.
Allgood, Edward	AE	0	0	0	
Alsup, Joseph	JW	0	0	0	
Amont, Obadiah	RM	-	-	-	See Gooch, John
Anderson, Capt.	AE	0	0	0	

NAME	LIST	Other white male tithes	Slaves	Acres	COMMENTS
John					
Anderson, Charles	JW	Anderson, James	1	175	
Anderson, Claiborne	JB	0	7	572	List
Anderson, Francis	JB	0	5	650	
Anderson, Francis	TT	0	13	700	
Anderson, Henry	JB	Hopkins, Peter	29	2568	1 riding chair
Anderson, Henry	JW	0	2	367	
Anderson, James	JW	-	-	-	see Anderson, Charles
Anderson, James Jr.	RM	0	1	100	
Anderson, John	JW	Hulm, Chas.	5	600	
Anderson, Pauling	TT	-	-	-	See Anderson, Richard
Anderson, Pauling	TT	Townsend, John Cavenar, Hugh	10	2221	List
Anderson, Richard	TT	Anderson, Pauling	4	0	
Anderson, West	JB	0	4	150	
Appling, John	JW	0	4	643	
Appling, Thomas	JW	0	0	321	no tithes listed
Archer, John	JB	-	-	-	See Archer, William
Archer, John	JB	Johnson, Jeremiah Haynes, Thomas	8	1200	"Patroler"; 1 riding chair
Archer, William	JB	Archer, John Mitchell, Evans Moon?, Lewis	14	1335	
Asselin, David	JB	0	3	282	1 riding chair
Atkinson, John	TT	0	0	0	
Atkinson, Thomas	JW	0	5	577	
Avory, George	JB	Avory, William	2	252	Also spelled Avery
Avory, William	JB	-	-	-	See Avory, George
Bagby, George Jr.	JW	0	0	200	Name MAY be BAGLEY
Bagby, John	TT	0	3	0	
Bagby, Robert Jr.	TT	0	0	200	
Bagby, Robert Sr.	TT	0	0	200	
Bagley, Geo.	JW2	Ligon, Richd.	4	600	
Bagley, James	AE	0	4	100	
Baily, Micager	AE	0	0	309	"Sussex Co."
Baldwin, George	JW2	-	-	-	See Baldwin, John
Baldwin, Jno.	JW	-	-	-	see Gilliam, Jno. Jr.
Baldwin, John	JW2	Baldwin, George	3	210	
Baldwin, John Jr.	JW	0	0	313	no tithes
Baldwin, William	JW	0	0	95	
Ball, Thomas Sr.	JW	0	2	150	
Ball, Thos. Jr.	JW	Trammell, Jno.	4	600	List

NAME	LIST	Other white male tithes	Slaves	Acres	COMMENTS
Ballard, Moreman	TT	-	-	-	See Jones, Robert
Ballard, Thomas	TT	-	-	-	See Barnett, James
Banden?, James	JW	-	-	-	see Smith, Richard
Barding, James	TT	-	-	-	See Williamson, Frances
Barding, James	TT	0	0	53	
Barker, Charles	AE	-	-	-	See Haynes, Anthony Est.
Barlow, Thomas	TT	-	-	-	See Booker, Edmund
Barnett, James	TT	Ballard, Thomas	2	100	List
Barry, Peter	TT	-	-	-	See Seay, Jacob
Bass, Alexander	TT	-	-	-	See Bass, Christopher
Bass, Christopher	TT	Bass, Alexander	4	400	List
Bass, Edward	TT	0	10	697	1 riding chair
Bass, John	JW	0	3	330	
Bass, William	TT	0	8	400	
Bates, Abner	JW2	0	2	303	
Beadle, Augustin	JW	-	-	-	see Ward, H. "est. of"
Beasley, Amb.	JW	Beasley, George Beasley, Richd.	1	200	
Beasley, George	JW	-	-	-	see Beasley, Amb.
Beasley, John P.	TT	-	-	-	See Tabb, Thomas
Beasley, Richd.	JW	0	4	203	
Beasley, Richd.	JW	-	-	-	see Beasley, Amb.
Beckley, Humphrey	TT	-	-	-	See Tabb, Thomas
Beedles, Abram	JW	Beedles, Thos.	0	184	
Beedles, Jno.	JW	0	0	116	
Beedles, Thos.	JW	-	-	-	Beedles, Abra.
Belcher, John	JB2	-	-	-	See Palmore, Reuben
Bentley, Samuel	AE	0	0	200	
Bently, John	JB2	Ware, William	7	452	
Bently, Samuel	AE	-	-	-	See Sallard, Charles
Bently, Samuel	TT	Walden, Mason	8	700	1 riding chair
Beuford, Henry	JW	-	-	-	see Hardy, Thomas
Beuford, Herman?	JW	0	1	0	List?; smudged
Beuford, James	JW	Beuford, Warren	5	383	
Beuford, Thomas	JW	0	2	100	
Beuford, Warren	JW	-	-	-	see Beuford, James
Bevill, Daniel	JB	Bevill, Thomas	4	241	
Bevill, Joell	JB	0	3	251	
Bevill, Thomas	JB	-	-	-	See Bevill, Daniel
Bibb, William	JB2	0	9	335	
Blanchett, Isaac	JB	0	0	30	
Bland, Col. Theo.	AE	0	0	0	List
Blankingship,	AE	0	0	0	

NAME	LIST	Other white male tithes	Slaves	Acres	COMMENTS
Thomas					
Bolling, Col. Alexr.	AE	Gun, James	5	0	List
Bolling, Col. Alexr.	JW2	Jeffries, Thomas	5		List
Bolling, Col. Alexr.	JW2	Ellis, Ellison	4	1672	List
Booker, Ann	JB2	0	13	1025	List; 1 riding chair
Booker, Capt. Edm.	JW2	McCubbing, Wm	1		List
Booker, Edmund	TT	Booker, Edmund Jr. Barlow, Thomas	11	1072	
Booker, Edward	JB	0	3	200	
Booker, Edward	TT	0	9	0	List?
Booker, George	JB2	-	-	-	See Booker, Martha
Booker, George	TT	0	7	973	1 riding chair
Booker, George & Lucy	JB2	Lockett, Stephen	9	335	List
Booker, John	JB	Couzins, William	4	386	"C.House"
Booker, John	JB	Jolly, Dudley	17	1403	1 riding chair
Booker, Lowry	JB2	-	-	-	See Booker, Mary
Booker, Martha	JB2	Booker, George Booker, Richard	3	835	List
Booker, Mary	JB2	Booker, William Booker, Lowry	7	218	List
Booker, Rachel	TT	Lee, Charles	12	512	List; 1 riding chair
Booker, Richard	JB2	-	-	-	See Booker, Martha
Booker, William	JB2	-	-	-	See Booker, Mary
Borrum, Edward	JB2	??	??	??	Large ink blot obscures his entry.
Borrum, James	JB2	0	0	0	
Borrum, Richard	JB2	0	1	475	
Bott, Miles	JB	0	5	752	
Bott, William	JB	0	2	648	
Bottom, Thomas	JB	Mann, Joseph	9	1450	
Bottom, Thos. Jr.	JW	Mann, Joseph	1	485	List
Boyd, George	AE	Burgs, William	3	450	
Boyd, Walter	AE	Butler, William	6	450	List
Brackett, Thomas	TT	Brackett, Thomas Jr.	6	918	
Bradberry, Wm.	JW	-	-	-	see Harriss, James
Bradley, James	AE	0	2	0	
Bradley, James	TT	Cooper, Francis	10	953	List
Bradshaw, William	RM	0	0	0	
Branch, Benj.	JB2	Jackson, William	6	318	List
Branch, Henry	JB	Clay, Martin Vassar, John Burton, Charles	3	0	
Branch, James	JW	-	-	-	see Whitlaw, Fra.

NAME	LIST	Other white male tithes	Slaves	Acres	COMMENTS
Branch, Thomas' Est.	JB	Mann, Cain	5	390	Estate List
Brannen?, William	JW2	0	0	0	
Branton?, James	JW	-	-	-	see Dupuy, Peter Jr.
Bridgforth, Benjamin	AE	0	6	800	
Brigendine, Isaac	JW2	Brigendine, Wm	2	502	
Brigendine, Wm	JW2	-	-	-	See Brigendine, Isaac
Brintle, William	AE	-	-	-	See Epes, Francis
Brookes, Thomas Jr.	JB	0	0	0	
Brooks, George	JB	0	0	0	
Brooks, John	JB2	0	0	0	
Brooks, Thomas Sr.	JB	Brooks, William	2	550	
Brooks, William	JB	-	-	-	See Brooks, Thomas Sr.
Brown, Alexander	JB2	0	3	200	
Brown, John	JB2	Sulavant, John	2	100	
Brown, Laurence	RM	Brown, Thos.	0	200	
Brown, Thos	RM	-	-	-	See Brown, Laurence
Bruce, Alexander	RM	Bruce, John Dixon, John	8	597	
Bruce, Alexander Sr.	RM	0	1	0	
Bruce, John	RM	-	-	-	See Bruce, Alexander
Brumfield, Major	TT	0	0	200	
Brunskill, John	JB2	0	3	400	List
Bryan, John	AE	0	0	400	
Bueford, Wm.	JW2	0	1	0	Also spelled BEUFORD
Buford, Henry	JW	Buford, William Buford, James Buford, LeRoy	10	300	
Buford, James	JW	-	-	-	see Buford, Henry
Buford, LeRoy	JW	-	-	-	see Buford, Henry
Buford, William	JW	-	-	-	see Buford, Henry
Bullington, John	JB	Bullington, Robert	0	100	
Bullington, Robert	JB	-	-	-	See Bullington, John
Burgs, Thomas	AE	Burgs, William	1	500	
Burgs, William	AE	-	-	-	See Boyd, George
Burgs, William	AE	-	-	-	See Burgs, Thomas
Burks, Richd.	JW	Cunningham, Joseph	3	686	List
Burton, Abraham	TT	0	3	84	
Burton, Charles	JB	-	-	-	See Branch, Henry

NAME	LIST	Other white male tithes	Slaves	Acres	COMMENTS
Burton, John	TT	Hudson, John	11	482	
Busby, Benjamin	RM	Westbrook, Amos	4	240	List?
Butler, William	AE	-	-	-	See Boyd, Walter
Butler, William	TT	0	1	267	
Cabaness, John	JW	-	-	-	see Cabaness, Matthew Sr.
Cabaness, Matthew Sr.	JW	Cabaness, John	0	612	
Cabbiness, George	AE	0	3	347	
Cabiniss, Matthew	RM	-	-	-	See Watson, William
Caldner??, John	JW2	Mudginger, Thos	10	1143	List (name illegible)
Callicoat, James	JB2	0	3	0	
Callicoat, William	JB2	0	2	1220	
Campbell, William	TT	0	0	0	
Candlemire, John Christ.	JB2	-	-	-	See Finnie, Mary
Carruthers, Dr. Joseph	AE	Glasy?, William	8	666	List
Carter, John? ___	JB	-	-	-	See Walker, Edmund
Cavenar, Hugh	TT	-	-	-	See Anderson, Pauling
Chambers, Hugh	JW	0	3	195	
Chapman, John	TT	0	1	400	
Chapman, Samuel	TT	0	2	0	
Chappell, Robt.	JW	??	8	435	List; smudged
Chapple, James	JB2	0	7	998	
Chavis, James	AE	-	-	-	See Featherston, Lewis
Cheatam, Archer	TT	-	-	-	See Clement, William Est.
Cheatam, Leonard	TT	0	5	300	
Cheatham, James	JB2	0	3	232	
Childress, Stephen	TT	-	-	-	See Christian, Anthony
Chislom (sic), John	AE	-	-	-	See Hooper, Zachariah CHISHOLM intended?
Christian, Anthony	TT	Childress, Stephen	6	106	
Chumley, John	TT	0	0	100	
Claiborn, Philip W.	AE	Lipscomb, Charles	9	1272	List
Clark, George	AE	0	0	100	
Clark, Henry	AE	Clark, William	2	0	
Clark, John	RM	0	3	612	
Clark, Peter	RM	0	0	100	
Clark, William	AE	-	-	-	See Clark, Henry
Clarke, James	JB2	0	6	0	
Clay, Charles	AE	Clay, Isham	1	150	
Clay, Henry	RM	0	0	0	

NAME	LIST	Other white male tithes	Slaves	Acres	COMMENTS
Clay, Isham	AE	-	-	-	See Clay, Charles
Clay, Martin	JB	-	-	-	See Branch, Henry
Clay, Peter	JB2	-	-	-	See Crawley, William
Claybrook, Peter	TT	0	2	222	
Clement, Isham	TT	Land, Epharim	0	0	
Clement, John	JB2	-	-	-	See Clement, Simon
Clement, John	TT	Tabb, Edward	8	300	
Clement, Simon	JB2	Clement, John	3	234	
Clement, William Est.	TT	Cheatam, Archer White, John	5	725	"Estate of"; List
Clement, Zephaniah	JB2	-	-	-	See Swan, Thompson
Clondas?, George	JB2	0	1	0	
Clough, Richard	TT	Foster, Richard	8	654	
Cock, Stephen	AE	0	4	0	
Cocke, Abraham	AE	0	2	0	
Cocke, John	AE	-	-	-	See Cocke, Mary
Cocke, Mary	AE	Cocke, Thomas Cocke, John	8	2518	List
Cocke, Thomas	AE	-	-	-	See Cocke, Mary
Combs, Frances	JB2	0	1	150	List
Combs, George	JB2	0	3	300	
Compton, Richard	TT	-	-	-	See Scott, John
Connelly, Charles	AE	0	2	200	
Cook, Chasteen	TT	-	-	-	See Farrar, Peter
Cook, James	TT	-	-	-	See Cook, Shem Sr.
Cook, James	TT	-	-	-	See Cook, John
Cook, John	TT	Cook, Joseph Cook, James	3	1074	
Cook, Joseph	TT	-	-	-	See Cook, John
Cook, Shem Sr.	TT	Cook, James	3	0	
Cooke?, James	JB	-	-	-	See Royall, John
Cornelius, Jesse	JW	-	-	-	see Cornelius, Rebecca
Cornelius, Rebecca	JW	Cornelius, Jesse	2	0	List
Couzins, William	JB	-	-	-	See Booker, John
Covington, Chas.	JW2	-	-	-	See Covington, Wm.
Covington, Wm.	JW2	Covington, Chas.	4	290	
Cox, George (Henrico)	TT	Raiborne, George	12	964	List
Cox, Henry Jr.	TT	Allen, Samuel	2	100	
Craddock, John	JW	0	3	250	
Craddock, Richard	JW	Vaughan, John	4	385	
Craddock, Wm. Cross	JW	0	2	325	

NAME	LIST	Other white male tithes	Slaves	Acres	COMMENTS
Crain, John	RM	0	0	0	
Crain, Philemon	RM	0	0	200	
Crain, Philo. Jr.	JW	0	0	0	
Crawley, David	JB2	-	-	-	See Crawley, William
Crawley, William	JB2	Crawley, David Ellington, David Morgan, John Clay, Peter	34	3924	1 riding chair
Creek?, Richd.	JW2	Nash, Thos.	1	246	
Crenshaw, Bartho.	JW	-	-	-	see Crenshaw, Cornelius
Crenshaw, Benjamin	TT	-	-	-	See Murray, James
Crenshaw, Cornelius	JW	Crenshaw, Bartho.	3	400	Name also sp. Chrenshaw
Crenshaw, Elkanah	TT	0	4	400	
Crenshaw, James (patroller)	JW2	-	-	-	See Crenshaw, Wm. Sr.
Crenshaw, John Jr.	JW	0	1	207	
Crenshaw, Robert	JW	0	2	200	
Crenshaw, William	AE	0	2	350	
Crenshaw, Wm. Jr.	JW2	0	0	200	
Crenshaw, Wm. Sr.	JW2	Crenshaw, James (patroller)	6	800	
Crittington, Henry	JB2	Crittinton, William	0	74	Surname spelled both ways
Crittinton, William	JB2	-	-	-	See Crittington, Henry
Crowder, William	JB2	0	2	150	
Crutchfield, Henry	TT	0	0	0	
Cryer, Robert	AE	??	??	??	Smudged entry
Cryer, William	AE	White, Daniel Winter, Henry	6	700	
Cumps?, Ambrose	JB	-	-	-	See Ford, Christopher
Cumpton, Caleb	TT	-	-	-	See Cumpton, John Jr.
Cumpton, John Jr.	TT	Cumpton, Caleb Cumpton, Meredith	3	300	
Cumpton, John Sr.	TT	0	1	100	
Cumpton, Meredith	TT	-	-	-	See Cumpton, John Jr.
Cuningham, Joseph	JW	-	-	-	see Birks, Richd.
Dalby, John	TT	0	1	0	
Dalby, Nightingale	TT	0	0	674	
Davinport, George	JW	0	2	230	
Davis, Gresset	TT	-	-	-	See Tabb, Thomas
Davis, Jacob	AE	Davis, William Davis, Thomas	3	210	

NAME	LIST	Other white male tithes	Slaves	Acres	COMMENTS
Davis, James	JW	-	-	-	see Davis, William
Davis, Robert	JW2	0	0	200	
Davis, Samuel	TT	-	-	-	See Mumford, Thomas
Davis, Thomas	AE	-	-	-	See Davis, Jacob
Davis, Thomas	TT	Jones, David	0	98	
Davis, William	AE	-	-	-	See Davis, Jacob
Davis, William	JW	Davis, James	2	465	
Dearing, John	JW2	0	0	0	
Dearing, Richd.	JW2	0	0	240	
Deaton, James	TT	Howlet, Harry	0	116	Patroler
Deaton, John	TT	Deaton, Levi	1	370	Patroler
Deaton, Levi	TT	-	-	-	See Deaton, John
Deaton, William	TT	0	0	0	
Dennice, Gower	RM	0	0	0	Dennis intended??
Dennis, Henry Jr.	JW	0	4	540	
Dennis, Richard Jr.	RM	0	3		See alson Dennice
Dixon, John	RM	-	-	-	See Bruce, Alexander
Dixon, Wm.	RM	-	-	-	See Watson, William
Dobson, Thos. Jr.	JW	0	1	200	
Dobson, Thos. Sr.	JW	0	3	200	
Draper, James	AE	Draper, Wm.	0	249	
Draper, Wm.	AE	-	-	-	See Draper, James
Drinkard, Frank	AE	0	4	250	
Drinkard, John	JB	0	3	0	
Drinkwater, John	TT	Drinkwater, Josiah	0	200	
Drinkwater, Josiah	TT	-	-	-	See Drinkwater, John
Dudley, __ Estate	TT	0	0	900	Probably Marlow Dudley
Dun, John	JW2	-	-	-	See Leaton, Hugh
Dunnant, William	TT	-	-	-	See Moulson, William
Dunnavant, Clement	TT	-	-	-	See Dunnavant, Hodge
Dunnavant, Hezekiah	TT	-	-	-	See Dunnivant, William
Dunnavant, Hodge	TT	Dunnavant, Thomas Dunnavant, Clement	2	250	
Dunnavant, John	TT	-	-	-	See Dunnivant, William
Dunnavant, Norvel	TT	-	-	-	See Dunnavant, Phillip
Dunnavant, Phillip	TT	Dunnavant, Shadrack Dunnavant, Norvel	0	250	
Dunnavant, Shadrack	TT	-	-	-	See Dunnavant, Phillip

NAME	LIST	Other white male tithes	Slaves	Acres	COMMENTS
Dunnavant, Thomas	TT	-	-	-	See Dunnavant, Hodge
Dunnivant, William	TT	Dunnavant, John Dunnavant, Hezekiah	4	200	
Dupuy, Bartholomew	JW	0	5	600	
Dupuy, James	JW	-	-	-	see Dupuy, Peter
Dupuy, Jno James	JW	0	0	400	List?; "Land"; no tithes
Dupuy, John B.	JW	Maddox, Robt.	5	197	
Dupuy, Peter Jr.	JW	Branton?, James	1	188	
Dupuy, Peter Sr.	JW	Dupuy, James	4	381	
Durham, Josua	AE	-	-	-	See Eckles, Robert
Dyer, Thomas	TT	0	0	150	
Eastice, Moses Jr.	JB	0	1	0	
Eastice, Moses Sr.	TT	0	0	138	
Eastice, William	TT	0	0	0	
Eastin, William	TT	Foster, James	0	0	
Eckles, Robert	AE	Durham, Josua	0	330	
Eckles, Thomas	AE	Morgan, Robt.	0	320	
Edmonds, Francis	JW	-	-	-	see Tunstill?, Col. Richd.
Eggleston, _(smudged)	TT	-	-	-	See Eggleston, Richard
Eggleston, Joseph	JB	0	15	1200	1 riding chair
Eggleston, Richard	TT	Eggleston, _(smudged)	7	800	List
Eggleston, William	JB	0	7	300	
Ellett?, John	JW	0	3	285	name smudged
Ellington, David	JB2	-	-	-	See Crawley, William
Ellington, David	JW2	Ellington, Josiah Ellington, Hezekiah	3	1883	
Ellington, David Jr.	JW	0	2	200	
Ellington, Hezekiah	JW2	-	-	-	See Ellington, David
Ellington, Jeremiah	JW	0	2	0	
Ellington, John	JB	Ellington, William	6	1138	
Ellington, John	JB	-	-	-	See Marshall, Robert
Ellington, Josiah	JW2	-	-	-	See Ellington, David
Ellington, William	JB	-	-	-	See Ellington, John
Ellis, Ambrose	JW2	-	-	-	See Ellis, Thomas
Ellis, Ellison	JW2	-	-	-	See Bolling, Col. Alexr.
Ellis, Harderess?	JW2	-	-	-	See Ellis, Thomas
Ellis, Richd.	JW2	-	-	-	See Ellis, Thomas
Ellis, Thomas	JW2	Ellis, Ambrose Ellis, Harderess?	2	273	

NAME	LIST	Other white male tithes	Slaves	Acres	COMMENTS
		Ellis, Richd.			
Ellis, Thomas	TT	0	0	108	Patroler
Elmore, Abijah	RM	0	0	0	
Elmore, Frank	AE	0	0	0	
Elmore, Susannah	TT	0	1	166	List
Emonson, Benj.	AE	0	1	254	
Emonson, Upton	AE	0	4	385	
Epes, Francis	AE	Hellum, John Shell, John Brintle, William	17	1697	
Epes, Peter	JW	Hardy, Thomas	7	670	List
Eppes, Richard's est.	JW	0	0	750	"Estate of"
Erskine, Alexr.	AE	Riggon, Moses	8	940	
Evans, Robt.	JW2	Shelton, Josiah	4	761	List
Fairis, James	JB2	-	-	-	See Henderson, James
Fallen, Charles	AE	-	-	-	See Mainyard, Edw.
Fannen, Laughling	AE	0	0	0	
Farley, Caser	JW2	-	-	-	See Farley, Wm.
Farley, Daniel	RM	0	0	200	"Constable"
Farley, Forrist	JB2	Harper, George	3	200	List
Farley, George	JB2	0	3	268	
Farley, John James	JB2	0	0	0	
Farley, Joseph	JB2	0	6	789	
Farley, Peter's Estate	JB2	Farley, Matthew Farley, Jeremiah	1	250	List
Farley, Stephen	TT	Geers, Robert	0	0	
Farley, Stewart	JB2	Farley, Stewart	1	250	List
Farley, Stewart	JB2	-	-	-	See Farley, Stewart
Farley, William	JB2	0	4	240	
Farley, Wm.	JW2	Farley, Caser	0	200	
Farrar, Peter	TT	Roberts, Step Cook, Chasteen	13	2980	
Featherston, Charles	TT	0	1	210	
Featherston, Lewis	AE	Chavis, James	0	0	
Featherston, William Grig	AE	0	0	200	
Featherston, William Jr.	AE	0	4	200	
Featherstone, Charles	JB2	0	0	0	
Fennen, Achales	AE	Fennen, William	0	140	
Fennen, William	AE	-	-	-	See Fennen, Achales

NAME	LIST	Other white male tithes	Slaves	Acres	COMMENTS
Ferguson, Daniel	TT	0	0	0	
Ferguson, Edward	JW	0	0	0	
Ferguson, Henry	TT	-	-	-	See Thompson, Roger
Ferguson, John	JB	0	6	500	
Ferguson, Richard	JB	Jackson, Nan Jackson, Tom	0	0	
Ferguson, Robert Jr.	TT	0	0	0	
Ferguson, Robert Sr.	JB	Foster, James	6	500	List
Fields, Robert	TT	0	2	0	
Finnie, Mary	JB2	Candlemire, John Christ. Worsham, Henry	11	1294	List
FitzGerrald, Capt. Wm	AE	FitzGerrald, Wm. Jr. Paythress, Edward Vallintine, Vasil	18	1998	
FitzGerrald, Wm. Jr.	AE	-	-	-	See FitzGerrald, Capt. Wm
Fleming, Robert	JW	0	0	200	
Fletcher, Nathan	JW	Matthews, Peter	3	429	
Foler?, Mark	AE	-	-	-	See Stokes, Nathan Jr.
Ford, Abraham	RM	0	0	200	
Ford, Christopher	JB	Cumps?, Ambrose	0	0	
Ford, Culverine	TT	Meanly, Absolom	3	200	
Ford, John	JB2	0	4	402	
Ford, John Jr.	TT	Ford, William	0	834	
Ford, Reuben	JB2	0	0	300	
Ford, William	RM	0	0	142	
Ford, William	TT	0	2	0	Constable
Ford, William	TT	-	-	-	See Ford, John Jr.
Forde, Absalom	AE	-	-	-	See Forde, George
Forde, Albery	AE	0	0	100	
Forde, Frederick	AE	Forde, John	1	255	
Forde, George	AE	Forde, Richd. Forde, Absalom	1	200	
Forde, John	AE	-	-	-	See Forde, Frederick
Forde, Nathanil	AE	Howard, Alexr.	2	480	
Forde, Richd.	AE	-	-	-	See Forde, George
Forrest, Abraham	RM	0	0	297	
Forrest, Abram Jr.	JW2	-	-	-	See Forrest, Abram Sr.
Forrest, Abram Sr.	JW2	Forrest, Abram Jr.	3	200	
Forrest, Jn. Jr.	JW2	0	0	0	
Forrest, John	JW2	-	-	-	See Hurt, Moses

NAME	LIST	Other white male tithes	Slaves	Acres	COMMENTS
Forrest, John Jr.	JW	0	0	381	
Forrest, Richard	RM	0	3	480	
Forster, James	JB2	0	0	0	
Forster, William	JB2	0	0	0	
Foster, Abram Forest	JW2	-	-	-	see Foster, Geo.
Foster, Anthony	TT	-	-	-	See Foster, George
Foster, Geo.	JW2	Foster, Abram Forest Foster, James	10	1003	Names of "sons" diff than those on JW
Foster, George	TT	Foster, George Jr. Foster, Anthony Foster, Wm.	0	147	
Foster, George F.C.	JW	Foster, James Forrest Foster, Richd.	10	1003	initials "F.C." after name; unsure of meaning
Foster, James	JW2	-	-	-	See Foster, Geo.
Foster, James	TT	-	-	-	See Eastin, William
Foster, James	TT	-	-	-	See Tinsley, Thomas
Foster, James Forrest	JW	-	-	-	see Foster, George F.C.
Foster, James Sr.?	JW	0	0	0	"Springings" beside name
Foster, John	TT	-	-	-	See Foster, William
Foster, John	TT	Foster, Robert	0	0	"son of Thomas"
Foster, John	TT	-	-	-	See Foster, William Sr.
Foster, Moses	TT	-	-	-	See Foster, Thomas
Foster, Richard	TT	-	-	-	See Clough, Richard
Foster, Richd.	JW	-	-	-	see Foster, George F.C.
Foster, Robert	TT	-	-	-	See Foster, John
Foster, Robt.	JW	-	-	-	see Trabue?, John
Foster, Thomas	TT	Foster, Thomas Jr. Foster, Moses	4	600	
Foster, William	JB2	-	-	-	See James, Thomas
Foster, William	TT	Foster, John	0	100	"Sto. Creek"
Foster, William	TT	0	0	50	
Foster, William Sr.	TT	Foster, John	6	793	
Foster, Wm.	TT	-	-	-	See Foster, George
Foulkes, Joseph	JW	0	3	400	
Fowlkes, Gabriel	JW	0	9	775	
Fowlkes, Jennings?	JW	-	-	-	see Fowlkes, John
Fowlkes, John	JW	Fowlkes, Jennings?	6	975	
Freeman, Gid.	TT	-	-	-	See Tabb, Thomas
Freeman, James	JB	-	-	-	See Royall, John

NAME	LIST	Other white male tithes	Slaves	Acres	COMMENTS
Friend, Thomas	TT	Walthall, Benjamin	6	200	List
Furguson, Peleg	AE	0	2	329	
Gaites, James	JB2	-	-	-	See Harden, Erasmus
Galloway, Bitt?	AE	-	-	-	See Stokes, Robert Sr.
Garrant, John	RM	0	0	200	
Geers, Robert	TT	-	-	-	See Farley, Stephen
Geers, Thomas	JB2	-	-	-	On another's list, name clipped from top of page
George, William	RM	Hundley, John Hundley, John (Jr.?)	1	478	
Gibbs, Mary	TT	Gibbs, William	4	200	
Gibbs, Matthew	JB	Webster, William	1	100	List
Gibbs, William	TT	-	-	-	See Gibbs, Mary
Giles, William	JB2	0	9	976	1 riding chair
Gill, John	JB2	0	0	0	"lived with James Callicoat"
Gilliam, Jno. Jr.	JW	Baldwin, Jno.	6	933	List
Gilliam, John Sr.	RM	0	3	0	
Gillington, Nicholas	JB2	0	1	300	
Glasy?, William	AE	-	-	-	See Carruthers, Dr. Joseph
Gooch, John	RM	Amont, Obadiah Moor, Ruben	0	0	
Gooch, Joseph	JB2	0	2	223	
Grant, Gregory	TT	-	-	-	See Murray, James
Gray, Joseph	JW	0	2	187	
Green, Henry	AE	Lawson, John	4	303	
Green, John	TT	-	-	-	See Green, Thomas
Green, Thomas	TT	Green, John Green, Thomas Jr.	0	150	
Green, William	JB2	0	2	625	
Greenhill, Capt. David	RM	0	2	0	List?
Greenwood, William	TT	-	-	-	See Tabb, Thomas
Grigg, Josiah	AE	0	3	186	
Gun, James	AE	-	-	-	See Bolling, Col. Alexr.
Gunn, Thomas	JW2	Gunn, Thomas Jr.	2	150	
Gunn, Thomas Jr.	JW2	-	-	-	See Gunn, Thomas
Ha_____, William	TT	0	0	0	Entry smudged; HAMM?
Hagard, John	RM	-	-	-	See Munford, Robert

NAME	LIST	Other white male tithes	Slaves	Acres	COMMENTS
Hall, John	JW	Hall, Stephen	4	529	
Hall, Stephen	JW	-	-	-	see Hall, John
Hall, Thomas	JB2	0	3	185	
Hall, William	JB2	0	5	275	
Ham, Thomas	TT	0	0	2??	Entry smudged
Hamack, Benadict	AE	0	0	90	
Hamack, Benadict Jr.	AE	0	0	0	
Hamer, Edward	AE	0	0	90	
Hamer, William	AE	Hamer, William Jr.	0	150	
Hames, John	AE	Hames, William	2	496	
Hames, William	AE	-	-	-	See Hames, John
Hamlin, William	AE	0	1	275	
Hamm, George Jr.	TT	0	0	0	
Hamm, George Sr.	TT	0	1	150	
Hamm, Thomas	TT	-	-	-	See Tabb, Thomas
Hammon, Joshua	AE	-	-	-	See Hammon, Lewis
Hammon, Lewis	AE	Hammon, Joshua	1	200	
Handcock, George	TT	0	8	220	
Hanks, James	AE	0	0	100	
Hanks, Richd.	AE	0	0	242	
Hanse, Hendrick	JB	0	6	0	
Hardaway, Col. Stith	RM	0	4	0	List
Hardaway, Daniel	JB	-	-	-	See Hardaway, Stith
Hardaway, Joseph	JB	Young, Stephen	3	290	List
Hardaway, Stith	JB	Hardaway, Daniel Hardaway, Stith Willson, Mumford	21	1538	
Hardaway, Stith	JB	-	-	-	See Hardaway, Stith
Harden, Erasmus	JB2	Gaites, James	3	150	List
Hardisay, James	JW2	Moore, William	3	300	List
Hardy, "Estate"	JW	Hardy, Covington	3	250	"Hardy's Est. Tithes"
Hardy, Covington	JW	-	-	-	see Hardy, "Estate"
Hardy, Thomas	JW	-	-	-	see Epes, Peter
Hardy, Thomas	JW	Beuford, Henry	0	100	List
Harper, Binah?'s List	JW	Harper, Jno. Patrolm.?	4	200	List
Harper, Jno. Patrolm.?	JW	-	-	-	see Harper, Binah?'s List
Harper, Joseph	AE	Smith, Matthew	1	200	List
Harper, William	JW	0	0	150	
Harris, Daniel	TT	-	-	-	See Wayles, John
Harris, John	TT	0	0	50	

NAME	LIST	Other white male tithes	Slaves	Acres	COMMENTS
Harris, William	TT	0	0	0	
Harrison, Nathaniel	JB	Roach, Millington	??	??	Entry smudged
Harrison, William	RM	Richardson, Ruler?	7	575	List
Harriss, James	JW	Bradberry, Wm.	1	200	
Hart, William	JB	Newbell, William	2	0	
Hasken, Joseph	TT	-	-	-	See Wood, William
Hatchett, Archibald	JB2	-	-	-	See Hatchett, William
Hatchett, John	JB2	Roberts, Thomas	2	50	
Hatchett, William	JB2	Hatchett, Archibald	3	150	
Hatchett, William	TT	-	-	-	See Tabb, Thomas
Hathway, Frank	AE	0	1	100	
Hatte?, James	RM	0	1	137	
Hawkins, Zaceriah	JB2	0	0	0	
Hayes, John	TT	-	-	-	See Mumford, Thomas
Haynes, Anthony Est.	AE	Barker, Charles	5	792	"Estate of"
Hellum, John	AE	-	-	-	See Epes, Francis
Henderson, James	JB2	Pride, Rowlett Fairis, James	3	0	
Hendrick, Benj. Jr.	JB	0	1	200	
Hendrick, Benj. Sr.	JB	Hendrick, Bernard	6	300	
Hendrick, Bernard	JB	-	-	-	See Hendrick, Benj. Sr.
Hendrick, Nathaniel	JW	0	1	200	
Herskine, Christopher	AE	Walthall, Francis	5	400	1 riding chair
Hicks, Alles	TT	-	-	-	See Southall, William
Hightower, Charles	RM	-	-	-	See Hightower, Joshua Sr.
Hightower, George	AE	Thorn, Thomas	2	376	
Hightower, John	AE	Hightower, Yapodee?	4	300	
Hightower, Joshua Jr.	AE	Kirkland, John	3	450	
Hightower, Joshua Sr.	RM	Hightower, Charles	5	200	
Hightower, Richd.	AE	-	3	250	
Hightower, Thomas	AE	0	2	100	
Hightower, Yapodee?	AE	-	-	-	See Hightower, John
Hill, Isaac	TT	0	0	0	
Hill, James Est.	TT	Robertson, George	11	1375	"Estate"; List
Hill, Joell	TT	0	0	0	
Hill, John Jr.	AE	0	1	200	

NAME	LIST	Other white male tithes	Slaves	Acres	COMMENTS
Hill, John Jr.	TT	0	0	0	
Hill, John Sr.	TT	0	1	0	
Hillsman, William	JB2	0	1	100	
Hines, James	JW	0	1	0	
Hinson, Nimrod	JW	-	-	-	see Shelton, Daniel
Hinton, Wood	RM	-	-	-	See Ragsdale, Robert
Hobs, Nathaniel	AE	Watts?, John	2	92	List; HOBBS intended?
Holland, Chales?	JW2	Holland, Joseph	3	*	"same land as last year"
Holland, George	JW2	-	-	-	See Sneed, Wm.
Holloway, William	AE	0	0	100	
Holt, David	JB	Young, Allen Ridley	8	290	List
Holt, David	JW	-	-	-	see Holt, Richd.
Holt, Dibdell	RM	Holt, William Cocke	3	200	List
Holt, Richd.	JW	Holt, David Holt, Shad(rack)	0	150	
Holt, Shad(rack)	JW	-	-	-	see Holt, Richd.
Holt, Thomas	JB2	-	-	-	See Worsham, Thomas
Holt, William Cocke	RM	-	-	-	See Holt, Dibdell
Hooper, Zachariah	AE	Irby, William Chislom (sic), John	0	0	
Hopkins, Francis	TT	0	3	0	
Hoskins?, John	JW2	0	1	108	
Howard, Alexr.	AE	-	-	-	See Forde, Nathanil
Howell, Stephen	TT	0	0	100	
Howlet, Harry	TT	-	-	-	See Deaton, James
Howlett, William	JB2	0	4	148	
Howson, John	JW	0	4	370	
Hubbard, Benjamin	TT	0	1	100	
Hubbard, John	TT	0	0	?	Entry smudged
Hubbard, Joseph	TT	0	1	140	
Huddleston, Tom	JB	-	-	-	See Morgan, John
Hudson, Christopher	TT	Matlock, George	17	0	Smudged entry
Hudson, Hall	RM	Hudson, Obadiah	2	530	
Hudson, James	JW	0	2	125	
Hudson, John	JW2	0	0	200	
Hudson, John	TT	-	-	-	See Burton, John
Hudson, Joshua	RM	0	0	0	
Hudson, Nicholas	TT	0	8	??	Entry clipped off
Hudson, Obadiah	RM	-	-	-	See Hudson, Hall
Hudson, Peter	JW	0	1	100	
Hudson, Richard	RM	0	0	0	
Hudson, Thomas	JW	0	0	200	

NAME	LIST	Other white male tithes	Slaves	Acres	COMMENTS
Hudson, Ward	RM	0	3	125	
Hughes, John	JB	Jones, William	5	200	List
Hughes, William	AE	0	0	200	
Hulm, Chas.	JW	-	-	-	see Anderson, John
Hundley, Anthony	JW	0	1	166	
Hundley, Charles Sr.	JW	Hundley, Chas. Jr.	4	322	
Hundley, Chas. Jr.	JW	-	-	-	see Hundley, Charles Sr.
Hundley, John	JW	0	1	260	
Hundley, John	RM	-	-	-	See George, William
Hundley, Josiah	JW	Nelson, Matthew	5	600	
Hurt, Abraham	TT	0	0	0	
Hurt, Benj.	JW	-	-	-	see Hurt, William
Hurt, Joel	JW	0	0	200	
Hurt, John	TT	0	0	200	
Hurt, Moses	JW2	Forrest, John	8	300	
Hurt, Moses Jr.	AE	0	0	160	
Hurt, William	JW	Hurt, Benj. Hurt, Wm.	4	200	
Hurt, William	TT	Smith, James	6	463	
Hurt, Wm.	JW	-	-	-	see Hurt, William
Hutchason, Charles	TT	-	-	-	See Tabb, Thomas
Hutchason, Drury	TT	-	-	-	See Hutchason, William
Hutchason, William	TT	Hutchason, Drury	0	100	
Hutcheson, Chas.	JW	Hutcheson, Peter	2	200	
Hutcheson, Peter	JW	-	-	-	see Hutcheson, Chas.
Irby, Charles	JW2	0	6	400	
Irby, Susanah	JW2	Sneed, Zack	6	560	List
Irby, William	AE	-	-	-	See Hooper, Zachariah
Jackson James	JW2	-	-	-	See Jackson, Thos.
Jackson, Arthur	JW2	0	0	0	
Jackson, Charles	AE	0	0	600	
Jackson, Daniel	AE	-	-	-	See Jackson, William
Jackson, Daniel	AE	-	-	-	See Jackson, Edward
Jackson, Danl.	JW2	-	-	-	See Jackson, John
Jackson, Edward	AE	Jackson, Daniel	2	884	
Jackson, Francis	JB2	Jackson, Josiah	0	200	
Jackson, Francis	TT	Jackson, Rowland Jackson, Josiah	1	160	
Jackson, Joell	JB2	Roberts, John	3	250	
Jackson, John	JW2	-	-	-	See Jackson, Martn?
Jackson, John	JW2	Jackson, Danl.	2	590	
Jackson, John	RM	-	-	-	See Jackson, Thos.
Jackson, John Jr.	JW2	0	0	0	

NAME	LIST	Other white male tithes	Slaves	Acres	COMMENTS
Jackson, Joseph	TT	0	0	200	
Jackson, Josiah	JB2	-	-	-	See Jackson, Francis
Jackson, Josiah	TT	-	-	-	See Jackson, Francis
Jackson, Martn?	JW2	Jackson, John	0	0	
Jackson, Matthew	JB2	Jackson, Matthew (Jr.?)	3	200	
Jackson, Nan	JB	-	-	-	See Ferguson, Richard
Jackson, Rowland	TT	-	-	-	See Jackson, Francis
Jackson, Thos.	JW2	Jackson James	0	200	
Jackson, Thos.	RM	Jackson, John	1	600	
Jackson, Tom	JB	-	-	-	See Ferguson, Richard
Jackson, William	AE	Jackson, William Jr. Jackson, Daniel	3	1131	
Jackson, William	TT	0	2	354	
James, Lucy	JB	0	4	0	No individuals listed
James, Thomas	JB2	Foster, William	2	200	
Jeffries, Thomas	JW2	-	-	-	See Bolling, Col. Alexr.
Jeffries, Thomas	JW2	Admerson?, John	6	449	List
Jenkins, James	TT	0	5	420	
Jennings, __	JW	-	-	-	see Jennings, William Sr.?
Jennings, James	JW	0	0	0	
Jennings, John	JW	Thompson, Robt.	8	320	
Jennings, William Sr.?	JW	Jennings, __	5	200	
Jesse, John	TT	-	-	-	See Kennon, Wm. Estate
Jeter, Oliver	JW	Jeter, Sam Jeter, Thomas	0	0	
Jeter, Sam	JW	-	-	-	see Jeter, Oliver
Jeter, Thomas	JW	-	-	-	see Jeter, Oliver
Johns, John	RM	Johns, John Jr.	3	300	
Johnson, Archer	TT	-	-	-	See Tabb, Thomas
Johnson, Ashley	JW2	0	1	125	
Johnson, Gerrard	JW2	0	1	425	
Johnson, Isham	TT	-	-	-	See Johnson, Richard
Johnson, James	JB2	-	-	-	See Worsham, John Berk?
Johnson, James	JW2	0	1	0	
Johnson, James?	TT	-	-	-	See Johnson, Richard
Johnson, Jesse	JW2	0	1	123	
Johnson, John	JB2	-	-	-	See Neal, David
Johnson, John	JW2	0	0	125	
Johnson, John	RM	-	-	-	See Osbern, William

NAME	LIST	Other white male tithes	Slaves	Acres	COMMENTS
Johnson, John	TT	-	-	-	See Phillis, Richard
Johnson, Richard	TT	Johnson, James? Johnson, Isham	0	0	
Johnson, Stephen	JW2	0	0	1	
Johnson, William	TT	0	4	300	
Jolly, Dudley	JB	-	-	-	See Booker, John
Jones, Benjamin	JW2	0	4	200	
Jones, David	TT	-	-	-	See Davis, Thomas
Jones, Field Thomas	JB2	0	0	0	
Jones, Henry	AE	0	1	0	
Jones, Maj. Richard	RM	Jones, Richard Jr. Wilson, Richard	19	1795	List
Jones, Nelson	AE	Shelton, James	8	0	1 riding chair
Jones, Nottoway	RM	-	-	-	See Jones, Thomas
Jones, Richard	TT	Jones, William Jones, Richard (Jr.?)	4	200	
Jones, Richard	TT	-	-	-	See Tabb, Thomas
Jones, Richard "Overseer"	TT	0	0	195	No tithe
Jones, Richard Jr.	RM	-	-	-	See Jones, Maj. Richard
Jones, Robert	TT	Ballard, Moreman	5	400	
Jones, Thomas	RM	Jones, Nottoway	3	200	
Jones, Thos.	JW	0	3	300	
Jones, Uriah	TT	-	-	-	See Tabb, Thomas
Jones, William	AE	0	5	393	
Jones, William	JB	-	-	-	See Hughes, John
Jones, William	JB2	0	0	0	
Jones, William	TT	-	-	-	See Jones, Richard
Jones, Wm.	JW2	0	0	0	
Jordan, __ Estate	AE	Phillips, Joseph	7	0	No given name;estate of
Jordan, Absolem	TT	0	0	0	
Jordan, Edward	JW2	0	0	400	
Jordan, Joseph	TT	0	0	430	
Jordan, Sam "Est"	JW	0	0	1110	"Est. of"
Jurdan, Samuel	AE	-	-	-	See Jurdan, William
Jurdan, William	AE	Jurdan, William Jr. Jurdan, Samuel	7	360	
Kennon, Wm. Estate	TT	Jesse, John	8	1000	List
Kincher, John	JB2	0	0	0	
King, John	TT	-	-	-	See Tabb, Thomas
Kinnon, Wm.	JW2	0	0	170	
Kirkland, John	AE	-	-	-	See Hightower, Joshua

NAME	LIST	Other white male tithes	Slaves	Acres	COMMENTS
					Jr.
Land, Epharim	TT	-	-	-	See Clement, Isham
Lankaster?, John	JW2	??	??	??	Smudged
Lawson, John	AE	-	-	-	See Green, Henry
Lawson, Robert	JW2	-	-	-	See Peachy, Thos. Griffin
Lea, William	JW2	0	6	662	
Leath, Arthur	AE	Waller, William	6	839	
Leath, Peter	AE	Pace, Frank	3	400	
Leaton, Hugh	JW2	Dun, John	0	350	
Lee, Charles	TT	-	-	-	Booker, Rachel
Lewis, David	AE	0	1	0	List
Lewis, Frank	AE	0	3	400	
Lewis, Griffin	AE	0	3	225	
Lewis, John	AE	0	1	360	
Lewis, John	AE	0	3	0	
Liggon, Robert	JB	-	-	-	See Liggon, William
Liggon, Thomas	JB	0	1	300	
Liggon, William	JB	Liggon, William Jr. Liggon, Robert	11	1115	
Liggon, William Jr.	JB	-	-	-	See Liggon, William
Ligon, Richd.	JW2	-	-	-	See Bagley, Geo.
Lipscomb, Ambrose	AE	0	0	144	
Lipscomb, Charles	AE	-	-	-	See Claiborn, Philip W.
Loafman, John	TT	-	-	-	See Walthall, Thomas
Lockett, Abraham	TT	-	-	-	See Lockett, Benjamin
Lockett, Benjamin	TT	Lockett, Abraham	2	239	
Lockett, James	JW	0	2	200	
Lockett, Stephen	JB2	-	-	-	See Booker, George-Lucy
Lockett, Thomas	TT	0	0	100	
Long, George	AE	0	1	375	
Lorton, John	TT	-	-	-	See Lorton, Thomas
Lorton, Thomas	TT	Lorton, John Walden, John	4	400	List
Lovell, David	JW2	0	0	100	
Lovesay, Bolling	AE	-	-	-	See Lovesay, Richd.
Lovesay, Richd.	AE	Lovesay, Bolling	1	150	
Loving, James	TT	0	0	0	
Loving, William	TT	0	0	100	
Lowry, Thomas	JW	-	-	-	see Tabb, Col. Thos.
Lowry, Thos.	JW	0	1	0	1 chair wheels; List
Lumkin, Dickerson	JW2	0	1	0	

NAME	LIST	Other white male tithes	Slaves	Acres	COMMENTS
Lumkin, Peter	JW2	0	1	200	
Maddox, Robt.	JW	-	-	-	see Dupuy, John B.
Mainyard, Edw.	AE	Mainyard, John Fallen, Charles	0	200	
Mainyard, John	AE	-	-	-	See Mainyard, Edw.
Major, Philip	JB	0	3	150	
Manier, John	AE	0	0	0	
Manior, William	AE	Manior, William Jr.	1	100	See also Manier
Mann, Cain	JB	-	-	-	See Branch, Thomas' Est.
Mann, Cattlet?	JW	Mann, James	3	390	
Mann, Charles	TT	0	0	0	
Mann, Field	JB	-	-	-	See Mann, Robert
Mann, James	JB	-	-	-	See Mann, Samuel
Mann, James	JW	-	-	-	see Mann, Cattlet?
Mann, Joseph	JB	-	-	-	See Bottom, Thomas
Mann, Joseph	JW	-	-	-	see Bottom, Thos. Jr.
Mann, Robert	JB	Mann, Field	1	150	
Mann, Samuel	JB	Mann, James	0	150	
Mann, Samuel Jr.	JB	0	0	0	
Marshall, Alexr.	JW	0	3	400	
Marshall, Robert	JB	Ellington, John	11	796	
Marshall, Wm	JB	0	3	400	
Marshall, Wm. Jr.	JB	0	4	400	
Martin, George	JW	0	5	200	
Martin, Thomas	JB	0	0	0	
Mason, John	TT	0	0	0	
Mason, Joseph	TT	0	2	0	
Matlock, George	TT	-	-	-	See Hudson, Christopher
Matthews, Peter	JW	-	-	-	see Fletcher, ___
May, Henry	AE	-	-	-	See May, William Jr.
May, James	RM	-	-	-	See May, John
May, John	AE	-	-	-	See May, William
May, John	RM	May, James	3	224	
May, William	AE	May, John	4	900	
May, William Jr.	AE	May, Henry	0	0	
Mayes, Daniel	JB	-	-	-	See Mayes, Gardner
Mayes, Gardner	JB	Mayes, Daniel	0	0	
Mayes, Matt	JW	0	0	200	
McCubbing, Wm	JW2	-	-	-	See Brooking, Capt. Edm.
McDearman, Bryan	RM	0	0	0	
McKinny, Francis	AE	0	0	125	

NAME	LIST	Other white male tithes	Slaves	Acres	COMMENTS
McNabb, Alexander	TT	-	-	-	See Tabb, Thomas
Meadow, ____	TT	(given name smudged)	-	-	See Wright, John
Meadow, Henry	TT	0	0	0	
Meadow, Jeremiah	TT	0	0	124	
Meadow, Jeremiah	TT	-	-	-	See Meadow, Joell
Meadow, Jeremiah	TT	-	-	-	See Wright, Thomas Sr.
Meadow, Joell	TT	Meadow, Joell Jr. Meadow, Jeremiah	0	225	
Meadow, John	TT	-	-	-	See Robertson, George
Meanly, Absolom	TT	-	-	-	See Ford, Culverine
Milliner, John Jr.	JW	-	-	-	see Milliner, John Sr.
Milliner, John Sr.	JW	Milliner, William Milliner, John Jr.	1	285	
Milliner, Richd.	JW	0	0	0	
Milliner, William	JW	-	-	-	see Milliner, John Sr.
Minor, James	TT	0	0	0	
Mitchel, Thomas	RM	0	0	0	
Mitchel, William	RM	0	0	0	
Mitchel?, James	JW	Mitchell, Anderson	3	500	
Mitchell, Anderson	JW	-	-	-	see Mitchel?, James
Mitchell, Evans	JB	-	-	-	See Archer, William
Mitchell, John	JW	0	1	200	
Moh___, Jno.	JW	-	-	-	see Smith, Covington
Moody, Arthur	JW	-	-	-	see Smith, Covington
Moody, Jas.	JW	-	-	-	see Smith, Covington
Moor, Ruben	RM	-	-	-	See Gooch, John
Moore, David	JW2	0	2	300	
Moore, William	JW2	-	-	-	See Hardisay, James
Moores, James	AE	0	1	0	
More, George	AE	-	-	-	
More, John	AE	More, William	0	275	
More, Mark	AE	0	0	0	
More, William	AE	-	-	-	See More, John
Morgan, Jacob	AE	Morgan, Jacob P. Whitworth, William	19	905	
Morgan, Jacob P.	AE	-	-	-	See Morgan, Jacob
Morgan, John	AE	0	0	45	
Morgan, John	JB	Huddleston, Tom	2	150	List
Morgan, John	JB2	-	-	-	See Crawley, William
Morgan, Robert	JW	-	-	-	see Royall, Richd.'s tithes
Morgan, Robt.	AE	-	-	-	See Eckles, Thomas

NAME	LIST	Other white male tithes	Slaves	Acres	COMMENTS
Morgan, Samuel	JB	Morgan, William	4	688	
Morgan, Thomas	AE	0	0	400	
Morgan, William	JB	-	-	-	See Morgan, Samuel
Morris, Isaac	TT	-	-	-	See Wayles, John
Morris, Mary	TT	Morris, Syl	6	1200	List
Morris, Syl	TT	-	-	-	See Morris, Mary
Motley, Joel	JW	-	-	-	see Motley, Joseph Sr.
Motley, Joseph Jr.	JW	0	6	691	
Motley, Joseph Sr.	JW	Motley, Joel	6	600	
Moulson, William	TT	Dunnant, William	16	1070	
Mudginger, Thos	JW2	-	-	-	See Ca____, John
Mumford, Thomas	TT	Davis, Samuel Hayes, John	12	1340	1 riding chair
Munford, Robert	RM	Piles, Williamson Hagard, John	16	1640	2 riding chairs
Munford, Thos. Ball	JW	Munford, William	11	743	List?
Munford, William	JW	-	-	-	see Munford, Thos. Ball
Murray, James	TT	Grant, Gregory Crenshaw, Benjamin	20	4622	List
Murry, Daniel	JB	0	0	0	
Name clipped	JB2	Geers, Thomas	11	1100	Clipped from top of page
Nance, Aplus?	JW	0	2	75	
Nance, David	JW	-	-	-	see Nance, John
Nance, John	JW	Nance, David	0	121	
Nash, Thos.	JW2	-	-	-	See Creek?, Richd.
Navier, James	JW	-	-	-	see Robertson, Henry
Neal, David	JB2	Johnson, John	5	200	
Neal, Joell	JB	-	-	-	See Neal, William??
Neal, John	JB	-	-	-	See Neal, William??
Neal, Stephen	JB2	0	2	100	
Neal, Thomas' Estate	JB2	0	0	266	
Neal, William??	JB	Neal, Joell Neal, John	??	??	Bottom line of entry cut off
Nelson, Matthew	JW	-	-	-	see Hundley, Josiah
Newbell, William	JB	-	-	-	See Hart, William
Nichola, Zachariah	TT	0	1	0	
Noble, Joseph	TT	0	0	200	
Norvele, Holdcraft	JB2	0	0	0	
Norvill, John	JW	0	2	202	
Oakley, Richd?	JW2	-	-	-	See Oakley, Thos.
Oakley, Thos, Jr.	JW2	-	-	-	See Oakley, Thos.

NAME	LIST	Other white male tithes	Slaves	Acres	COMMENTS
Oakley, Thos.	JW2	Oakley, Richd? Oakley, Thos, Jr.	0	100	
Oasley?, Thomas	JB	-	-	-	See Walker, Edmund
Ogilby, John	JB2	0	6	611	
Oliver, Isaac	RM	-	-	-	See Oliver, James
Oliver, James	RM	Oliver, Isaac	8	1000	
Ormsby, Matthew	AE	0	0	25	
Osbern, William	RM	Johnson, John	6	0	Osborne intended?
Osborne, Francis	JB2	Westbrook, William	4	400	List
Osborne, George	TT	0	0	0	
Osborne, Joseph	JB2	0	7	850	
Osborne, William	JB2	Osborne, William Jr.	11	1170	
Osborne, William Jr	JB2	-	-	-	See Osborne, William
Osburn?, Thos.	JW2	0	2	0	Illegible
Overstreet, Thomas	JW	0	0	0	
Overton, Jno.	JW	-	-	-	see Overton, Moses
Overton, Moses	JW	Overton, Jno.	2	365	
Owen, Natt	JW2	0	0	0	
Pace, Frank	AE	-	-	-	See Leath, Peter
Pace, William	JW2	0	1	497	"Patroler"? next to name
Page, John	JW	-	-	-	see Vaughn, Thomas
Page, Nat	JW	0	1	396	
Palmore, Reuben	JB2	Belcher, John	2	324	
Parrott, John	JW2	0	0	100	
Pavory, Thomas	AE	0	1	100	
Payne, Thomas	JW	0	2	334	
Paythress, Capt. Peter	AE	Morton, John	7	585	List
Paythress, Edward	AE	-	-	-	See FitzGerrald, Capt. Wm
Peachy, Thos. Griffin	JW2	Lawson, Robert Spain, David	8	1720	1 riding chair
Pendleton, Jno.	JW	0	0	400	
Perdue, Josiah	AE	0	0	0	
Perkinson, Jeremiah	JB2	-	-	-	See Perkinson, Seth
Perkinson, Matthew	JB2	0	0	231	
Perkinson, Ralph	JB2	0	1	187	
Perkinson, Seth	JB2	Perkinson, Jeremiah	1	242	"Constable"
Phillips, John	JW2	-	-	-	See Phillips, Thomas
Phillips, Joseph	AE	-	-	-	See Jordan, ___ Estate
Phillips, Thomas	JW2	Phillips, John	0	800	
Phillis, Richard	TT	Johnson, John	3	150	
Piles, Williamson	RM	-	-	-	See Munford, Robert

NAME	LIST	Other white male tithes	Slaves	Acres	COMMENTS
Pincham, Peter	RM	0	5	200	
Pincham, Samuel	JB2	0	3	816	
Pincham, Samuel	RM	0	3	268	List?
Pinnix?, Joseph	JW	0	0	204	no tithe listed
Pollard, Henry	TT	0	2	0	
Pollard, Joseph	TT	0	1	140	
Pollard, Thomas	TT	0	2	150	
Ponton, William	TT	-	-	-	See Williamson, Frances
Porter, James	TT	0	0	100	
Powel, John	AE	0	0	222	
Powell, Henry Estate	TT	0	0	160	
Powell, Thomas	AE	-	-	-	See Wilkerson, Rev. Thomas
Powell, Thomas	TT	0	2	200	
Presnall, James	JW	Presnall, James Jr.	2	250	
Presnall, James Jr.	JW	-	-	-	see Presnall, James
Pride, Francis	JB2	-	-	-	See Pride, John
Pride, John	JB2	Pride, Francis	5	400	
Pride, John Jr.	JB2	Stone, Elijah	7	386	List
Pride, Rowlett	JB2	-	-	-	See Henderson, James
Pride, William	JB2	0	1	300	
Pringle, Richard	TT	-	-	-	See Tabb, Thomas
Pryor, John "Richmond"	RM	Ward, Thomas	8	550	2 riding chairs
Pucket, Edward	RM	-	-	-	See Tomson, Isham
Puckett, James	TT	-	-	-	See Puckett, Richard
Puckett, Richard	TT	Puckett, James	2	100	
Pulliam, Jennings	JW	-	-	-	see Pulliam, William
Pulliam, William	JW	Pulliam, Jennings	2	340	
Purdie, Aaron	JW	-	-	-	see Smith, Covington
Quarles, Richard	AE	0	0	100	
Quisingbary, John	RM	-	-	-	See Quisingbary, Nicholas
Quisingbary, Nicholas	RM	Quisingbary, John	1	0	
Radford, Andrew	RM	0	6	200	
Ragsdale, George	TT	0	1	100	
Ragsdale, Robert	RM	Short, Thomas Hinton, Wood Tomson, Thos.	11	600	List?
Raiborne, George	TT	-	-	-	See Cox, George (Henrico)
Randolph, Henry	JB	0	19	1053	1 riding chair
Ray, James	RM	-	-	-	See Ray, John

NAME	LIST	Other white male tithes	Slaves	Acres	COMMENTS
Ray, John	RM	Ray, James	0	0	
Rea, James	JW2	0	0	396	
Reams, Frederick	JB	-	-	-	See Reams, Thomas
Reams, Thomas	JB	Reams, Frederick	1	150	
Renolds, Thomas	RM	0	0	0	
Richardson, Ruler?	RM	-	-	-	See Harrison, William
Riggon, Moses	AE	-	-	-	See Erskine, Alexr.
Roach, Millington	JB	-	-	-	See Harrison, Nathaniel
Roberts, Francis	JB	Roberts, John	2	250	
Roberts, John	JB	-	-	-	See Roberts, Francis
Roberts, John	JB2	-	-	-	See Jackson, Joell
Roberts, Sarah	JB	Willshire, Henry	2	300	List
Roberts, Step	TT	-	-	-	See Farrar, Peter
Roberts, Thomas	JB2	-	-	-	See Hatchett, John
Roberts, William	JB	0	0	0	
Robertson, Christopher	JW	-	-	-	see Robertson, Henry
Robertson, Edward	JW	Robertson, John	5	410	
Robertson, George	TT	-	-	-	See Hill, James Est.
Robertson, George	TT	Meadow, John	4	558	List
Robertson, Henry	JW	Navier, James Robertson, Christopher	5	1812	
Robertson, James	TT	Stewart, William	14	1461	Estate; List
Robertson, John	JW	-	-	-	see Robertson, Edward
Robertson, John Est.	TT	Sears, Thomas	11	1600	List
Robertson, Natha	JW2	Robertson, Richd.	6	1061	"Cons__" by name
Robertson, Robert	TT	0	0	0	
Rowlett, George	JB	0	0	116.5	
Royall, John	JB	Cooke?, James Freeman, James	10	960	
Royall, Joseph	JB	Truehill, Levy	5	400	List
Royall, Richd.'s tithes	JW	Morgan, Robert	4	0	LIST
Rucker, Elisha	JB	-	-	-	See Rucker, William Sr.
Rucker, James	JB	-	-	-	See Rucker, William Jr.
Rucker, Joshua	JB	-	-	-	See Rucker, William Jr.
Rucker, Mordaca	JB	-	-	-	See Rucker, William Sr.
Rucker, William Jr.	JB	Rucker, Joshua Rucker, James	0	0	
Rucker, William Sr.	JB	Rucker, Elisha Rucker, Mordaca	4	600	
Sadler, John	TT	0	2	0	

NAME	LIST	Other white male tithes	Slaves	Acres	COMMENTS
Sallard, Charles	AE	Bently, Samuel	11	1000	
Scott, George	JB2	0	0	0	
Scott, John	TT	Compton, Richard	9	1400	
Scott, John & Company	TT	0	0	96	
Scott, Roger	JB2	Truly, Peter	2	957	
Seamon, John	AE	0	0	96	
Sears, Thomas	TT	-	-	-	See Robertson, John Est
Seay, Jacob	TT	Barry, Peter	5	545	
Seay, James	RM	0	0	150	
Seay, James Sr.	TT	0	2	393	
Seay, Moses	TT	0	1	200	
See, Gideon	JB2	-	-	-	See See, Jese
See, Jese (sic)	JB2	See, Gideon	3	200	
Shannon, William	JB2	0	0	200	"Deceased"
Sharratt, John	RM	0	0	100	
Shell, John	AE	-	-	-	See Epes, Francis
Shelton, Ben Jr.	AE	-	-	-	See Shelton, James
Shelton, Benjamin	JW	0	0	100	
Shelton, Beverly	JW	-	-	-	see Shelton, Crispin
Shelton, Crispin	JW	Shelton, Beverly	4	362	
Shelton, Daniel	JW	Hinson, Nimrod	1	140	
Shelton, James	AE	-	-	-	See Jones, Nelson
Shelton, James	AE	Shelton, Ben Jr.	2	109	List
Shelton, John	JW	0	1	169	
Shelton, Josiah	JW2	-	-	-	See Evans, Robt.
Sherwin, Sam	RM	Ward, Richd.	8	801	
Short, Thomas	RM	-	-	-	See Ragsdale, Robert
Simmons, Benj.	AE	Simmons, Thos.	2	183	
Simmons, John	AE	0	0	0	
Simmons, Thos.	AE	-	-	-	See Simmons, Benj.
Smith, ____	JB2	Smith, John	6	224	Name clipped
Smith, Capt. Abraham	AE	Muse, William	4	444	List
Smith, Covington	JW	Purdie, Aaron Moody, Jas. Moh___, Jno. Moody, Arthur	1	300	
Smith, George	JB	0	0	0	
Smith, George	JW	0	1	0	
Smith, Griffin	JW2	-	-	-	See Smith, Saml.
Smith, Isaac	JW2	-	-	-	See Smith, Saml.
Smith, James	TT	-	-	-	See Hurt, William
Smith, Jno. Fors.	JW	0	3	0	
Smith, John	JB2	-	-	-	See Walthall, William Jr.

NAME	LIST	Other white male tithes	Slaves	Acres	COMMENTS
Smith, John	JW	Smith, Owen	2	200	
Smith, Matthew	AE	-	-	-	See Harper, Joseph
Smith, Owen	JW	-	-	-	see Smith, John
Smith, Richard	JW	Swinney, Thomas Swinney, Joseph Banden?, James	2	112	
Smith, Saml.	JW2	Smith, Griffin Smith, Isaac	7	960	
Smith, Thomas	JW2	0	0	0	
Snead, James	AE	-	-	-	See Stokes, Robert Sr.
Sneed, Wm.	JW2	Holland, George Thompson, Nedcip?	0	25	"Patroler" by name; exempt from his tithe
Sneed, Zack	JW2	-	-	-	See Irby, Susanah
Solomon, John	JB	-	-	-	See Wily, William
Southall, James	JB	0	0	0	
Southall, John	TT	-	-	-	See Southall, William
Southall, William	TT	Southall, John Hicks, Alles	0	255	
Spain, David	JW2	-	-	-	See Peachy, Thos. Griffin
St. John, William	AE	0	3	600	
Standley, Joshua	JW	-	-	-	see Standley, William
Standley, Thomas	JW2	0	0	0	
Standley, William	JW	Standley, Joshua	2	150	
Standly, James	AE	0	1	0	
Starn, Ann	TT	0	6	370	List
Starn, John	TT	0	0	0	
Stearman, Valentine	TT	0	0	0	
Stearman, Wm.	JB	-	-	-	See Walthall, Daniel
Still, George Jr.	AE	0	0	289	
Stoe, William	AE	Stoe, Jack	0	120	STOW intended?
Stokes, Mathew	AE	0	0	281	
Stokes, Nathan Jr.	AE	Foler?, Mark	0	0	
Stokes, Robert Sr.	AE	Snead, James Galloway, Bitt?	0	300	List
Stone, Elijah	JB2	-	-	-	See Pride, John Jr.
Stubblefield, Joel	RM	0	0	0	
Stuert, Charles	RM	0	0	192	
Stuert, John	RM	0	1	150	
Stuert, John Jr.	RM	0	0	0	
Stuert, Little Barry	RM	0	0	0	
Sulavant, John	JB2	-	-	-	See Brown, John
Swan, Thompson	JB2	Clement, Zephaniah	4	300	List
Swinney, Joseph	JW	-	-	-	see Smith, Richard

NAME	LIST	Other white male tithes	Slaves	Acres	COMMENTS
Swinney, Thomas	JW	-	-	-	see Smith, Richard
Tabb, Col. Thos.	JW	Whitworth, Jno. Adams, Charles Lowry, Thomas	12	0	LIST
Tabb, Edward	TT	-	-	-	See Clement, John
Tabb, John	TT	0	0	955	
Tabb, Thomas	TT	Pringle, Richard McNabb, Alexander Davis, Gresset Hamm, Thomas Hutchason, Charles Johnson, Archer Greenwood, William Beasley, John P. Jones, Richard Jones, Uriah Hatchett, William Beckley, Humphrey Freeman, Gid. King, John	91	8612	1 chariot & 1 chair; 6 wheels
Tanner, Branch	JB2	0	9	327	1 riding chair
Tanner, Joel	RM	0	2	400	
Tanner, Joseph	JB2	0	1	230	
Tanner, Lodowick	JB2	0	10	572	1 riding chair
Taylor, Daniel	AE	-	-	-	See Taylor, Robt.
Taylor, Robt.	AE	Taylor, Daniel	2	200	
Thomas, Athenasus	AE	-	-	-	See Thomas, Samuel
Thomas, Athenasus	AE	-	-	-	See Thomas, William
Thomas, Samuel	AE	Thomas, Athenasus	4	775	
Thomas, William	AE	Thomas, William Jr. Thomas, Athenasus	0	200	
Thompson, David	JW	0	1	0	
Thompson, Nedcip?	JW2	-	-	-	See Sneed, Wm.
Thompson, Peter	JB2	0	6	400	
Thompson, Robert	JB2	0	0	0	
Thompson, Robt.	JW	-	-	-	see Jennings, John
Thompson, Roger	TT	Ferguson, Henry	3	0	
Thompson, Saml.	JW	0	3	452	
Thompson, William	TT	Wilkinson, William	0	0	
Thorn, Thomas	AE	-	-	-	See Hightower, George
Thorp, Charles	JB2	0	0	0	
Thorp, James	JB2	-	-	-	See Thorp, William
Thorp, John	TT	0	2	150	
Thorp, William	JB2	Thorp, James	0	150	

NAME	LIST	Other white male tithes	Slaves	Acres	COMMENTS
Thurston, John	JB2	-	-	-	See Thurston, Seth
Thurston, Plumer??	JB2	-	-	-	See Thurston, Seth
Thurston, Seth	JB2	Thurston, Plumer?? Thurston, John	0	0	
Tinsley, David	TT	-	-	-	See Tinsley, Isaac
Tinsley, Isaac	TT	Tinsley, David	4	200	
Tinsley, Thomas	TT	Foster, James	0	0	
Tomas, Mark	RM	0	0	0	Thomas intended?
Tomson, Isham	RM	Pucket, Edward	2	800	List?
Tomson, Thos.	RM	-	-	-	See Ragsdale, Robert
Townes, James	JB2	0	5	545	
Townsend, John	TT	-	-	-	See Anderson, Pauling
Trabue?, John	JW	Foster, Robt.	3	200	List?
Truehill, Levy	JB	-	-	-	See Royall, Joseph
Truly, Peter	JB2	-	-	-	See Scott, Roger
Tucker, John	AE	0	0	200	
Tucker, Lewis	RM	0	0	0	
Tucker, William	AE	0	1	333	
Tunbull, Amey?	JW	0	0	500	
Tunstill?, Col. Richd.	JW	Edmonds, Francis	10	1328	
Turner, William	AE	0	1	200	
Vaden, Henry	JB	0	0	0	
Vallintine, Vasil	AE	-	-	-	See FitzGerrald, Capt. Wm
Vassar, Abraham	TT	0	0	300	
Vassar, Jesse	JB	-	-	-	See Vassar, Mary
Vassar, John	JB	-	-	-	See Branch, Henry
Vassar, Mary	JB	Vassar, William Vassar, Jesse	3	362	
Vassar, William	JB	-	-	-	See Vassar, Mary
Vaughan, Jesse	JB	-	-	-	See Vaughan, Lewis
Vaughan, John	JB	0	0	0	
Vaughan, John	JW	-	-	-	see Craddock, Richard
Vaughan, Lewis	JB	Vaughan, Jesse	3	0	
Vaughan, Nicholas	JB	0	0	0	
Vaughan, Robt. Jr.	JW	0	3	283	
Vaughn, Benjamin	RM	0	0	0	
Vaughn, Frederick	RM	-	-	-	See Vaugnh, Isham
Vaughn, Isham	AE	Vaughn, John	0	0	
Vaughn, James	JB2	0	1	0	
Vaughn, Jane	JB2	Worsham, George	1	652	List
Vaughn, John	AE	-	-	-	See Vaughn, Isham
Vaughn, Nicholas	TT	-	-	-	See Vaughn, Robert Sr.

NAME	LIST	Other white male tithes	Slaves	Acres	COMMENTS
Vaughn, Robert Sr.	TT	Vaughn, Nicholas	2	500	
Vaughn, Samuel	RM	Vaughn, Samuel (Jr.?) Vaughn, Silvister Vaughn, Stephen	0	353	
Vaughn, Samuel (Jr.?)	RM	-	-	-	See Vaughn, Samuel
Vaughn, Silvister	RM	-	-	-	See Vaughn, Samuel
Vaughn, Stephen	RM	-	-	-	See Vaughn, Samuel
Vaughn, Thomas	JW	Page, John	1	133	
Vaugnh, Isham	RM	Vaughn, Frederick	0	600	
Wainwright, Mary	AE	0	0	210	
Walden, John	TT	-	-	-	See Lorton, Thomas
Walden, Mason	TT	-	-	-	See Bently, Samuel
Walker, Alexander	0	0	3	0	
Walker, Asaph	TT	-	-	-	See Ward, Benjamin
Walker, Charles	JB	0	0	0	
Walker, Edmund	JB	Walker, Edmund Jr. Carter, John? ___ Oasley?, Thomas	15	800	1 riding chair
Walker, Edmund Jr.	JB	-	-	-	See Walker, Edmund
Walker, Henry	AE	-	-	-	See Walker, Thomas Sr.
Walker, John	AE	-	-	-	See Walker, Thomas
Walker, Samuel	TT	Walker, Thomas Walker, Samuel (Jr.?)	4		
Walker, Thomas	AE	Walker, John	1	0	
Walker, Thomas	TT	-	-	-	See Walker, Samuel
Walker, Thomas Sr.	AE	Walker, Henry	5	360	
Walker, Thos.	AE	-	-	-	See Williams, Thomas
Waller, William	AE	-	-	-	See Leath, Arthur
Wallice, Frank	AE	Wallice, Michall (sic)	0	200	
Wallice, Michall (sic)	AE	-	-	-	See Wallice, Frank
Walls, John	JW	0	0	0	
Walthall, Benjamin	TT	-	-	-	See Friend, Thomas
Walthall, Christopher	JB2	Walthall, Christopher Jr.	6	500	
Walthall, Christopher Jr.	JB2	-	-	-	See Walthall, Christopher
Walthall, Daniel	JB	Stearman, Wm.	2	202	
Walthall, Francis	AE	-	-	-	See Herskine, Christopher
Walthall, Henry	JB2	0	6	400	
Walthall, Thomas	TT	Loafman, John	12	803	

NAME	LIST	Other white male tithes	Slaves	Acres	COMMENTS
Walthall, William Jr.	JB	0	4	388	
Walthall, William Jr.	JB2	Smith, John	6	367	
Walton, George	JW	0	3	377	
Ward, Ben	JW	-	-	-	see Ward, H. "est. of"
Ward, Benjamin	TT	Walker, Asaph	12	???	Page torn along margin; 1 riding chair
Ward, H. (estate of)	JW	Ward, Ben Beadle, Augustin	6	803	Estate of H. Ward
Ward, Richd.	RM	-	-	-	See Sherwin, Sam
Ward, Rowland	JB	0	9	992	
Ward, Thomas	RM	-	-	-	See Pryor, John
Ware, William	JB	0	0	150	
Ware, William	JB2	-	-	-	See Bently, John
Waters, Wm.	TT	0	6	500	
Watkins, Stephen Est.	TT	0	0	465	Estate
Watson, Luke	JB	0	0	0	
Watson, Simeon	JW2	Watson, Wm.	2	270	
Watson, William	RM	Cabiniss, Matthew Dixon, Wm.	17	928	
Watson, Wm.	JW2	-	-	-	See Watson, Simeon
Watts?, John	AE	-	-	-	Hobs, Nathaniel Name difficult to read
Wayles, John	TT	Morris, Isaac Harris, Daniel	10	1021	
We__, John	JW	0	0	100	smudged
Webster, Anthony	JB2	-	-	-	See Webster, Peter Sr.
Webster, George	TT	0	0	100	
Webster, John	TT	0	0	0	
Webster, LaGeorge?	TT	0	0	100	
Webster, Peter Jr.	JB	0	1	0	
Webster, Peter Sr.	JB2	Webster, Anthony	3	780	
Webster, Thomas	JB2	Webster, Thomas (Jr.?)	2	450	
Webster, William	JB	-	-	-	See Gibbs, Matthew
Wells, Abraham	AE	0	1	100	
Wells, Burrel	AE	0	0	0	
Wells, Fedrick (sic)	AE	0	0	0	
Wells, Mathew	AE	0	0	0	
Wesbrook, Charles	AE	Wesbrook, Henry	1	197	
Wesbrook, Henry	AE	-	-	-	See Wesbrook, Charles
Wesbrook, James	AE	0	0	50	
Wesbrook, Thos.	AE	0	0	70	

NAME	LIST	Other white male tithes	Slaves	Acres	COMMENTS
Westbrook, Amos	RM	-	-	-	See Busby, Benjamin
Westbrook, William	JB2	-	-	-	See Osborne, Francis
White, Daniel	AE	-	-	-	See Cryer, William
White, Francis	JW2	-	-	-	See White, John
White, George Christopher	TT	0	7	0	
White, John	JW2	White, Francis	2	0	
White, John	TT	-	-	-	See Clement, William Est.
White, Joseph	AE	0	0	200	
Whitlaw, Fra.	JW	Branch, James	6	999	
Whitlaw, Henry	JW	0	0	0	
Whitworth, Abraham	TT	0	3	300	
Whitworth, Jno.	JW	-	-	-	see Tabb, Col. Thos.
Whitworth, Samuel	TT	0	2	166	
Whitworth, Thomas	TT	Whitworth, Thom. Jr.	0	282	"land for his father-232"
Whitworth, William	AE	-	-	-	See Morgan, Jacob
Wilke, John	RM	0	2	250	
Wilkerson, Rev. Thomas	AE	Powell, Thomas	9	500	1 riding chair
Wilkinson, Joseph	JB	0	7	300	
Wilkinson, Martin	JB	0	6	553	
Wilkinson, William	TT	-	-	-	See Thompson, William
Wilkinson, Wm. Est.	JB2	0	0	200	"Estate of"
Williams, Billington	RM	0	0	270	
Williams, Charles	AE	0	1	253	
Williams, Edward	JB	0	2	674	
Williams, Philip	JW	Williams, Philip Jr.	4	400	
Williams, Philip Jr.	JW	-	-	-	see Williams, Philip
Williams, Reuben	JW2	0	0	239	
Williams, Thomas	AE	Walker, Thos.	23	4031	1 riding chair
Williams, Thomas Sr.	AE	Williams, William	4	600	
Williams, William	AE	-	-	-	See Williams, Thomas Sr.
Williamson, Frances	TT	Barding, James	3	240	List
Williamson, Frances	TT	Ponton, William	7	296	List
Williamson, Jacob	TT	0	6	300	
Williamson, Joseph	AE	0	3	0	

NAME	LIST	Other white male tithes	Slaves	Acres	COMMENTS
Williamson, Lewellling	AE	0	2	0	
Wills, Rubin	AE	0	0	0	
Willshire, Henry	JB	-	-	-	See Roberts, Sarah
Willson, Capt. Daniel	JB2	0	6	689	
Willson, George	JB2	0	2	266	
Willson, Mumford	JB	-	-	-	See Hardaway, Stith
Willson, Richd.	JW	0	0	203	
Willson, Thomas Branch	JB2	0	7	900	1 riding chair
Wilson, Richard	RM	-	-	-	See Jones, Maj. Richard
Wilson, William	RM	0	2	100	
Wily, William	JB	Solomon, John	6	318	
Winfry, Gideon	JW	0	3	389	
Wingo, James	TT	Wingo, John	0	104	
Wingo, John	TT	0	0	200	
Wingo, John	TT	-	-	-	See Wingo, James
Wingo, Sarah	TT	0	0	140	List
Wingo, Thomas	TT	0	0	6?	Page torn
Winn, John	JW2	Winn, John Jr.	14	740	
Winn, John	JW2	-	-	-	See Winn, John
Winter, Henry	AE	-	-	-	See Cryer, William
Wood, James (Carpenter)	TT	0	0	?	Page torn
Wood, James Estate	TT	0	2	2??	Page torn
Wood, William	JW2	0	0	0	
Wood, William	TT	Hasken, Joseph	5	0	
Worsham, Daniel	JB2	0	6	819	
Worsham, George	JB2	-	-	-	See Vaughn, Jane
Worsham, George	JB2	Worsham, Joshua	6	200	
Worsham, Henry	JB2	-	-	-	See Finnie, Mary
Worsham, John Berk?	JB2	Johnson, James	5	0	List;
Worsham, Joshua	JB2	-	-	-	See Worsham, George
Worsham, Thomas	JB2	Holt, Thomas	3	646	List
Worsham, William	JB2	0	2	100	
Wortham, Edw.	JW	0	0	375	
Wright, Edward	AE	0	0	0	
Wright, John	TT	Meadow, ____	5	539	List
Wright, John	TT	-	-	-	See Wright, Thomas Sr.
Wright, Thomas Jr.	TT	0	0	100	
Wright, Thomas Sr.	TT	Wright, John	9	316	

NAME	LIST	Other white male tithes	Slaves	Acres	COMMENTS
		Meadow, Jeremiah			
Yarbrough, Jordan	JW	-	-	-	see Yarbrough, Thomas
Yarbrough, Saml.	JW2	0	0	572	
Yarbrough, Thomas	JW	Yarbrough, Jordan	7	600	
Young, Allen Ridley	JB	-	-	-	See Holt, David
Young, Ellison	JB2	-	-	-	See Young, Samuel
Young, Samuel	JB2	Young, Samuel (Jr.?) Young, Ellison	1	290	
Young, Stephen	JB	-	-	-	See Hardaway, Joseph
Zachary, Bartho.	JW	Buttery?, Zachary	3	153	

The 1769 AMELIA COUNTY, VIRGINIA TITHE LISTS

EXPLANATION OF COLUMN HEADINGS

NAME: the name of the person paying the Tithe

LIST: The initials of the person who compiled the tithe list on which the individual appears (an indication of the geographic area and the parish where these individuals lived.

OTHER WHITE MALE TITHES: The names of other men above the age of 16, whose tithe was paid by the taxpayer. When of the same surname, these were usually sons of the taxpayer. Otherwise, they were guests, overseers or other employees.

THE TAX "COMMISSIONERS" FOR 1769, AND THEIR AREA/PARISH

JB = John Booker of Raleigh Parish
SC = Stephen Cocke, of Nottoway Parish
TM = Thomas Munford of Raleigh Parish
TW = Thomas Williams of Nottoway Parish
VB = Vivion Brooking, the lower part of Raleigh Parish

COMMENTS

Land = individual taxed only for land, not for self; exempt for some reason.
List = individual named not taxed for self; exempt, or taxed personally elsewhere.
List? = number of individuals named is one more than number taxed; List implied but not stated.

NAME	LIST	Other white male tithes	Slaves	Acres	COMMENTS
Adams, David	VB	0	2	0	
Adams, William	VB	-	-	-	see Clay, John
Adkinson, John	JB	0	0	0	
Algood, Jno.	SC	-	-	-	see Fannin, Laughlin
Allen, Daniel	VB	0	3	392	
Allen, Edmund	VB	-	-	-	see Ford, John
Allen, John	TW	-	-	-	see Bridgeforth, Ben.
Allin, David	TM	-	-	-	see Gillington, Nicholas
Allin, John	SC	0	1	0	
Allin, Samuel	TM	-	-	-	see Walker, Alexander
Anderson, Charles	JB	-	-	-	see Willson, Daniel Jr.
Anderson, Charles	TW	Anderson, James Butry, Zach.	2	0	
Anderson, Claiborne	JB	Morgan Sam	9	572	List
Anderson, Frances	TM	Walding, John	12	700	
Anderson, Henry	TW	0	2	0	
Anderson, James	TW	-	-	-	see Anderson, Charles
Anderson, James	TW	0	1	0	
Anderson, Paulin	TM	Bohannon, Henry Bagby, James	12	2221	1 riding chair
Applin, Thomas	JB	-	-	-	see Clement, William
Archer, John	JB	0	2	0	
Archer, John	JB	-	-	-	see Archer, William
Archer, William	JB	Archer, John Cock, Chastain Archer, William Jr.	16	0	

NAME	LIST	Other white male tithes	Slaves	Acres	COMMENTS
Archer, William Jr.	JB	-	-	-	see Archer, William
Asslin, Dr. David	TM	0	3	288	
Asslin, Larrance	TM	-	-	-	see Ford, Christopher
Avery, John	VB	Mayton?, Jo__? Hood, William	0	180	
Bagby, Henry	JB	0	0	200	Land
Bagby, James	TM	-	-	-	see Anderson, Paulin
Bagby, John	JB	0	3	200	
Bagley, James	TW	Johnston, William	3	0	
Bailey, John	SC	0	3	0	
Bailey, Micajah	SC	0	0	389	
Bardin, James	TM	0	0	102	
Barker, Charles	SC	0	1	253	List
Barker, Charles	SC	-	-	-	see Hanes, Anthony Est.
Bass, Christopher	JB	Bass, William	4	410	
Bass, Edward	JB	0	10	743	1 riding chair
Bass, William	JB	-	-	-	see Bass, Christopher
Bass, William Sr.	JB	0	10	470	
Bates, Abner	TW	0	2	225	
Belcher, John Sr.	JB	Belcher, Thomas	0	0	
Belcher, Thomas	JB	-	-	-	see Belcher, John Sr.
Bell, John	TM	-	-	-	see Whales, John
Bennett, Benj.	VB	Bennett, William Bennett, Benj. Jr.	0	282	
Bennett, Benj. Jr.	VB	-	-	-	see Bennett, Benj.
Bennett, William	VB	-	-	-	see Bennett, Benj.
Bennit, Robert	TM	-	-	-	see Davis, Thomas
Bentley, Jno.	SC	-	-	-	see Bentley, Samuel
Bentley, Saml. Jr.	SC	-	-	-	see Bentley, Samuel
Bentley, Samuel	SC	Bentley, Saml. Jr. Bentley, Jno.	0	0	
Bentley, Samuel	TM	Bentley, Samuel Jr.	8	700	1 riding chair
Bentley, Samuel Jr.	TM	-	-	-	see Bentley, Samuel
Berry, Thos.	VB	0	2	240	
Bevil, Hezekiah	VB	0	0	100	
Bevil, James	VB	Worsham, George	4	300	
Bevill, Abraham	VB	0	0	0	
Bevill, Archer	JB	0	0	0	
Bevill, Essex	JB	0	0	150	
Bevill, Joel	JB	0	3	200	
Bevill, Jos.?	VB	0	1	200	
Bevill, Robert	VB	0	1	200	
Bevill, Robert Jr.	VB	0	1	100	
Bevill, Thomas	JB	0	2	241	
Bevill, William	VB	0	2	0	
Billington, John	JB	0	0	100	"Land"
Blanchet, Henry	JB	-	-	-	see Hall, William
Blanchett, Isaac	JB	0	0	30	

NAME	LIST	Other white male tithes	Slaves	Acres	COMMENTS
Bland, Doctor	TW	Brown, William	8	0	List
Bohannon, Henry	TM	-	-	-	see Anderson, Paulin
Bollen, John	VB	-	-	-	see Jones, Peter Sr.
Bolling, Col. Alex. Est.	SC	Gunn, James	5	1672	"Estate of"
Bolling, Col. Robert	VB	Kidd, George Freeman, Allen Mitchell, Evan	54	0	List?
Booker, Ann	JB	Thackston, William	11	1025	List
Booker, Edward	JB	Dunnivant, Hezekiah	10	0	
Booker, Edward	TM	0	2	200	
Booker, George	TM	Booker, Samuel	8	973	1 riding chair
Booker, George	TM	-	-	-	see Ford, Christopher
Booker, John	TM	0	3	150	
Booker, Rachel	TM	McHamy?, James	12	511	List
Booker, Samuel	TM	-	-	-	see Booker, George
Booth, George	VB	-	-	-	see Booth, Judith
Booth, Jas.	VB	-	-	-	see Booth, Thomas
Booth, Judith	VB	Booth, Nathaniel Booth, George	5	230	
Booth, Nathaniel	JB	0	2	336	
Booth, Nathaniel	VB	-	-	-	see Booth, Judith
Booth, Thomas	VB	Booth, Jas.	1	382	
Booth, William	VB	0	2	252	
Booth, William Jr.	VB	0	0	100	
Boothe, John	JB	0	6	556	
Borough, Peter	VB	-	-	-	see Wills, Laurence
Borum, Edmund	TW	Davis, Ishmael	0	0	
Bott, Miles	JB	0	5	752	
Bott, William	JB	0	3	646	
Bottom, Thomas	JB	0	9	970	
Boyd, Walter	SC	McCutcheon, Jno. Moor, Wm.	9	0	List
Brackett, Benjamin	JB	-	-	-	see Brackett, Thomas
Brackett, Thomas	JB	Brackett, Thos. Jr. Brackett, Benjamin	6	910	
Brackett, Thos. Jr.	JB	-	-	-	see Brackett, Thomas
Bradley, James	SC	-	-	-	see Epes, Francis
Bradley, James	TW	Bradley, James Jr.	1	0	
Bradley, James Jr.	TW	-	-	-	see Bradley, James
Bradshaw, Richard	TM	0	0	0	
Bridgeforth, Ben.	TW	Allen, John	8	0	
Brintle, Wm.	SC	-	-	-	see Epes, Francis
Brookes, George	JB	0	0	100	
Brookes, Joell	JB	-	-	-	see Brookes, Thomas
Brookes, Thomas	JB	Brookes, Joell	0	150	
Brookes, William	JB	0	3	0	
Brooking, Vivion	VB	Fowler, Bullard	26	2217	List? 1 riding chair

NAME	LIST	Other white male tithes	Slaves	Acres	COMMENTS
Brown, Alexander	JB	0	2	0	
Brown, Archiball	TM	-	-	-	see Fargusson, John
Brown, William	TW	-	-	-	see Bland, Doctor
Brumbelow, Edward	SC	0	0	0	
Brumfield, Majer	TM	00	0	200	
Brumskill, Rev. John	TM	0	3	400	List
Bryan, Frederick	JB	-	-	-	see Scott, Joseph
Burton, Abel	VB	0	2	200	
Burton, Peter	VB	0	1	173	
Butler, William	TM	0	1	267	
Butler, Wm.	JB	-	-	-	see Scott, John
Butry, Zach.	TW	-	-	-	see Anderson, Charles
Cabiness, George	SC	0	3	0	
Cabiness, Matt.	VB	-	-	-	see Osborne, William
Callicot, James	JB	0	2	0	
Callicot, William	JB	0	2	1220	
Candlemire, John X.	JB	-	-	-	see Finnie, Mary
Cape, John	JB	0	0	150	
Cary, Robert	JB	Dunnivant, Thomas	7	0	
Caudle, Jno.	VB	-	-	-	see Jones, Peter
Caudle, William	VB	0	0	0	
Cavender, Hugh	TM	0	0	150	
Chaffin, Joshua	JB	-	-	-	see Walker, Edward
Chambers, Thomas	SC	Chambers, William	6	290	
Chambers, William	SC	-	-	-	see Chambers, Thomas
Chapman, John	TM	0	1	400	
Chapman, Samuel	TM	0	3	0	
Chappel, James	JB	Standley, John	12	996	
Chappel, Jno. Jr.	VB	-	-	-	see Chappel, John
Chappel, John	VB	Chappel, Robt. Chappel, Jno. Jr.	5	492	
Chappel, Patty	SC	0	0	435	"Estate"
Chappel, Robt.	VB	-	-	-	see Chappel, John
Chappel, Wm.	JB	-	-	-	see Tabb, Thomas
Cheatam, Archer	JB	-	-	-	see Tabb, Thomas
Chetam, James	TM	0	3	0	
Claiborne, T.W.	SC	Lipscomb, Ambrose	12	0	List?
Clardy, Benj.	VB	Clardy, Benj. Jr.	4	526	
Clardy, Benj. Jr.	VB	-	-	-	see Clardy, Benj.
Clardy, Jas.	JB	-	-	-	see Hays, Richd.
Clardy, John	JB	-	-	-	see Finnie, Mary
Clardy, John	VB	0	0	100	
Clardy, Michael	VB	0	0	175	
Clardy, Richd.	JB	-	-	-	see Hardaway, Daniel
Clark, Henry	SC	Clark, Thos. Clark, Henry Jr.	1	0	
Clark, Henry Jr.	SC	-	-	-	see Clark, Henry
Clark, Peter	SC	0	0	100	

NAME	LIST	Other white male tithes	Slaves	Acres	COMMENTS
Clark, Thomas	VB	0	1	200	
Clark, Thos.	SC	-	-	-	see Clark, Henry
Clay, Caleb	VB	-	-	-	see Powell, Robert
Clay, Charles	SC	Clay, Joshua	1	150	
Clay, Charles	VB	Clay, Daniel	1	150	
Clay, Daniel	VB	-	-	-	see Clay, Charles
Clay, Elijah	VB	-	-	-	see Clay, Thos.
Clay, Jno. Jr.	VB	-	-	-	see Clay, John
Clay, John	VB	Clay, Jno. Jr. Adams, William	6	400	
Clay, Joshua	SC	-	-	-	see Clay, Charles
Clay, Peter	JB	-	-	-	see Crawley, William
Clay, Solomon	VB	-	-	-	see Clay, Thos.
Clay, Thos.	VB	Clay, Elijah Clay, Solomon	0	150	
Clement, William	JB	Applin, Thomas	2	510	
Clements, Isham	TM	Clements, William Duglas, John	1	435	
Clements, John	TM	Tabb, Edward	8	300	
Clements, William	TM	-	-	-	see Clements, Isham
Clough, Elizabeth	JB	Foster, Richard	10	0	List
Cock, Chastain	JB	-	-	-	see Archer, William
Cock, Stephen	JB	-	-	-	see Farrar, Peter
Cocke, John	SC	0	2	0	
Cocke, Stephen	SC	Portwood, Page Mays, Abraham	6	0	
Cocke, Thomas	SC	0	4	0	
Cocke, Wm.	SC	0	2	0	
Coleman, Abraham	VB	Coleman, Jeremiah	1	94	
Coleman, Daniel	VB	Coleman, Jesse	5	662	
Coleman, Daniel Jr.	VB	0	1	292	
Coleman, Francis	VB	-	-	-	see Coleman, John
Coleman, Hezekiah	JB	Hudson, Daniel	3	168	
Coleman, Jeremiah	VB	-	-	-	see Coleman, Abraham
Coleman, Jesse	VB	-	-	-	see Coleman, Daniel
Coleman, John	VB	Coleman, Francis	0	100	
Coleman, Jos. Jr.	VB	0	0	75	
Coleman, Joseph	VB	Coleman, Sutton Coleman, Page	0	96	
Coleman, Page	VB	-	-	-	see Coleman, Joseph
Coleman, Peter	JB	-	-	-	see Morgan, John
Coleman, Peter	VB	0	0	150	
Coleman, Sutton	VB	-	-	-	see Coleman, Joseph
Colly, David	VB	-	-	-	see Couvens?, George
Connally, Charles	SC	Connally, George	3	0	
Connally, George	SC	-	-	-	see Connally, Charles
Cornelius, Jesse	JB	-	-	-	see Sturdivant, James
Cousens, John	VB	Tucker, Geo.	5	590	

NAME	LIST	Other white male tithes	Slaves	Acres	COMMENTS
Cousens, Robt.	VB	Ragland, Jos. Ragland, Benj.	9	678	
Cousens, William	VB	Hancock, Annanias Hanks, Thos.	5	948	
Cousens, William Jr.	VB	0	3	578	
Cousens?, George	VB	Colly, David	6	1000	List?
Cowles, Thos.	VB	Weekes, Richard	7	1084	List?
Cox, George	TM	0	0	0	
Cox, Henry	TM	Tunstall, Richard	2	100	
Craddock, Moses	SC	-	-	-	see Craddock, Wm. "Const."
Craddock, Wm. "Const."	SC	Craddock, Moses	2	650	"Constable"
Cranshaw, Elkanah	TM	0	6	400	
Crawley, David	JB	-	-	-	see Crawley, William
Crawley, William	JB	Crawley, David Morgan, John Clay, Peter Ellington, William	44	3984	
Creel, Absolom	SC	-	-	-	see Ellis, Richard
Crenshaw, William Jr.	SC	0	2	350	
Critington, Wm.	VB	-	-	-	see Jones, Col. Wood
Cross, Charles	SC	-	-	-	see Cross, William
Cross, Richd.	SC	-	-	-	see Cross, William
Cross, William	SC	Cross, Richd. Cross, Charles	9	0	
Crowder, John	JB	0	0	300	
Crowder, Jos.	VB	0	2	0	
Cryer, Robt.	SC	0	0	173	"P. George Co."
Cryer, Wm. Jr.	SC	Elder, Peter	7	800	
Cumpton, Zachariah	JB	-	-	-	see Tabb, Thomas
Cumton, Ambros	TM	0	0	0	Cumpton intended?
Cumton, Jehu	TM	-	-	-	see Cumton, John
Cumton, John	TM	Cumton, Joshua	3	300	
Cumton, John	TM	Cumton, Jehu	1	100	
Cumton, Joshua	TM	-	-	-	see Cumton, John
Daniel, Benj.	JB	-	-	-	see Scott, John
Davis, Ishmael	TW	-	-	-	see Borum, Edmund
Davis, Jacob	SC	Davis, Wm. Davis, Thos.	3	0	
Davis, Thomas	TM	Worsham, Charles Bennit, Robert	2	90	
Davis, Thos.	SC	-	-	-	see Davis, Jacob
Davis, Wm.	SC	-	-	-	see Davis, Jacob
Deaton, Iabe?	JB	-	-	-	see Roberts, Sarah
Deaton, James	JB	0	0	116	
Deaton, John	TM	0	3	170	
Deaton, William	JB	0	0	0	
Degraffenried, Frances	TM	-	-	-	see Ford, Christopher

NAME	LIST	Other white male tithes	Slaves	Acres	COMMENTS
Dennis, Henry	TW	0	7	0	
Dennis, Richard	TW	0	4	400	
Dixon, Benj.	VB	0	6	156	
Dixon, Wm.	SC	-	-	-	see Smith, Samuel
Dodson, Edward	VB	-	-	-	see Dodson, John
Dodson, John	VB	Dodson, Edward	2	100	
Draper, James	SC	Draper, Wm.	0	0	
Draper, Wm.	SC	-	-	-	see Draper, James
Dudley, Edward	VB	Dudley, Jas.	8	0	
Dudley, Jas.	VB	-	-	-	see Dudley, Edward
Duglas, John	TM	-	-	-	see Clements, Isham
Dun, Jno.	VB	0	0	0	
Dunnavant, Clem	JB	-	-	-	see Dunnavant, Hodge
Dunnavant, Daniel	JB	-	-	-	see Dunnavant, William Sr.
Dunnavant, Hodge	JB	Dunnavant, Clem	5	250	
Dunnavant, John	JB	-	-	-	see Dunnavant, William Sr.
Dunnavant, Phillip	TM	Dunnavant, Shadrick	3	250	
Dunnavant, Shadrick	TM	-	-	-	see Dunnavant, Phillip
Dunnavant, William Sr.	JB	Dunnavant, John Dunnavant, Daniel	3	200	
Dunnivant, Hezekiah	JB	-	-	-	see Booker, Edward
Dunnivant, Thomas	JB	-	-	-	see Cary, Robert
Durham, Joshua	SC	0	0	0	
Dyan, Ann	JB	0	0	150	Land
Eckles, James	SC	-	-	-	see Leath, Arthur
Eckles, Robt.	SC	0	1	0	
Eckles, Thomas	SC	0	1	0	
Edmondson, Benj.	SC	0	2	0	
Edmondson, Upton	SC	0	2	0	
Eggleston, Joseph	TM	0	0	2100	1 riding chair
Eggleston, Richard	TM	Sadler, Thomas	6	750	
Elam, John Jr.	JB	0	0	0	
Elder, Peter	SC	-	-	-	see Cryer, Wm. Jr.
Elington, Daniel	JB	-	-	-	see Elington, John
Elington, John	JB	Elington, Daniel	7	1130	
Ellington, David	TW	Ellington, Josiah Ellington, Ward	5	0	
Ellington, John	JB	-	-	-	see Marshall, Robert's Est.
Ellington, Josiah	TW	-	-	-	see Ellington, David
Ellington, Ward	TW	-	-	-	see Ellington, David
Ellington, William	JB	-	-	-	see Crawley, William
Ellis, Richard	SC	Creel, Absolom	30	1952	List?; 1 riding chair
Elmor, Jno.	SC	-	-	-	see Seaman, John
Elmor, Wm.	SC	-	-	-	see Powel, John
Epes, Francis	SC	Brintle, Wm. Ward, Richd. Bradley, James	25	0	List 1 riding chair
Epes, Peter	SC	Harrison, Moses	9	675	

NAME	LIST	Other white male tithes	Slaves	Acres	COMMENTS
Erskine, Alex. Estate of	TW	Hinton, Ally	4	0	"Estate of"
Estes, William	TM	0	0	0	
Fannen, Archalus	SC	Fannen, Wm.	0	0	
Fannen, Laughlin	SC	Algood, Jno.	0	0	
Fannen, Wm.	SC	-	-	-	see Fannen, Archalus
Fargusson, Ann	TM	0	1	0	List
Fargusson, Daniel	TM	0	2	0	
Fargusson, James Jr.	TM	0	0	100	
Fargusson, John	TM	Fargusson, Robin Brown, Archiball Jackson, ???	11	500	
Fargusson, Richard	TM	Jackson, Tom	0	0	
Fargusson, Robin	TM	-	-	-	see Fargusson, John
Farley, John	TM	-	-	-	see Farley, Sarah
Farley, Joseph	VB	0	6	689	
Farley, Sarah	TM	Farley, John	0	243	
Farley, Stephen	TM	Gears, Robert	0	0	
Farley, William	TM	0	5	243	
Farlie, Jeremiah	JB	-	-	-	see Farlie, Mary Amelia
Farlie, Mary Amelia	JB	Farlie, Jeremiah	4	200	List; "of Amelia" intended?
Farlie, Matthew	JB	0	3	250	
Farrar, Peter	JB	Cock, Stephen Roberts, Step	18	2771	
Featherston, Jesse	SC	-	-	-	see Featherston, Wm. Grigg
Featherston, Lewis	SC	0	1	0	
Featherston, Wm. Grigg	SC	Featherston, Jesse	5	400	
Featherstone, Charles	JB	0	2	210	
Ferguson, Peleg	SC	0	2	0	
Ferguson, Thomas	JB	-	-	-	see Jones, William
Field, Robert	JB	0	0	0	
Finnie, Mary	JB	Finnie, William Clardy, John Candlemire, John X.	13	1274	List
Finnie, William	JB	-	-	-	see Finnie, Mary
Fluellen, Freeman	SC	-	-	-	see Jones, Nelson
Fontaine, Joseph	JB	-	-	-	see Scott, Joseph
Ford, Billy	TM	0	1	0	
Ford, Christopher	TM	Whitworth, John Degraffenried, Frances Asslin, Larrance Booker, George	10	1001	1 riding chair
Ford, Culvin	TM	0	3	200	
Ford, John	VB	Allen, Edmund	7	437	
Ford, Reuben	VB	0	0	300	List? (no tithe)
Ford, William	TM	Hurt, James	5	318	

NAME	LIST	Other white male tithes	Slaves	Acres	COMMENTS
Forde, Abraham	TW	0	0	0	
Forde, Albury	TW	0	0	100	
Forde, Frederick	TW	Forde, John	0	355	
Forde, George	TW	0	1	200	
Forde, Henry	TW	-	-	-	see Williams, Thomas
Forde, Hezekiah	TW	-	-	-	see Forde, Nathaniel
Forde, John	TW	-	-	-	see Forde, Frederick
Forde, Nathaniel	TW	Forde, Hezekiah	3	0	
Fortin?, Jos.	SC	-	-	-	see Shelton, Danl.
Foster, Antony	TM	-	-	-	see Foster, George
Foster, Antony	TM	0	0	0	
Foster, George	TM	Foster, George Pollard Foster, Antony Foster, Joseph	0	147	
Foster, George Pollard	TM	-	-	-	see Foster, George
Foster, James	TM	0	0	0	"son of James"
Foster, James	TM	-	-	-	see Wright, Thomas
Foster, John	JB	-	-	-	see Tabb, Thomas
Foster, John	TM	0	0	0	"son of William"
Foster, Joseph	TM	-	-	-	see Foster, George
Foster, Richard	JB	-	-	-	see Clough, Elizabeth
Foster, Robert	JB	-	-	-	see Hill, Isaac
Foster, Robert	TM	-	-	-	see Foster, Thomas
Foster, Thomas	TM	Foster, Robert	6	600	
Foster, Thomas	TM	0	0	0	
Foster, William Jr.	TM	-	-	-	see Foster, William Sr.
Foster, William Sr.	TM	Foster, William Jr.	0	0	
Foulkes, John	JB	-	-	-	see Worsham, John's Est.
Fowler, Bullard	VB	-	-	-	see Brooking, Vivion
Frank, Jack	VB	-	-	-	see Spain, Joshua
Freeman, Allen	VB	-	-	-	see Bolling, Col. Robert
Furguson, Edward	TW	King, Andrew	0	0	
Gallamore, Edw.	VB	-	-	-	see Jones, Henry
Gallamore, Elizabeth	VB	-	-	-	see Jones, Henry
Gallamore, Geo.	VB	-	-	-	see Jones, Henry
Gates, James?	JB	-	-	-	see Williamson, Jacob
Gears, Robert	TM	-	-	-	see Farley, Stephen
Gibbs, Matt.	JB	0	2	200	List
Gibbs, Thos.	JB	-	-	-	see Webster, Peter Jr.
Giles, William	TM	0	10	976	
Gill, John	JB	0	0	0	
Gilliam, John Jr.	VB	0	3	0	List?
Gilliam, John Sr.	VB	Winfield, Robt.	14	1240	List?
Gillington, Nicholas	TM	Allin, David	1	300	
Gorham, John	VB	-	-	-	see Walthall, William
Gray, Alexander	SC	Gray, Jos.	0	145	

NAME	LIST	Other white male tithes	Slaves	Acres	COMMENTS
Gray, John	VB	0	3	100	
Gray, Jos.	SC	-	-	-	see Gray, Alexander
Green, Abra.	VB	-	-	-	see Green, Thomas
Green, Abraham	VB	-	-	-	see Green, Abraham Jr.
Green, Abraham Jr.	VB	Green, Abraham Green, Mat. Pitchford, Will. Tucker, Micheal	19	1750	1 riding chair
Green, Henry	SC	Green, Jno.	4	0	
Green, Jno.	SC	-	-	-	see Green, Henry
Green, John	TM	0	0	0	
Green, Mat.	VB	-	-	-	see Green, Abraham Jr.
Green, Thomas	TM	0	0	150	
Green, Thomas	VB	Green, Abra.	1	268	
Green, William	VB	0	5	652	
Greenhill, Capt. David	SC	0	2	0	List
Greenhill, David	VB	Wilson, William Wilie, Solomon Smart, James	24	1541	
Greenwood, William	JB	-	-	-	see Tabb, Thomas
Greggs, James	SC	0	0	0	
Gunn, James	SC	-	-	-	see Bolling, Col. Alex. Est.
Gunn, James	SC	0	4	0	List
Hall, Ambrose	VB	0	0	0	
Hall, Henry	VB	0	0	0	
Hall, Lionard	VB	0	0	0	
Hall, Thomas	JB	0	4	125	
Hall, William	JB	Blanchet, Henry	5	275	
Hall?, George	JB	-	-	-	see Hudson, Christopher
Ham, Thos.	TM	0	0	274	
Hamblin, Charles	VB	0	11	366	List?
Hamblin, John	VB	Mallory, Francis	7	0	List? 1 riding chair
Hamblin, Stephen	VB	Roach, William	6	0	List?
Hames, Edmund	SC	0	0	0	
Hames, John	SC	Hames, Wm.	3	0	could be HARRIS
Hames, Wm.	SC	-	-	-	see Hames, John
Hames, Wm. Jr.	SC	0	0	0	
Hamlin, Wm.	SC	0	2	0	
Hamm, George Sr.	JB	0	2	150	
Hamm, Thomas	JB	-	-	-	see Tabb, Thomas
Hamm, William	JB	0	0	125	Land
Hammond, Wm.	SC	0	1	0	
Hancock, Annanias	VB	-	-	-	see Cousens, William
Hancock, Edward	TM	-	-	-	see Hancock, George
Hancock, George	TM	Hancock, Edward	7	220	
Hanes, Anthony Est.	SC	Barker, Charles	4	792	"Estate"; List?
Hanks, Thos.	VB	-	-	-	see Cousens, William

NAME	LIST	Other white male tithes	Slaves	Acres	COMMENTS
Hardaway, Daniel	JB	Clardy, Richd. Totty, Abner	20	1238	1 riding chair
Hardaway, Joseph	JB	Smith, Henry	4	290	List
Hardin, Erasmus	JB	Hastings, John	3	150	List
Harper?, Henry	TM	0	0	50	name faded
Harris, James	TM	-	-	-	see Harris, John
Harris, John	TM	Harris, James	0	0	
Harris, William	TM	0	0	0	
Harris, William	TM	-	-	-	see Munford, Thomas
Harrison, Moses	SC	-	-	-	see Epes, Peter
Harrison, William	JB	-	-	-	see Scott, Joseph
Hart?, William	TM	Walker, Thos	3	0	name faded and faint
Haskew, Joseph	JB	-	-	-	see Tabb, Thomas
Haskins, Christopher	SC	Moor, Mark	6	0	1 riding chair
Hastings, John	JB	-	-	-	see Hardin, Erasmus
Hastings, John	JB	0	0	200	Land
Hatchett, Abraham	JB	-	-	-	see Hatchett, William Sr.
Hatchett, William Sr.	JB	Hatchett, Abraham	4	150	
Hawke, George	VB	-	-	-	see Hawke, Joshua
Hawke, Joshua	VB	Hawke, George	3	531	
Hawke, Richard	VB	0	0	0	
Hawkins, David	VB	0	2	200	
Hawting, William	VB	0	1	0	
Hawting, Zachariah	VB	0	0	0	
Hays, Richd.	JB	Hays, Wm. Clardy, Jas.	9	797	
Hays, Wm.	JB	-	-	-	see Hays, Richd.
Hendrick, Barnit	TM	-	-	-	see Hendrick, Benjamin Sr.
Hendrick, Benjamin Jr.	TM	0	1	200	
Hendrick, Benjamin Sr.	TM	Hendrick, Barnit	8	475	
Hendrick, Hans	TM	0	8	0	
Higgins, Solomon	JB	-	-	-	see Walthall, Thomas
Hightower, Charnel	SC	-	-	-	see Jones, William
Hightower, Hannah	SC	Hoskins, Thos.	1	200	List
Hightower, Joshua Jr.	SC	Hightower, Thos.	4	610	
Hightower, Thos.	SC	-	-	-	see Hightower, Joshua Jr.
Hightower, Wm.	SC	-	-	-	see Hurt, Moses Jr.
Hill, Isaac	JB	Foster, Robert	0	0	
Hill, John Jr.	TM	-	-	-	see Hill, John Sr.
Hill, John Sr.	TM	Hill, John Jr.	1		
Hill, Moses	JB	0	0	0	
Hilsman, Mathew	TM	0	1	200	
Hilsman, William	TM	0	2	100	
Hinson, Jonas	TM	-	-	-	see Starn, Ann
Hinton, Ally	TW	-	-	-	see Erskine, Alex. Estate of
Hix, Allis	TM	-	-	-	see Southall, William

NAME	LIST	Other white male tithes	Slaves	Acres	COMMENTS
Hobkins, Francis	TM	0	3	215	
Holt, David	VB	-	-	-	see Munford, William
Holt, Dixdale?	SC	0	1	200	
Hood, Abraham	VB	0	0	240	
Hood, John	SC	0	0	0	
Hood, John	VB	Hood, Thos.	3	372	
Hood, Robert	VB	0	0	75	
Hood, Thos.	VB	-	-	-	see Hood, John
Hood, Tucker	VB	0	0	0	
Hood, William	VB	-	-	-	see Avery, John
Hood, William	VB	0	0	75	
Hood, Wm.	SC	-	-	-	see Williams, Charles
Hooper, Zachariah	SC	0	2	0	
Hoskins, Thos.	SC	-	-	-	see Hightower, Hannah
Howlett, William	JB	0	3	140	
Hubbard, Joseph	TM	0	0	140	
Hubbart, John	TM	Majer, George	0	106	
Hudleston, Thos.	VB	0	1	195	
Hudson, Christopher	JB	Hall?, George	17	1500	1 riding chair
Hudson, Daniel	JB	-	-	-	see Coleman, Hezekiah
Hudson, John	VB	0	0	0	
Hudson, Peter	VB	-	-	-	see Tucker, Daniel
Hughes, Wm.	SC	0	0	0	
Hughs, John	TM	Jones, William Hundley, Charles	12	875	Hughes intended?
Hundley, Charles	TM	-	-	-	see Hughs, John
Hurt, James	TM	-	-	-	see Ford, William
Hurt, Moses	SC	Hurt, Zacheus West, Absolum	9	300	
Hurt, Moses Jr.	SC	Hightower, Wm.	0	0	"Constable"
Hurt, William	TM	0	0	0	"son of John"
Hurt, Zacheus	SC	-	-	-	see Hurt, Moses
Hutchason, Charles	JB	-	-	-	see Tabb, Thomas
Hutcherson, Elkanah	TM	-	-	-	see Hutcherson, William
Hutcherson, John	TM	-	-	-	see Molson, William Sr.
Hutcherson, William	TM	Hutcherson, Elkanah	1	100	
Jackson, ???	TM	-	-	-	see Fargusson, John
Jackson, Ben	JB	-	-	-	see Jackson, Francis
Jackson, Burwell	JB	-	-	-	see Jackson, Francis
Jackson, Charles	SC	Jackson, Philip	0	0	
Jackson, Edward	SC	0	2	0	
Jackson, Francis	JB	Jackson, Burwell Jackson, Ben	1	200	
Jackson, Francis	TM	0	1	260	
Jackson, Isaac	VB	Lawson, Claibourne W. Lawson, Benj.	2	196	
Jackson, Joel	JB	0	3	250	

NAME	LIST	Other white male tithes	Slaves	Acres	COMMENTS
Jackson, John	SC	0	0	0	
Jackson, John	SC	0	0	0	
Jackson, Joseph	TM	0	1	200	
Jackson, Matt.	JB	-	-	-	see Wilkinson, Joseph Est.
Jackson, Matthew	JB	0	3	200	
Jackson, Philip	SC	-	-	-	see Jackson, Charles
Jackson, Samuel	TM	-	-	-	see Jackson, William
Jackson, Thomas	SC	0	1	0	
Jackson, Tom	TM	-	-	-	see Fargusson, Richard
Jackson, William	JB	0	1	0	"son of Mat"
Jackson, William	TM	Jackson, Samuel	2	354	
Jackson, Wm. Jr.	SC	0	0	0	
Jackson, Wm. Sr.	SC	0	3	0	
James, Thomas Jr.	TM	-	-	-	see James, Thomas Sr.
James, Thomas Sr.	TM	James, Thomas Jr.	2	200	
Jesse, John	JB	-	-	-	see Tabb, Thomas
Jeter, Henry	JB	-	-	-	see Tabb, Thomas
Jinkins, James	TM	Southall, James White, David	6	420	
Johnson, William	TM	Ray, John	2	400	
Johnston, William	TW	-	-	-	see Bagley, James
Jones, Adam	SC	Jones, Benj.	9	400	
Jones, Agnis	TM	0	4	0	List
Jones, Benj.	SC	-	-	-	see Jones, Adam
Jones, Branch	TW	-	-	-	see Jones, Peter
Jones, Capt. Robert	TM	Southall, John	7	400	
Jones, Col. Wood	VB	Jones, Phil Critington, Wm.	12	0	
Jones, Daniel	JB	Jones, Daniel Jr.	12	1341	
Jones, Daniel Jr.	JB	-	-	-	see Jones, Daniel
Jones, Dorothy	VB	Varsor, Wm.	9	500	List?
Jones, Edw.	TM	-	-	-	see Wood, William
Jones, Henry	VB	Gallamore, Edw. Gallamore, Geo. Gallamore, Elizabeth	4	1303	List?
Jones, John	VB	Nance, David	3	1000	
Jones, Maj. Richard	TM	Sammons, Thomas	6	0	List
Jones, Nelson	SC	Fluellen, Freeman	6	0	1 riding chair
Jones, Peter	TW	Jones, Branch Willington, William	7	0	
Jones, Peter	VB	Caudle, Jno.	8	784	
Jones, Peter Sr.	VB	Bollen, John	13	3750	
Jones, Phil	VB	-	-	-	see Jones, Col. Wood
Jones, Richard	JB	Oliver, John	4	572	
Jones, Richard	JB	-	-	-	see Tabb, Thomas
Jones, Richard Jr.	TM	-	-	-	see Jones, Richard Sr.
Jones, Richard Sr.	TM	Jones, Richard Jr.	4	150	
Jones, Sarah	VB	0	6	0	List?

NAME	LIST	Other white male tithes	Slaves	Acres	COMMENTS
Jones, Sheriff Peter	VB	0	3	0	
Jones, Thomas	JB	Oliver, Ben Watne?, Richd.	9	572	
Jones, Thomas	SC	0	4	200	
Jones, Thomas Field	VB	0	0	100	
Jones, Uriah	JB	-	-	-	see Tabb, Thomas
Jones, William	JB	Ferguson, Thomas	4	744	
Jones, William	SC	Hightower, Charnel	4	0	"Huricane Creek" by name
Jones, William	TM	-	-	-	see Hughs, John
Jordan, Jonas	JB	0	1	273	
Jordan, Saml.?	SC	-	-	-	see Jordan, Wm.
Jordan, Wm.	SC	Jordan, Saml.? Young, Wm.	8	360	
Kidd, George	VB	-	-	-	see Bolling, Col. Robert
King, Andrew	TW	-	-	-	see Furguson, Edward
King, John	JB	-	-	-	see Tabb, Thomas
Kinnon, Robert	VB	0	9	0	List
Lang, George	SC	0	1	370	
Lawson, Benj.	VB	-	-	-	see Jackson, Isaac
Lawson, Claibourne W.	VB	-	-	-	see Jackson, Isaac
Leath, Arthur	SC	Eckles, James	7	839	
Leaveston, Alex.	TW	-	-	-	see Williams, Thomas
Legg, Bartholemy	TM	-	-	-	see White, John
Lewis, Francis	SC	0	3	0	
Lewis, Griffin	SC	0	3	295	
Ligan, John	VB	0	0	0	
Liggin, Thomas	TM	0	1	0	
Ligon, Robert	JB	0	1	230	
Ligon, William	JB	Williams, Sam	6	400	
Ligon, William Jr.	JB	0	2	230	
Lipscomb, Ambrose	SC	0	3	0	
Lister?, Jeremiah	VB	0	1	100	
Livesie, Bolling	SC	-	-	-	see Livesie, Richard
Livesie, Richard	SC	Livesie, Bolling Livesie, Shadrack	1	0	
Livesie, Shadrack	SC	-	-	-	see Livesie, Richard
Loafman, John	JB	-	-	-	see Walthall, Christopher Jr.
Lockit, Stephen	TM	0	4	0	
Lorton, John	TM	-	-	-	see Lorton, Thomas
Lorton, Thomas	TM	Lorton, John	5	0	
Loving, Moses	TM	0	0	150	
Loving, William	JB	0	0	100	
Lowry, Richard	JB	-	-	-	see Tabb, Thomas
Majer, George	TM	-	-	-	see Hubbart, John
Mallory, Francis	VB	-	-	-	see Hamblin, John
Malone, Isham	JB	0	0	0	
Manire?, Jno.	SC	0	0	0	

NAME	LIST	Other white male tithes	Slaves	Acres	COMMENTS
Mann, Caine	JB	-	-	-	see Tanner, Branch
Mann, Field	JB	-	-	-	see Mann, Robert
Mann, James	JB	-	-	-	see Mann, Samuel Sr.
Mann, Robert	JB	Mann, Field	2	150	
Mann, Robert	JB	-	-	-	see Mann, Samuel Sr.
Mann, Samuel Sr.	JB	Mann, James Mann, Robert	0	150	
Marshall, John	JB	-	-	-	see Marshall, Robert's Est.
Marshall, Robert's Est.	JB	Marshall, Wm. Marshall, John Ellington, John	13	798	
Marshall, William Jr.	JB	Woods, Jos.	2	400	
Marshall, Wm.	JB	-	-	-	see Marshall, Robert's Est.
May, William Jr.	SC	0	4	0	
Mays, Abraham	SC	-	-	-	see Cocke, Stephen
Mayton?, Jo__?	VB	-	-	-	see Avery, John
McCutcheon, Jno.	SC	-	-	-	see Boyd, Walter
McHamy?, James	TM	-	-	-	see Booker, Rachel
McKinney, Laverne?	SC	0	0	0	
McLacklin, John Jr.	VB	0	1	0	
McNabb, Alexander	JB	-	-	-	see Tabb, Thomas
Meadow, James	TM	-	-	-	see Meadows, Joel
Meadow, Jehu	JB	-	-	-	see Robertson, George
Meadows, Benjamin	JB	0	0	100	
Meadows, Henry	TM	0	0	100	
Meadows, Joel	JB	0	2	174	
Meadows, Joel	TM	Meadow, James	2	0	
Meredith, Sampson	VB	0	3	0	
Merimoon, David	VB	0	0	100	
Miner, Nicholas	TW	-	-	-	see Stokes, Robt. Jr.
Minor, Daniel	SC	-	-	-	see Quarles, Richard
Mitchell, Evan	VB	-	-	-	see Bolling, Col. Robert
Molson, William Jr.	TM	-	-	-	see Molson, William Sr.
Molson, William Sr.	TM	Molson, William Jr. Hutcherson, John	13	1008	1 riding chair
Moodey, Blanks	JB	-	-	-	see Vaughan, Nicholas
Moody, Auther	TM	0	0	0	
Moor, Drury?	SC	-	-	-	see Moor, Wm.
Moor, George	SC	0	0	75	
Moor, James	TW	0	1	200	List
Moor, John	SC	0	0	100	
Moor, Mark	SC	-	-	-	see Haskins, Christopher
Moor, William	JB	-	-	-	see Tabb, Thomas
Moor, Wm.	SC	-	-	-	see Boyd, Walter
Moor, Wm.	SC	Moor, Drury?	0	100	
Moore, Robt.	JB	-	-	-	see Smith, John
Moore, William	JB	-	-	-	see Tabb, Thomas
Morgan Sam	JB	-	-	-	see Anderson, Claiborne

NAME	LIST	Other white male tithes	Slaves	Acres	COMMENTS
Morgan, Jac___	SC	-	-	-	see Morgan, Jacob
Morgan, Jacob	SC	Morgan, Jac___ Morgan, Samuel	18	0	
Morgan, Jno.	SC	0	0	0	
Morgan, John	JB	-	-	-	see Crawley, William
Morgan, John	JB	Coleman, Peter	2	100	List
Morgan, Joshua	JB	0	0	0	
Morgan, Sam Sr.	JB	Morgan, William Morgan, Simon	4	432	
Morgan, Samuel	SC	-	-	-	see Morgan, Jacob
Morgan, Simon	JB	-	-	-	see Morgan, Sam Sr.
Morgan, Thos.	SC	0	0	0	
Morgan, William	JB	-	-	-	see Morgan, Sam Sr.
Mumford, Edward	TM	-	-	-	see Munford, Thomas
Mundford, Robert	TW	Quesenbury, Aron	15	0	
Munford, Thomas	TM	Mumford, Edward Harris, William Ware, William	13	1051	1 riding chair
Munford, William	VB	Holt, David	8	1000	
Murray, Daniel	JB	0	0	0	
Murry, James	TM	Worsham, Henry	13	1465	List
Nance, David	VB	-	-	-	see Jones, John
Neal, David	JB	0	5	100	
Neal, Joel	JB	-	-	-	see Neal, William Sr.
Neal, John	JB	-	-	-	see Neal, William Sr.
Neal, John's Est.	JB	0	0	266	Estate of
Neal, Roger	JB	0	1	100	
Neal, Stephen	JB	0	3	100	
Neal, William Sr.	JB	Neal, Joel Neal, John	5	351	
Neal, Wm. Jr.	JB	0	5	100	List
Newman, Richard	VB	Walker, Vinson Tabb, Hampton	1	1186	
Norvell, Holtcroft Bates	JB	0	0	0	
Ogilby, John	JB	0	6	811	
Old, Jas.	VB	-	-	-	see Old, Mary
Old, Mary	VB	Old, Jas.	6	895	List?
Oliver, Ben	JB	-	-	-	see Jones, Thomas
Oliver, John	JB	-	-	-	see Jones, Richard
Osborne, Abner	VB	-	-	-	see Osborne, William
Osborne, Francis	JB	Powers, Sampson	3	400	List
Osborne, Joseph	JB	0	10	850	
Osborne, William	VB	Osborne, Wm. Jr. Osborne, Abner Cabiness, Matt.	14	1570	
Osborne, Wm. Jr.	VB	-	-	-	see Osborne, William
Ozely, Thomas	TM	0	0	109	

NAME	LIST	Other white male tithes	Slaves	Acres	COMMENTS
Palmore, Reuben	JB	0	3	200	
Parham, Gower	VB	0	2	100	
Parham, James	VB	0	2	150	
Parham, William	VB	0	3	230	
Parriot, John	SC	-	-	-	see Vaughn, Isham
Patterson, Benj. Jr.	VB	-	-	-	see Patterson, Benjamin
Patterson, Benjamin	VB	Patterson, Benj. Jr.	2	0	
Patterson, John	VB	0	0	300	
Peachy, Thos. Griffin	SC	Piles, Williamson	6	0	
Perdue, William	VB	0	1	150	
Phillips, Richard	TM	0	3	200	
Piles, Williamson	SC	-	-	-	see Peachy, Thos. Griffin
Pincham, Peter	SC	0	6	0	
Pitchford, Daniel	JB	0	0	50	
Pitchford, Will.	VB	-	-	-	see Green, Abraham Jr.
Pollard, Isack	TM	-	-	-	see Pollard, Joseph
Pollard, Joseph	TM	Pollard, Isack	1	140	
Pollard, Thomas Jr.	TM	-	-	-	see Pollard, Thomas Sr.
Pollard, Thomas Sr.	TM	Pollard, Thomas Jr.	2	140	
Ponton, Wm.	JB	-	-	-	see Royall, John
Portwood, Page	SC	-	-	-	see Cocke, Stephen
Powel, John	SC	Elmor, Wm.	0	0	
Powell, James	JB	0	0	0	
Powell, John	VB	0	1	200	
Powell, Mary	VB	0	2	0	List?
Powell, Robert	VB	Clay, Caleb	2	200	
Powers, Sampson	JB	-	-	-	see Osborne, Francis
Pride, Rowlett	JB	-	-	-	see Tabb, Thomas
Pride, William	JB	0	2	300	
Pringle, Parrot	JB	0	0	0	
Pringle, Richard	JB	-	-	-	see Tabb, Thomas
Puckett, Edward	JB	0	0	0	
Puckett, James	JB	0	0	0	
Puckett, John	JB	-	-	-	see Puckett, Richd.
Puckett, Richd.	JB	Puckett, John	2	100	
Puckett, Thomas	JB	-	-	-	see Willson, Daniel Jr.
Purkinson, Isham	JB	0	0	0	
Purkinson, Ralph	JB	0	1	232	
Purkinson, T___?	JB	0	1	0	name smudged, illegible
Quarles, Richard	SC	Minor, Daniel	0	0	
Quesenbury, Aron	TW	-	-	-	see Mundford, Robert
Quisenbury, John	VB	-	-	-	see Quisenbury, Nicholas
Quisenbury, Nicholas	VB	Quisenbury, John	0	0	
Ragland, Benj.	VB	-	-	-	see Cousens, Robt.
Ragland, Jos.	VB	-	-	-	see Cousens, Robt.
Ragsdale, George	JB	0	1	116.5	
Randolph, John	JB	0	17	1053	
Ray, John	TM	-	-	-	see Johnson, William

NAME	LIST	Other white male tithes	Slaves	Acres	COMMENTS
Ray, Joseph	TM	-	-	-	see Ray, William
Ray, William	TM	Ray, Joseph	0	0	
Reams, Frederick	JB	0	0	0	
Reams, Thos.	JB	0	1	150	
Rice, John	JB	-	-	-	see Robertson, John's Est.
Riggon, Moses	TW	0	0	0	
Right, William	TM	-	-	-	see Wright, John
Roach, William	VB	-	-	-	see Hamblin, Stephen
Roberson, James' Est.	TM	Stewart, William	13	1461	"Estate of"
Roberson, Robert	TM	0	0	0	
Roberts, Sarah	JB	Deaton, Iabe?	2	0	List
Roberts, Step	JB	-	-	-	see Farrar, Peter
Robertson, Bridge	JB	-	-	-	see Robertson, Wm.
Robertson, George	JB	Meadow, Jehu	5	558	List
Robertson, John's Est.	JB	Rice, John	3	0	Estate of
Robertson, Wm.	JB	Robertson, Bridge	0	0	
Royall, John	JB	Royall, Joseph Ponton, Wm.	12	960	1 riding chair
Royall, Joseph	JB	-	-	-	see Royall, John
Royall, Joseph	VB	0	7	400	
Rucker, Elisha	TM	-	-	-	see Rucker, William Sr.
Rucker, James	TM	0	0	150	
Rucker, Joshua	TM	Rucker, Mordacai	0	80	
Rucker, Mordacai	TM	-	-	-	see Rucker, Joshua
Rucker, William Jr.	TM	0	0	100	
Rucker, William Sr.	TM	Rucker, Elisha	3	170	
Sadler, Thomas	TM	-	-	-	see Eggleston, Richard
Sallard, Charles	SC	0	9	0	
Sammons, Thomas	TM	-	-	-	see Jones, Maj. Richard
Scott, John	JB	Daniel, Benj. Butler, Wm.	10	1400	
Scott, Joseph	JB	Harrison, William Bryan, Frederick Woodson, Joseph Fontaine, Joseph	1	0	
Seaman, John	SC	Elmor, Jno.	0	0	
Seay, Gidion	TM	0	0	0	
Seay, Jacob	TM	0	5	545	
Seay, James	TM	0	2	392	
Seay, Jesse	TM	Seay, Sargius	4	0	
Seay, Moses	TM	0	2	200	List?
Seay, Sargius	TM	-	-	-	see Seay, Jesse
Shelton, Benjamin	SC	0	1	0	
Shelton, Danl.	SC	Fortin?, Jos.	3	0	
Short, Thomas	TW	0	7	600	
Smart, James	VB	-	-	-	see Greenhill, David

NAME	LIST	Other white male tithes	Slaves	Acres	COMMENTS
Smith, Henry	JB	-	-	-	see Hardaway, Joseph
Smith, Jno.	VB	-	-	-	see Walthall, William
Smith, John	JB	Moore, Robt.	3	0	List
Smith, Mathew	SC	0	0	0	
Smith, Samuel	SC	Dixon, Wm.	7	0	
Smith, William	VB	0	1	125	
Southall, James	TM	-	-	-	see Jinkins, James
Southall, James	VB	0	1	100	
Southall, John	TM	-	-	-	see Jones, Capt. Robert
Southall, William	TM	Hix, Allis	1	255	
Southerland, Fendall	VB	Turner, Martin	13	1447	List?
Spain, Frederick	VB	0	1	100	
Spain, Joshua	VB	Frank, Jack	0	284	
St. John, Wm.	SC	0	3	0	
Standback, Peter	TW	0	1	0	
Standley, John	JB	-	-	-	see Chappel, James
Starn, Ann	TM	Hinson, Jonas	7	370	List
Stern, Francis	VB	0	5	346	
Stewart, William	TM	-	-	-	see Roberson, James' Est.
Still, George	SC	0	1	189	
Stokes, Mathew	SC	0	0	0	
Stokes, Robt. Jr.	TW	Miner, Nicholas	-	-	
Stokes, Robt. Sr.	TW	0	2	300	
Stow, Joel	SC	0	0	0	
Stow, William	SC	0	0	0	
Sturdivant, James	JB	Cornelius, Jesse	6	200	
Sturdivant, James	VB	0	3	200	
Sudsbury, David	JB	0	1	0	
Symonds, Benjamin	SC	0	0	0	
Tabb, Edward	TM	-	-	-	see Clements, John
Tabb, Hampton	VB	-	-	-	see Newman, Richard
Tabb, Langhorn	JB	-	-	-	see Tabb, Thomas
Tabb, Thomas	JB	Pringle, Richard Lowry, Richard Moore, William Hamm, Thomas Hutchason, Charles Chappel, Wm. McNabb, Alexander King, John Pride, Rowlett Tabb, Langhorn Cumpton, Zachariah Cheatam, Archer Jeter, Henry Moor, William Haskew, Joseph Jones, Richard	125	11,02 0	1 chariot 1 riding chair 2 wheels

NAME	LIST	Other white male tithes	Slaves	Acres	COMMENTS
		Greenwood, William Jesse, John Jones, Uriah Foster, John			
Talley, Daniel	VB	-	-	-	see Talley, Lodwick
Talley, Jessee	VB	-	-	-	see Talley, Lodwick
Talley, Lodwick	VB	Talley, Daniel Talley, Jessee	0	200	
Talley, Tucker	VB	0	3	325	
Talley, William	VB	0	2	165	
Talley, William	VB	0	0	0	
Tanner, Ann	JB	0	6	0	List
Tanner, Branch	JB	Mann, Caine	10	717	List
Tanner, Edward	VB	Tanner, Jeremiah	0	170	
Tanner, Jeremiah	VB	-	-	-	see Tanner, Edward
Tanner, Lodwick	JB	0	11	572	
Tanner, Robt.	VB	0	0	160	
Taylor, Daniel	SC	-	-	-	see Taylor, Robt.
Taylor, Robt.	SC	Taylor, Daniel	2	0	
Thackston, William	JB	-	-	-	see Booker, Ann
Thomas, Atha.	SC	-	-	-	see Thomas, Samuel
Thomas, David	SC	0	0	0	
Thomas, Samuel	SC	Thomas, Atha. Thomas, Woodliff	4	775	
Thomas, Wm. Jr.	SC	0	0	0	
Thomas, Wm. Sr.	SC	0	0	0	
Thomas, Woodliff	SC	-	-	-	see Thomas, Samuel
Thompson, Drury	JB	0	13	600	
Thompson, Peter	JB	0	8	532	
Thompson, William Jr.	VB	0	12	746	
Tinsly, Isack	TM	0	4	200	
Tinsly, Thomas	TM	0	1	0	
Toney, Jezzey	VB	-	-	-	see Toney, Peggy
Toney, John	VB	-	-	-	see Toney, Peggy
Toney, Peggy	VB	Toney, Jezzey Toney, John	0	0	
Totty, Abner	JB	-	-	-	see Hardaway, Daniel
Townes, Thomas	TM	-	-	-	see Townes, William
Townes, William	TM	Townes, Thomas	4	150	
Tucker, Absolam	VB	0	0	0	
Tucker, Daniel	VB	0	0	0	"son of William"
Tucker, Daniel	VB	Tucker, Robt.	2	200	
Tucker, Daniel	VB	Hudson, Peter	0	258	
Tucker, Danl.	VB	0	0	0	"son of John"
Tucker, David	VB	0	0	65	
Tucker, Frances	VB	Tucker, Godfrey	5	275	List?
Tucker, Francis Jr.	VB	0	0	0	

NAME	LIST	Other white male tithes	Slaves	Acres	COMMENTS
Tucker, Francis Sr.	VB	0	1	0	
Tucker, Geo.	VB	-	-	-	see Cousens, John
Tucker, George	VB	Tucker, Jos.	2	200	
Tucker, Godfrey	VB	-	-	-	see Tucker, Frances
Tucker, Henry	VB	0	0	25	
Tucker, Jno.	SC	-	-	-	see Tucker, Wm.
Tucker, John	SC	0	0	0	
Tucker, John	VB	-	-	-	see Tucker, William Sr.
Tucker, John	VB	Waller, Wm.	1	166	
Tucker, John	VB	-	-	-	see Tucker, John "Waller"
Tucker, John "Waller"	VB	Tucker, John	1	200	
Tucker, Jos.	VB	-	-	-	see Tucker, Robert
Tucker, Jos.	VB	-	-	-	see Tucker, George
Tucker, Joseph Jr.	VB	-	-	-	see Tucker, Joseph Sr.
Tucker, Joseph Sr.	VB	Tucker, Joseph Jr.	2	190	
Tucker, Lewis	SC	0	0	0	
Tucker, Matthew Jr.	VB	0	0	116	
Tucker, Matthew Sr.	VB	0	0	100	
Tucker, Micheal	VB	-	-	-	see Green, Abraham Jr.
Tucker, Robert	VB	Tucker, Jos.	1	478	
Tucker, Robt	VB	-	-	-	see Tucker, William Sr.
Tucker, Robt.	VB	-	-	-	see Tucker, Daniel
Tucker, Thomas	VB	0	0	84	
Tucker, William	VB	0	0	0	"son of William"
Tucker, William	VB	0	0	0	"son of Jno."
Tucker, William	VB	0	0	100	
Tucker, William Sr.	VB	Tucker, John Tucker, Robt.	3	844	
Tucker, Wm.	SC	Tucker, Jno.	1	0	
Tunstall, Richard	TM	-	-	-	see Cox, Henry
Turner, Martin	VB	-	-	-	see Southerland, Fendall
Vaden, Henry	JB	0	1	350	
Varsor, Wm.	VB	-	-	-	see Jones, Dorothy
Vassar, George	JB	-	-	-	see Vassar, Richard
Vassar, Richard	JB	Vassar, George	2	360	
Vaughan, Nicholas	JB	Moodey, Blanks	0	0	
Vaughn, David	SC	-	-	-	see Vaughn, Isham
Vaughn, Isham	SC	Vaughn, David Vaughn, Randolph Parriot, John	0	128	
Vaughn, Randolph	SC	-	-	-	see Vaughn, Isham
Vaughn, Samuel	SC	0	0	353	
Vaughn, Stephen	SC	0	0	0	
Verser, Abraham	TM	0	0	0	
Verser, Jesse	SC	-	-	-	see Verser, Jonas Est.
Verser, Jonas Est.	SC	Verser, Jesse	0	125	"Estate"
Walding, John	TM	-	-	-	see Anderson, Frances

NAME	LIST	Other white male tithes	Slaves	Acres	COMMENTS
Walke, Thomas	JB	West, Littleburry	3	0	
Walker, Alexander	TM	Allin, Samuel	2	0	
Walker, Edward	JB	Chaffin, Joshua	13	800	1 riding chair
Walker, Thomas	TW	-	-	-	see Williams, Thomas
Walker, Thos	TM	-	-	-	see Hart?, William
Walker, Vinson	VB	-	-	-	see Newman, Richard
Waller, Wm.	VB	-	-	-	see Tucker, John
Walthall, Christopher Jr.	JB	0	2	140	
Walthall, Christopher Jr.	JB	Loafman, John	6	400	
Walthall, Henry	JB	0	5	600	
Walthall, Richd.	VB	-	-	-	see Walthall, William
Walthall, Thomas	JB	Higgins, Solomon	14	803	
Walthall, William	VB	Gorham, John Walthall, Richd. Smith, Jno.	7	368	
Walthrop, Joseph	VB	Walthrop, Luke	0	400	
Walthrop, Luke	VB	-	-	-	see Walthrop, Joseph
Walthrop, Michael	VB	0	0	0	
Ward, Richd.	SC	-	-	-	see Epes, Francis
Ware, William	TM	-	-	-	see Munford, Thomas
Ware, William	TM	0	0	517	
Watne?, Richd.	JB	-	-	-	see Jones, Thomas
Watson, Luke	JB	0	0	0	
Webster, Anthony	VB	-	-	-	see Wilson, William Jr.
Webster, Peter Jr.	JB	Gibbs, Thos.	2	0	
Webster, Peter Sr.	JB	Webster, Wm.	5	700	
Webster, Thos.	JB	Webster, Thos. Jr.	4	450	
Webster, Thos. Jr.	JB	-	-	-	see Webster, Thos.
Webster, Wm.	JB	-	-	-	see Webster, Peter Sr.
Weekes, Emanuel	VB	0	0	0	
Weekes, Emmanuel	VB	-	-	-	see Wills, Willis
Weekes, Richard	VB	-	-	-	see Cowles, Thos.
West, Absolum	SC	-	-	-	see Hurt, Moses
West, Littleburry	JB	-	-	-	see Walke, Thomas
Westbrook, Chas.	SC	-	-	-	see Westbrook, Thos.
Westbrook, Henry	SC	-	-	-	see Westbrook, Thos.
Westbrook, Jos.	SC	-	-	-	see Westbrook, Thos.
Westbrook, Thos.	SC	Westbrook, Jos. Westbrook, Henry Westbrook, Chas.	1	0	
Whales, John	TM	Bell, John	13	0	List
White, David	TM	-	-	-	see Jinkins, James
White, Francis	SC	-	-	-	see White, John
White, George Christopher	TM	0	8	360	
White, John	SC	White, Francis	1	0	

NAME	LIST	Other white male tithes	Slaves	Acres	COMMENTS
White, John	TM	Legg, Bartholemy	2	290	
White, Joseph	SC	0	0	0	
Whitworth, Abraham	JB	0	2	300	
Whitworth, John	TM	-	-	-	see Ford, Christopher
Whitworth, Samuel	TM	Whitworth, Erasmus	2	291	
Whitworth, Thomas Jr.	TM	-	-	-	see Whitworth, Thomas Sr.
Whitworth, Thos. Sr.	TM	Whitworth, Thos. Jr.	1	282	
Whitworth, William	SC	0	0	0	
Wilie, Solomon	VB	-	-	-	see Greenhill, David
Wilkinson, Joseph Est.	JB	Jackson, Matt.	8	400	Estate of
Willas?, Danl.	SC	-	-	-	see Willas?, John
Willas?, John	SC	Willas?, Danl.	0	0	
Williams, Billington	SC	0	0	0	
Williams, Charles	SC	Hood, Wm.	1	0	
Williams, Sam	JB	-	-	-	see Ligon, William
Williams, Thomas	TW	Walker, Thomas Forde, Henry Leaveston, Alex.	25	0	
Williamson, Jacob	JB	Gates, James?	11	1016	
Williamson, Lew.	TW	0	5	0	
Willington, William	TW	-	-	-	see Jones, Peter
Wills, Burwell	SC	0	1	0	
Wills, Edmund	VB	0	1	0	
Wills, Edmund Jr.	VB	-	-	-	see Wills, Elias
Wills, Elias	VB	Wills, Edmund Jr.	8	1119	List?
Wills, Frederick	SC	0	0	100	
Wills, Laurence	VB	Wills, Thos. Tabb Borough, Peter	7	588	
Wills, Thos. Tabb	VB	-	-	-	see Wills, Laurence
Wills, Willis	VB	Weekes, Emmanuel	3	509	List?
Willson, Daniel Jr.	JB	0	5	0	
Willson, Daniel Jr.	JB	Anderson, Charles Puckett, Thomas	7	609	
Willson, Thomas B.	JB	0	18	1150	
Wilson, Charles	VB	-	-	-	see Wilson, John Sr.
Wilson, John Jr.	VB	0	2	507	
Wilson, John Sr.	VB	Wilson, Charles	6	300	
Wilson, William	VB	-	-	-	see Greenhill, David
Wilson, William Jr.	VB	Webster, Anthony	4	577	
Winfield, Robt.	VB	-	-	-	see Gilliam, John Sr.
Wingo, James	TM	Wingo, John	0	104	
Wingo, John	TM	0	0	200	
Wingo, John	TM	-	-	-	see Wingo, James
Wingo, Thomas	TM	0	0	60	
Winn, John	TW	0	1	0	
Winston, William	TM	0	3	420	

NAME	LIST	Other white male tithes	Slaves	Acres	COMMENTS
Wood, William	TM	Jones, Edw.	4	400	
Wood, William	TM	0	0	0	
Woods, Jos.	JB	-	-	-	see Marshall, William Jr.
Woodson, Joseph	JB	-	-	-	see Scott, Joseph
Worhsan, Henry	TM	0	0	40	
Worsham, Charles	TM	-	-	-	see Davis, Thomas
Worsham, Daniel	JB	0	11	719	
Worsham, George	VB	-	-	-	see Bevil, James
Worsham, Henry	TM	-	-	-	see Murry, James
Worsham, Henry (Gully)	JB	Worsham, Kemion?	2	150	
Worsham, John's Est.	JB	Foulkes, John	5	400	Estate of
Worsham, Kemion?	JB	-	-	-	see Worsham, Henry (Gully)
Worsham, William	JB	0	1	100	
Wright, Edward	SC	0	0	0	
Wright, John	TM	Right, William	5	630	List
Wright, John	TM	-	-	-	see Wright, Thomas
Wright, Thomas	TM	Wright, John Foster, James	10	300	
Young, Wm.	SC	-	-	-	see Jordan, Wm.

The 1770 AMELIA COUNTY TITHE LISTS – Note: two different formats (explained below)

EXPLANATION OF COLUMN HEADINGS

NAME: the name of the person paying the Tithe

LIST: The initials of the person who compiled the tithe list on which the individual appears (an indication of the geographic area and the parish where these individuals lived.

THE TAX "COMMISSIONERS" FOR 1770, AND THEIR AREA/PARISH

CF = Christopher Ford, Raleigh Parish
BW = Ben Ward, Raleigh Parish
JB = John Booker, Raleigh Parish
SC = Stephen Cocke, Nottoway Parish
TM = Thomas Munford of Raleigh Parish
TW = Thomas Williams, Nottoway Parish
VB = Vivion Brooking, the lower part of Raleigh Parish; this list was *very* difficult to read (**smudged, blurred data listed as "X" in Tables**)

In 1770, three of the commissioners (JB, VB & SC) used the same column headings as previous tithe lists, whereas the other 4 commissioners ceased to list the acres (if any) that each taxpayer owned, and instead listed Total Tithes. Thus, this year's tithe list is divided into **TWO tables**, to reflect and different formats.

OTHER WHITE MALE TITHES: The names of other men above the age of 16, whose tithe was paid by the taxpayer. When of the same surname, these were usually sons of the taxpayer. Otherwise, they were guests, overseers or other employees.

COMMENTS

Land = individual taxed only for land, not for self; exempt for some reason.
List = individual named not taxed for self; exempt, or taxed personally elsewhere.
List? = number of individuals named is one more than number taxed; List implied but not stated.

1770 TITHE LISTS, PART ONE

NAME	LIST	Other white male tithes	Slaves	Acres	COMMENTS
Adams, Wm.	VB	-	-	-	see Clay, John
Allen, Daniel	VB	0	3	X	
Allen, John	SC	0	1	0	
Anderson, Henry	JB	Clay, Jesse Puckett, James Puckett, Edward Johnson, Richard	50	3568	
Anderson, John	SC	0	1	100	
Appling, Thomas	JB	-	-	-	see Hardaway, Daniel
Archer, John	JB	-	-	-	see Archer, William
Archer, William	JB	Archer, John Archer, William Jr.	16	0	
Archer, William Jr.	JB	-	-	-	see Archer, William
Avery, John	VB	Mayton, Jno.	0	0	

NAME	LIST	Other white male tithes	Slaves	Acres	COMMENTS
		Hood, William			
Ballie, John	SC	0	3	0	(Bailey intended?)
Barker, Charles	SC	0	3	243	List
Bass, William Sr.	JB	0	10	0	
Batte, Thomas	SC	0	3	0	last name could be BALLE
Bennett, Benj.	VB	Bennett, William	1	283	
Bennett, Benj. Jr.	VB	0	0	0	
Bennett, Walter	JB	0	3	0	List?
Bennett, William	VB	-	-	-	see Bennett, Benj.
Bentley, John	SC	-	-	-	see Taylor, Robert
Bentley, Samuel Jr.	SC	0	0	0	
Bentley, Samuel Sr.	SC	0	0	0	
Bevil, Archer	VB	-	-	-	see Bevil, James
Bevil, James	VB	Bevil, Archer Bevil, Jas. Jr.	4	300	
Bevil, Jas. Jr.	VB	-	-	-	see Bevil, James
Bevil, Joseph	VB	0	1	X	
Bevil, Robt.	VB	0	1	200	
Bevil, Robt.	VB	0	1	200	(2nd man by same name)
Bevil, William	VB	0	2	100	
Bibb, William	JB	Taylor, Edmund	11	0	
Biggers, John	JB	-	-	-	see Booker, George & Lucy
Bird, Bob	SC	-	-	-	see Davis, Jacob
Bolling, Col. Robert	VB	Kidd, George	58	X	"Estate"
Bollings, Col. Alex.	SC	Gunn, Thomas	4	0	"Estate"
Booker, Ann	JB	0	12	0	List
Booker, Edmund	JB	Rice, James	13	0	1 riding chair
Booker, Edward	JB	0	12	1025	
Booker, Edward	JB	0	2	0	
Booker, George & Lucy	JB	Biggers, John	8	0	List
Booker, John	JB	Samson, Richard	20	1403	1 riding chair
Booker, John Jr.	JB	Watson, Luke	0	0	
Booker, Rachel	JB	Booker, Wm. Marshall	13	1023	"Estate of"
Booker, Wm. Marshall	JB	-	-	-	see Booker, Rachel
Booth, Benj.	VB	-	-	-	see Booth, Thomas
Booth, George	VB	Booth, Nath'l. Booth, George	2	450	
Booth, George	VB	-	-	-	see Booth, George
Booth, Jane	VB	0	2	0	List?
Booth, Jas.	VB	-	-	-	see Booth, Thomas
Booth, John	VB	0	6	360	
Booth, Nath'l.	VB	-	-	-	see Booth, George
Booth, Nathaniel	VB	0	3	336	
Booth, Thomas	VB	Booth, Jas. Booth, Benj.	1	X	
Booth, William	VB	Clardy, Jno.	3	X	

NAME	LIST	Other white male tithes	Slaves	Acres	COMMENTS
Borough?, Peter	VB	-	-	-	see Munford, William
Borum, Richard Sr.	JB	0	1	0	
Bradfute, Robt.	VB	-	-	-	see McKie, John
Bridgeforth, Benjamin	SC	Bridgeforth, Thomas	7	300	
Bridgeforth, Thomas	SC	-	-	-	see Bridgeforth, Benjamin
Brooking, Vivion	VB	Roach, William	27	2912?	1 riding chair
Brushill, Rev. Mr. John	JB	0	3	0	List?
Bryan, Frederick	JB	-	-	-	see Scott, Joseph
Burton, Peter?	VB	Clark, Jas.	1	170	
Caudle, William	VB	0	0	0	
Chaffin, Joshua	JB	-	-	-	see Walker, Edmund
Chambers, Mr. Thomas	SC	0	6	290	List?
Chapple, Martha	SC	0	0	135	"Estate"
Childress, Rips	JB	-	-	-	see Hill, James' Est.
Christian, Anthony	JB	Watkins, Stephen	7	0	
Claiborne, Phill. W.	SC	Lipscomb, Ambrose	12	1272	
Clardy, Benj.	VB	Clardy, James	4	526	
Clardy, James	VB	-	-	-	see Clardy, Benj.
Clardy, Jno.	VB	-	-	-	see Booth, William
Clardy, Michael	VB	0	2	175	
Clark, Jas.	VB	-	-	-	see Burton, Peter?
Clark, Thos.	VB	0	1	200	
Clay, Caleb	VB	-	-	-	see Wills, Willis
Clay, Charles	VB	Clay, Daniel	1	150	
Clay, Daniel	VB	-	-	-	see Clay, Charles
Clay, Elijah	VB	-	-	-	see Clay, Thos.
Clay, Jesse	JB	-	-	-	see Anderson, Henry
Clay, John	VB	Adams, Wm.	6	400	
Clay, John Jr.	VB	0	1	0	
Clay, Peter	VB	-	-	-	see Crawley, William
Clay, Shadrack	VB	-	-	-	see Clay, Thos.
Clay, Thos.	VB	Clay, Elijah Clay, Shadrack	0	152	
Clerk, Henry Jr.	SC	-	-	-	see Clerk, Henry Sr.
Clerk, Henry Sr.	SC	Clerk, Henry Jr. Clerk, Thos.	2	381	
Clerk, Peter Jr.	SC	-	-	-	see Clerk, Peter Sr.
Clerk, Peter Sr.	SC	Clerk, Peter Jr.	0	100	
Clerk, Thos.	SC	-	-	-	see Clerk, Henry Sr.
Cobb, John C.	JB	Cumpton, Richard	13	0	
Cobb, Theodocia	JB	0	1	0	1 riding chair; List
Cocke, John	SC	0	3	0	
Cocke, Stephen	SC	Mays, Abram	5	1010	
Cocke, Thomas	SC	0	3	0	

NAME	LIST	Other white male tithes	Slaves	Acres	COMMENTS
Cocke, William	SC	Portwood, Page	4	0	
Coleman, Abraham	VB	Coleman, Jeremiah	1	97	
Coleman, Daniel Jr.	VB	0	2	297	
Coleman, Daniel Sr.	VB	Coleman, Francis	6	461	
Coleman, Francis	VB	-	-	-	see Coleman, Daniel Sr.
Coleman, Jeremiah	VB	-	-	-	see Coleman, Abraham
Coleman, Jesse	VB	0	0	200	
Coleman, Jesse?	VB	-	-	-	see Coleman, Peter
Coleman, John	VB	0	0	100	
Coleman, John	VB	-	-	-	see Coleman, Peter
Coleman, Jos.	VB	0	0	75	
Coleman, Joseph Sr.	VB	Coleman, Sutton Coleman, Page	0	96	
Coleman, Page	VB	-	-	-	see Coleman, Joseph Sr.
Coleman, Peter	VB	Coleman, Jesse? Coleman, John	0	150	
Coleman, Sutton	VB	-	-	-	see Coleman, Joseph Sr.
Collee, David	VB	-	-	-	see Cuzzins, George
Combs, Francis	JB	Combs, Samuel	0	0	List
Combs, Samuel	JB	-	-	-	see Combs, Francis
Connally, Charles	SC	Connally, George	4		
Connally, George	SC	-	-	-	see Connally, Charles
Cousins, John	VB	0	6	643	
Cousins, Thos.	VB	0	0	0	
Cousins, William Jr.	VB	0	3	578	
Cousins, William Sr.	VB	Hanks, Thos.	5	1148	
Cowles, Thos.	VB	Weeks, Richd.	7	1084	"Estate"
Crawley, Da(vid)	VB	-	-	-	see Crawley, William
Crawley, William	VB	Crawley, Da(vid) Morgan, John Clay, Peter Ellington, William	46	3984	
Crenshaw, William Jr.	SC	0	2	330	
Cross, Charles	SC	-	-	-	see Cross, William
Cross, Richard	SC	0	3	0	
Cross, William	SC	Cross, Charles	7	0	
Crowder, John	VB	-	-	300	
Crowder, Joseph	VB	0	1	200	
Cumpton, Richard	JB	-	-	-	Cobb, John C.
Cuzzins, George	VB	Collee, David	6	1000	"Estate"
Davis, Jacob	SC	Davis, Thomas Bird, Bob	3	300	
Davis, Thomas	JB	Worsham, Charles	3	0	
Davis, Thomas	SC	-	-	-	see Davis, Jacob
Deaton, Tabby	JB	-	-	-	see Roberts, Sarah
Dodson, Edward	VB	-	-	-	see Dodson, John
Dodson, John	VB	Dodson, Edward	2	100	

NAME	LIST	Other white male tithes	Slaves	Acres	COMMENTS
Draper, James	SC	Draper, William Draper, Thomas	0	0	
Draper, Thomas	SC	-	-	-	see Draper, James
Draper, William	SC	-	-	-	see Draper, James
Dudley, Edward	VB	Dudley, Jas.	8	X	
Dudley, Jas.	VB	-	-	-	see Dudley, Edward
Dunn, John	VB	0	0	X	large ink blot
Durham, Joshua	SC	0	0	0	
Eckles, James	SC	0	0	331	
Eckles, Robert	SC	0	0	330	
Eggleston, Joseph	JB	______, William	22	2100	1 riding chair
Eggleston, William	JB	0	5	600	1 riding chair
Ellington, Daniel	JB	-	-	-	see Ellington, John
Ellington, John	JB	Ellington, Daniel	8	1138	
Ellington, William	VB	-	-	-	see Crawley, William
Ellington, William	VB	0	0	96	
Elmore, John	SC	-	-	-	see Lipscomb, Ambrose
Fairlie, James	JB	Haskins, Aaron	1	100	
Featherston, Lewis	SC	0	0	0	
Featherstone, Charles	JB	0	3	0	
Ferguson, John	JB	Ferguson, Robert	12	500	List?
Ferguson, Peleg	SC	0	3	325	
Ferguson, Richard	JB	0	1	0	
Ferguson, Robert	JB	-	-	-	see Ferguson, John
Ferguson, Thomas	JB	-	-	-	see Jones, William
Field, Robert	JB	0	1	0	
Ford, Abraham	SC	0	0	0	
Foster, Ann	JB	Foster, Richard	2	0	List
Foster, Richard	JB	-	-	-	see Foster, Ann
Fountain, Joseph	JB	-	-	-	see Scott, Joseph
Friend, Edward's Est.	JB	Power, Samson	6	0	"Estate"
Friend, Nathaniel?	JB	____, Robert	3	0	surnames obscured; List
Gallimore, Betty	VB	-	-	-	see Jones, Henry
Gallimore, Edward	VB	-	-	-	see Jones, Henry
Gallimore, George	VB	-	-	-	see Jones, Henry
Gates, James	JB	-	-	-	see Williamson, Jacob
Giles, William	JB	0	11	0	1 riding chair
Glasby, William	SC	-	-	-	see Morgan, Jacob
Gorham, John	VB	-	-	-	see Walthall, William
Green, Abraham	VB	Green, Abraham Jr. Green, Matthew Pitchford, Wm. Wilkerson, Peter	17	1750	1 riding chair
Green, Abraham	VB	-	-	-	see Green, Thomas
Green, Abraham Jr.	VB	-	-	-	see Green, Abraham

NAME	LIST	Other white male tithes	Slaves	Acres	COMMENTS
Green, Henry	SC	XX	4?	300	page torn, illegible
Green, John	VB	-	-	-	see Green, Thomas
Green, Matthew	VB	-	-	-	see Green, Abraham
Green, Thomas	VB	Green, Abraham Green, John	1	268	
Green, William	VB	McGinnis, Alexander	4	652	
Greenhill, David	VB	Greenhill, Jos. Wilson, Wm Wiles, Sol.	26	X	
Greenhill, Jos.	VB	-	-	-	see Greenhill, David
Gun, James	SC	0	5	1672	
Gunn, James	SC	King, George	6	200	List
Gunn, Thomas	SC	-	-	-	see Bollings, Col. Alex.
H____, _____	SC	Hurt, Zachariah Hurt, Absolom	8	300	Name cbscured; possibly Moses Hurt????
Haistings, William	VB	0	1	200	
Hall, Henry	VB	0	0	0	
Hames, John	SC	Hames, Will'm	3	0	
Hames, Will'm	SC	-	-	-	see Hames, John
Hamlin, Charles	VB	0	10	0	
Hamlin, John	VB	Moody, Phil.	9	148	
Hamlin, Stephen	VB	Roach, William	7	0	"Estate"
Hammock, Robert	SC	0	0	81	
Hammond, Lewis Jr.	SC	-	-	-	see Hammond, Lewis Sr.
Hammond, Lewis Sr.	SC	Hammond, William Hammond, Lewis Jr.	1	0	
Hammond, William	SC	-	-	-	see Hammond, Lewis Sr.
Hancock, Ananias	JB	-	-	-	see Lockett, Stephen
Hanks, Thos.	VB	-	-	-	Cousins, William Sr.
Hardaway, Daniel	JB	Parham, Francis Appling, Thomas	21	1238	"Pattroler"; 1 riding chair
Harper, Drury	SC	-	-	-	see Harper, Joseph
Harper, Joseph	SC	Harper, Drury Wood, Wm.	1		
Haskins, Aaron	JB	-	-	-	see Fairlie, James
Hawkins, David	VB	0	2	200	
Hawks, ___	VB	Hawks, Geo.	3	531	name blurred; prob. Joshua
Hawks, Geo.	VB	-	-	-	see Hawks, ___
Hawks, Richard	VB	0	0	0	
Hightower, Charnel	SC	-	-	-	see Hightower, Joshua Sr.
Hightower, Charnel	SC	-	-	-	see St. John, William
Hightower, George	SC	Hightower, Rich'd	6	0	
Hightower, Joshua Sr.	SC	Hightower, Charnel	5	0	
Hightower, Rich'd	SC	-	-	-	see Hightower, George

NAME	LIST	Other white male tithes	Slaves	Acres	COMMENTS
Hightower, Wm.	SC	-	-	-	see Hurt, Moses Jr.
Hill, Ann	JB	0	2	0	List
Hill, George	SC	0	0	200	List?
Hill, James' Est.	JB	Childress, Rips	5	0	"Estate"
Hillsman, Mathew	JB	0	1	0	
Hinton, Wood	SC	-	-	-	see Mays, Mathew
Hood, Abraham	VB	0	0	240	
Hood, John	VB	Hood, Thos.	3	472	
Hood, Robert	VB	0	0	75	
Hood, Thos.	VB	-	-	-	see Hood, John
Hood, William	VB	-	-	-	see Avery, John
Hood, William	VB	0	0	75	
Hooper, Zachariah	SC	0	1	0	
Hubbard, Benjamin	JB	0	1	100	
Huddleston, Thomas	VB	0	1	X	
Hudson, ____'s List	JB	Rice, John	6	0	List; names obscured
Hudson, Daniel?	VB	-	-	-	see Walthrop, Joseph
Hudson, John	VB	-	-	-	see Newman, Richard
Hudson, Peter	VB	-	-	-	see Tucker, Robert
Hughs, William	SC	0	0	200	
Hurt, Absolom	SC	-	-	-	see H____, _____
Hurt, Moses Jr.	SC	Hightower, Wm.	1	160	
Hurt, Zachariah	SC	-	-	-	see H____, _____
Irby, William	SC	0	2	145	
Jackson, Charles	SC	Jackson, Phillip	0	0	
Jackson, Dan'l	SC	-	-	-	see Manire, John
Jackson, Daniel	SC	0	2	0	
Jackson, Edward Jr.	SC	-	-	-	see Jackson, Edward Sr.
Jackson, Edward Sr.	SC	Jackson, Edward Jr.	2	653	
Jackson, Isaac	SC	-	-	-	see Jackson, William Sr.
Jackson, Isaac	VB	0	1	196	
Jackson, John	SC	0	0	50	
Jackson, Phillip	SC	-	-	-	see Jackson, Charles
Jackson, Thomas	SC	0	1	0	
Jackson, William Sr.	SC	Jackson, Isaac	3	0	
Johnson, Richard	JB	-	-	-	see Anderson, Henry
Jones, Adam	SC	Jones, Benjamin	9	400	
Jones, Benjamin	SC	-	-	-	see Jones, Adam
Jones, Charles	JB	0	2	0	
Jones, Col. Wood	VB	Jones, Philip Jones, Wood	12	0	1 chair
Jones, Daniel Jr.	VB	0	5		
Jones, Daniel Sr.	VB	Quisenbury, Aaron	17	1341	
Jones, Henry	SC	0	3	0	List?
Jones, Henry	VB	Gallimore,	6	1345	"Estate"

NAME	LIST	Other white male tithes	Slaves	Acres	COMMENTS
		George Gallimore, Edward Gallimore, Betty			
Jones, Peter	VB	0	8	784	
Jones, Philip	VB	-	-	-	see Jones, Col. Wood
Jones, Repes?? Sr.	SC	0	0	517	
Jones, Richard	JB	0	3	572	"Patroller"
Jones, Ripes Jr.	SC	0	0	0	
Jones, Sarah	VB	0	5	0	List?
Jones, Thomas	JB	Walne, Richard	9	572	
Jones, William	JB	Ferguson, Thomas	4	744	
Jones, William	SC	0	4	393	
Jones, Wood	VB	-	-	-	see Jones, Col. Wood
Jordan, Thomas	SC	-	-	-	see Jordan, William
Jordan, William	SC	Jordan, Thomas	8	360	
Kidd, George	VB	-	-	-	see Bolling, Col. Robert
King, George	SC	-	-	-	see Gunn, James
King, Henry	VB	0	1		
Lawson, Benj.	VB	-	-	-	see Lawson, Claiborne
Lawson, Claiborne	VB	Lawson, Benj.	0	0	
Lewis, Griffin	SC	0	3	295	
Lewis, Henry	VB	0	1	0	
Lewis, John	SC	0	2	220	
Liggan, John	VB	0	0	0	
Lipscomb, Ambrose	SC	-	-	-	see Claiborne, Phill. W.
Lipscomb, Ambrose	SC	Elmore, John	3	104	List
Lister, Jeremiah	VB	0	1	100	
Loafman, John	JB	-	-	-	see Ogilsby, John
Lockett, Arch'd	JB	-	-	-	see R___, Francis
Lockett, Stephen	JB	Hancock, Ananias	4	0	
Manire, John	SC	Jackson, Dan'l	0	0	
May, John	SC	0	1	0	
Mayes, P___'s List	JB	0	1	0	List; name blurred
Mays, Abram	SC	-	-	-	see Cocke, Stephen
Mays, Daniel Jr.	SC	-	-	-	see Mays, Daniel Sr.
Mays, Daniel Sr.	SC	Mays, Daniel Jr.	2	0	
Mays, Mathew	SC	Hinton, Wood	9	0	
Mayton, Jno.	VB	-	-	-	see Avery, John
McGinnis, Alexander	VB	-	-	-	see Green, William
McKenzie, Traverse	SC	0	0	0	
McKie, John	VB	Bradfute, Robt. McLeod, James	1	0	
McLachlin, John	VB	0	1	0	
McLeod, James	VB	-	-	-	see McKie, John
Meadows, Jehu	JB	-	-	-	see Robertson, George

NAME	LIST	Other white male tithes	Slaves	Acres	COMMENTS
Meredith, Sampson	VB	0	1	0	
Minire, William	SC	0	0	0	
Minor, Daniel	SC	-	-	-	see Stocker, Robert
Moody, Phil.	VB	-	-	-	see Hamlin, John
Moor, Drury?	SC	-	-	-	see Moor, William
Moor, George	SC	0	0	75	
Moor, John	SC	0	0	100	
Moor, William	SC	Moor, Drury?	0	100	
Moreans, Samuel	SC	-	-	-	see Morgan, Jacob
Morgan, Jacob	SC	Glasby, William Morgan, Jacob P. Moreans, Samuel	18	0	
Morgan, Jacob P.	SC	-	-	-	see Morgan, Jacob
Morgan, John	VB	-	-	-	see Crawley, William
Munford, William	VB	Borough?, Peter	8	1000	1 chair
Newman, Richard	VB	Hudson, John	4	1186	"Estate"
Ogilsby, John	JB	Loafman, John	8	0	
Old, James	VB	-	-	-	see Old, Mary
Old, Mary	VB	Old, James	X	X	large ink blot!
Pardue, William	VB	0	1	0	
Parham, Francis	JB	-	-	-	see Hardaway, Daniel
Parham, Gower	VB	0	2	100	
Parham, James	VB	0	2	163?	
Parram, William	VB	0	3	218	Parham intended?
Peavery, Mary	SC	0	1	100	List
Pitchford, Wm.	VB	-	-	-	see Green, Abraham
Ponton, William	JB	-	-	-	see Royall, John
Porter, John P.	SC	-	-	-	see Vaghn, Isham
Portwood, Page	SC	-	-	-	see Cocke, William
Powell, John	SC	0	0	222	
Powell, John	VB	0	1	200	
Powell, Mary	VB	0	2	0	List?
Powell, Robert	VB	0	2	200	"Patroller"
Power, Samson	JB	-	-	-	see Friend, Edward's Est.
Pride, Francis	JB	-	-	-	see Pride, John
Pride, John	JB	Pride, Francis	7	400	
Puckett, Edward	JB	-	-	-	see Anderson, Henry
Puckett, James	JB	-	-	-	see Anderson, Henry
Puckett, John	JB	-	-	-	see Puckett, Richard
Puckett, Richard	JB	Puckett, John	2	0	
Quarles, Richard	SC	0	1	0	
Quisenbury, Aaron	VB	-	-	-	see Jones, Daniel Sr.
R___, Francis	JB	Lockett, Arch'd	4	0	surname obscured
Rice, James	JB	-	-	-	see Booker, Edmund
Rice, John	JB	-	-	-	see Hudson, ____'s List
Roach, Millington	VB	0	0	400	"Patroller"
Roach, William	VB	-	-	-	see Brooking, Vivion

NAME	LIST	Other white male tithes	Slaves	Acres	COMMENTS
Roach, William	VB	-	-	-	see Hamlin, Stephen
Roberts, Sarah	JB	Deaton, Tabby	3	200	List
Robertson, George	JB	Meadows, Jehu	5	0	List
Robertson, James Est.	JB	Stewart, Wm.	13	0	"Estate of"
Robertson, William	JB	0	2	600	
Rodgers, John	SC	0	2	206	
Royall, John	JB	Royall, Joseph Ponton, William	11	0	1 riding chair
Royall, Joseph	JB	-	-	-	see Royall, John
Sallard, Charles	SC	0	9	710	
Samson, Richard	JB	-	-	-	see Booker, John
Scott, Joseph	JB	Fountain, Joseph Bryan, Frederick Woodson, Joseph	2		
Simmons, John	SC	0	0	100	
Simmons, Thomas	SC	0	1	0	
Smith, ____	VB	0	1	0	large ink blot!
Smith, John	VB	-	-	-	see Walthall, William
Southall, James	VB	0	1	100	
Southerland, Tindall	VB	Turner, Martin	12	1447	"Estate"
Spain, ___ (Joshua?)	VB	Spain, Newman	3	284	large ink blot!
Spain, Newman	VB	-	-	-	see Spain, ___ (Joshua?)
St. John, William	SC	Hightower, Charnel	4	263	
Starr, Jacob	SC	-	-	-	see Starr, William
Starr, Joel	SC	-	-	-	see Starr, William
Starr, William	SC	Starr, Joel Starr, Jacob	0	0	
Starr, William	SC	-	-	-	see Taylor, Robert
Stern, Francis	VB	0	3	346	large ink blot
Stewart, Wm.	JB	-	-	-	see Robertson, James Est.
Stocker, Mathew	SC	0	2	0	
Stocker, Robert	SC	Minor, Daniel	2	0	List of Tithes
Stocker, Robert Jr.	SC	0	0	0	
Sturdivant, Jas.	VB	0	3	200	"P.George" (county?)
Talley, Dan'l?	VB	-	-	-	see Talley, William
Talley, Frederick	VB	-	-	-	see Talley, Tucker
Talley, Jesse	VB	-	-	-	see Talley, Lodowick
Talley, John	VB	-	-	-	see Talley, Lodowick
Talley, Lodowick	VB	Talley, Jesse Talley, John	0	200	
Talley, Richard	VB	0	0	300?	smudged entry, blurry
Talley, Tucker	VB	Talley, Frederick	2	200	
Talley, William	VB	Talley, Dan'l?	0	0	"Patroller"
Talley, William	VB	0	2	163	
Tanner, Jeremiah	VB	0	0	170	
Tanner, Joseph	JB	Tanner, Thos.	1	0	

NAME	LIST	Other white male tithes	Slaves	Acres	COMMENTS
Tanner, Robert	VB	0	0	160	
Tanner, Thos.	JB	-	-	-	see Tanner, Joseph
Taylor, Edmund	JB	-	-	-	see Bibb, William
Taylor, James	JB	0	3	0	
Taylor, Robert	SC	Taylor, Daniel Bentley, John	2	0	
Thomas, Athan.	SC	-	-	-	see Thomas, Sam'l
Thomas, David	SC	-	-	-	see Thomas, William
Thomas, Jos.	SC	-	-	-	see Thomas, Sam'l
Thomas, Sam'l	SC	Thomas, Jos. Thomas, Athan. Thomas, Woodl.	4	948?	torn page
Thomas, William	SC	Thomas, David	0	0	
Thomas, William Jr.	SC	0	0	0	
Thomas, Woodl.	SC	-	-	-	see Thomas, Sam'l
Thompson, Roger	JB	0	2	0	
Trebeu, James	JB	0	2	0	
Tucker, ___	VB	0	0	400	large ink blot!
Tucker, Absolom	VB	0	0	0	
Tucker, Daniel	VB	0	0	258	
Tucker, Daniel	VB	0	0	190	"son of John"
Tucker, Daniel	VB	0	2	0	"son of William"
Tucker, Daniel Sr.	VB	Tucker, Robert	1	200	
Tucker, David	VB	0	0	65	
Tucker, Frances	VB	0	2	75	List?
Tucker, Francis	VB	Tucker, Godfrey	4	275	"Patroller"
Tucker, Francis	VB	0	1	X	
Tucker, George	VB	Tucker, George Jr. Tucker, Jos.	2	200	
Tucker, George Jr.	VB	-	-	-	see Tucker, George
Tucker, Godfrey	VB	-	-	-	see Tucker, Francis
Tucker, Henry	VB	0	0	25	
Tucker, Jno.	SC	-	-	-	see Tucker, William
Tucker, Jno.	VB	-	-	-	see Tucker, William Sr.
Tucker, Jno.	VB	-	-	-	see Wills, Elias
Tucker, John	VB	0	1	200	
Tucker, Jos.	VB	-	-	-	see Tucker, George
Tucker, Jos.	VB	-	-	-	Tucker, Joseph Sr.
Tucker, Joseph Sr.	VB	Tucker, Jos.	2	190	
Tucker, Matthew	VB	0	0	100	
Tucker, Matthew Jr.	VB	0	1	116	
Tucker, Robert	VB	Hudson, Peter	3	278	
Tucker, Robert	VB	-	-	-	see Tucker, Daniel Sr.
Tucker, Robt.	VB	-	-	-	see Tucker, William Sr.
Tucker, Thomas	VB	0	0	84	
Tucker, William	SC	Tucker, Jno.	1	0	
Tucker, William	VB	0	0	0	"son of Wm."

NAME	LIST	Other white male tithes	Slaves	Acres	COMMENTS
Tucker, William	VB	0	0	166	"son of John"
Tucker, William Sr.	VB	Tucker, Jno. Tucker, Robt.	3	844	
Turner, Martin	VB	-	-	-	see Southerland, Tindall
Vaghn, Daniel	SC	-	-	-	see Vaghn, Isham
Vaghn, Isham	SC	Vaghn, Daniel Vaghn, Rand. Vaughn, Robt. Porter, John P.	0	0	name spelled both ways in this entry!
Vaghn, Rand.	SC	-	-	-	see Vaghn, Isham
Vaughan, Cert?	JB	0	4		
Vaughn, Robt.	SC	-	-	-	see Vaghn, Isham
Walke, Thomas	JB	West, Littlebury	5	200	
Walker, Edmund	JB	Chaffin, Joshua	13	0	1 riding chair
Walker, Vincent	VB	0	0	0	
Wallace, Francis	SC	-	-	-	see Wallace, Mial?
Wallace, Mial?	SC	Wallace, Francis Wallace, Theodore	0	200	
Wallace, Theodore	SC	-	-	-	see Wallace, Mial?
Walne, Richard	JB	-	-	-	see Jones, Thomas
Walthall, William	VB	Gorham, John Smith, John	5	368	
Walthrop, Joseph	VB	Hudson, Daniel?	0	400	
Walthrop, Luke	VB	0	0	0	
Walthrop, Michael	VB	0	0	0	
Ward, Willey	SC	0	0	0	
Wathol, Richard	SC	0	3	276	
Watkins, Stephen	JB	-	-	-	see Christian, Anthony
Watson, Luke	JB	-	-	-	see Booker, John Jr.
Weeks, __?	VB	-	-	-	see Wills, Elias
Weeks, Emmanuel	VB	0	0	150	
Weeks, Richd.	VB	-	-	-	see Cowles, Thos.
West, Littlebury	JB	-	-	-	see Walke, Thomas
White, Joseph	SC	0	0	100	
Wiles, Sol.	VB	-	-	-	see Greenhill, David
Wilkerson, Peter	VB	-	-	-	see Green, Abraham
Williams, David	VB	0	0	125	
Williamson, Jacob	JB	Gates, James	12	794	
Wills, Abram	SC	Wills, Mathew	1	0	
Wills, Elias	VB	Weeks, __? Tucker, Jno.	7?	1322	"Estate" Large ink blot obscures
Wills, Laurence	VB	Wills, Thos. J.	9	788	
Wills, Mathew	SC	-	-	-	see Wills, Abram
Wills, Thos. J.	VB	-	-	-	see Wills, Laurence
Wills, Willis	VB	Clay, Caleb	4	509	"Estate"
Wilson, Chas.	VB	-	-	-	see Wilson, John Sr.

NAME	LIST	Other white male tithes	Slaves	Acres	COMMENTS
Wilson, John Jr.	VB	0	2	50?	
Wilson, John Sr.	VB	Wilson, Chas.	6	300	
Wilson, William	VB	0	8	580	
Wilson, Wm.	VB	-	-	-	see Greenhill, David
Wood, Wm.	SC	-	-	-	see Harper, Joseph
Woodson, Joseph	JB	-	-	-	see Scott, Joseph
Worsham, Charles	JB	-	-	-	see Davis, Thomas
Worsham, George	VB	0	3	240	

1770 TITHE LISTS, PART TWO

TAXPAYER	LIST	OTHER WMTs	Slaves	Total tithes	COMMENTS
____, Col. Theo.'s List	TW	North?, Thomas	17	18	
Adkinson, John	CF	-	-	1	
Algood, Edward	TW	-	-	1	
Algood, John	TW	-	-	1	
Allen, Samuel	CF	-	-	1	
Alsop, Joseph	BW	-	-	1	
Alsop, Samuel	BW	-	-	1	
Alsop. William	BW	-	-	1	
Anderson, Chas	BW				see Daniel Wilson
Anderson, Francis Jr.	CF	Oliver, John	10	12	
Anderson, Francis Sr.	CF	Waldin, John	14	16	
Anderson, Paulin's List	CF	Bagby, James Bohannon, Henry	15	17	
Anderson, Richard	CF	Hill, Joel	5	7	
Archer, John	BW	-	1	2	
Archer, John	JT				see John Tabb
Archer, John's List *	BW	Cloudas, George	5	6	"Chesterfield" (Co.)
Asselin, David	CF	-	3	4	one riding chair
Asselin, Laurence	CF				see Christopher Ford
Avery, George	BW	Avery, William	2	4	
Avery, William	BW				see George Avery
Bagby, James	CF				see Paulin Anderson's List
Bagby, John	CF	-	3	4	
Ballie?, Anvil?	BW				see Richard Hayes
Bass, Edward	JT	Burton, Charles	10	12	one riding chair
Bass, William Sr.	JT	-	5	6	
Beaufort, Thomas	TW	-	2	3	
Belcher, John	BW	Belcher, Thos.	-	2	-
Belcher, John Jr.	BW	-	-	1	-
Belcher, Thos.	BW				see John Belcher
Bell, George	JT				see Christopher Hudson
Bell, John	CF				see Thomas Wright
Bently, Samuel Sr.	CF	Bently, Samuel Jr.	9	11	
Besseley, Peter	BW	Young, Saml.	17	19	1400 acres
Bevel, Abraham	BW	-	-	1	

Bevel, Essia	BW	-	1	2	150 acres
Bevel, Joel	BW	-	4	5	251 acres
Bevel, Thomas	BW	-	1	2	251 acres
Blaikley, James	CF	-	1	2	
Blake, William	CF				see John Drinkwater Sr.
Blanchett, Henry	BW				see Thomas Hall
Blanchett, Isaac	BW	-	-	1	30 acres
Bland, Dr. Thk.'s List	TW	Brown, William	11	12	given name abbreviated
Bohannon, Henry	CF				see Paulin Anderson's List
Bonner, Thomas	BW	-	-	1	106 acres
Booker, George	CF				see Christopher Ford
Booker, John	CF	Whitworth, John	4	6	
Bott, Miles	BW	Brown, Wm.	5	7	752 acres
Bott, William	BW	-	2	3	646 acres
Bottom, Thomas	BW	-	9	10	970 acres
Boyd, Walter's List	TW	McCutchion, John Moore, William	11	13	
Brackett, Benjamin	JT				see Thomas Brackett
Brackett, Thomas	JT	Brackett, Thos. Jr. Brackett, Benj. Rhodes, John	7	11	
Bradley, James	TW	-	1	2	
Bradley, James' Tithes	JT	Cooper, Francis	13	14	
Bradshaw, Richard	CF	-	2	3	
Brintle, Jacob	BW				see Thomas Walthall
Brooks, George	BW	-	-	1	100 acres
Brooks, Joel	BW				see Thomas Brooks
Brooks, Thomas	BW	Brooks, Joel	-	2	150 acres
Brooks, Wiliam	BW	-	1	2	150 acres
Brown, William	TW				see Dr. Bland's list
Brown, Wm.	BW				see Miles Bott
Bullington, John *	BW	-	-	-	"Constable"; 100 acres
Burkes, Thomas	JT				see Bolling Eldridge
Burton, Charles	JT				see Edward Bass
Burton, John	CF	Hudson, Robert	12	14	one riding chair
Butler, Calup	CF				see Alexander Kelley
Butler, William	CF	-	1	2	
Ca_idlomer?, John C.	CF				see John Finney; surname very difficult to interpret
Callicoat, James	BW	-	2	3	-
Callicoat, William	BW	-	2	3	1220 acres
Carr, Robert	BW	Dunnivant, Thos.	7	9	surname could be CARRY
Cavinder, Hugh	CF	-	1	2	
Chapman, John	CF	-	-	1	
Chapman, Samuel	CF	-	3	4	
Chappell, James	BW	Stanley, Jno.	14	16	996 acres
Chappell, John	BW	Chappell, John Jr.	4	6	496 acres
Chappell, Robert	BW	-	1	2	-
Chappell, William	JT				see John Tabb
Cheatam, Archer	JT				see John Tabb

Cheatham, James	BW	-	2	3	-
Cheatham, Leonard	BW	-	6	7	300 acres
Chumley, John	CF	-	1	2	
Claibrook, John	CF	-	-	1	
Claibrook, Peter	CF	-	2	3	
Clardy, Benj.	BW				see Richard Denniss
Clardy, John	CF				see John Finney
Clardy, John Jr.'s List	BW	-	1	1	
Clement, Isham	CF	Duglass, John Clement, Wm.	2	5	
Clement, John	CF	-	6	7	
Clement, John	CF				see Simon Clement Sr.
Clement, Simon Sr.	CF	Clement, Simon Jr Clement, John Clement, Stephen	4	8	
Clement, Stephen	CF				see Simon Clement Sr.
Clement, William	BW	-	2	3	518 acres
Clement, William	CF				see Isham Clement
Cloudas, George	BW				see John Archer's List (Ch.)
Cloudas, George's List	BW	-	1	1	-
Clough, Richard's Estate	BW	-	12	12	654 acres
Cock, Stephen	BW				see Peter Farrar
Cole, John	BW				Neal, William Jr.'s List
Coleman, Peter	BW				see John Morgin's List
Compton, Ambrose	CF	-	-	1	
Cook, James	CF	-	-	1	
Cooper, Francis	JT				see James Bradley's Tithes
Cooper, Francis' tithes	JT	-	1	1	
Cox, George	CF	-	1	2	
Cox, George of Henrico	BW	Raiborn, George	12	13	964 acres
Cox, Henry	CF	-	4	4	
Crenshaw, Elkanah	CF	-	3	4	
Crowder, William	CF	-	2	3	
Cumpton, Jehu	JT				see John Cumpton Sr.
Cumpton, John Jr.	JT	Cumpton, Joshua	4	6	
Cumpton, John Sr.	JT	Cumpton, Jehu	1	3	
Cumpton, Joshua	JT				see John Cumpton Jr.
Cumpton, Zachariah	JT				see John Tabb
Daniel, Benjamin	JT				see J__ Scott
Deaton, Levi	JT				see Edward Mead
Dennis, Henry	TW	-	6	7	
Dennis, Richard Jr.	TW	-	3	4	
Denniss, Richard	BW	Clardy, Benj.	11	13	350 acres
Deton, James	BW	-	2	3	-
Deton, John	BW	-	3	4	180 acres; "Deaton"?
Deton, William	BW	-	1	2	-
Dixon?, William	TW				see Joseph Phillips' List
Dowdee, John	CF				see John Hughs
Drinkard, John	BW	Wilkinson, James	2	4	186 acres
Drinkhard, Jno.	BW				see William Wilkinson's Est.

Drinkwater, John Sr.	CF	Drinkwater, John Jr. Blake, William	-	3	
Drinkwater, Josiah	CF				Lockitt,Benjamin
Duglass, John	CF				see Isham Clement
Dunnivant, Clement	BW				see Hogis Dunivant
Dunnivant, Danl.	BW				see William Dunnivant
Dunnivant, Hogis	BW	Dunnivant, Clement	4	6	250 acres
Dunnivant, John	BW				see William Dunnivant
Dunnivant, Phillip	BW	Dunnivant, Shadrick Dunnivant, Norrell Dunnivant, Phillip Jr.	-	4	250 acres
Dunnivant, Thos.	BW				see Robert Carr
Dunnivant, William	BW	Dunnivant, John Dunnivant, Danl.	3	6	200 acres
Dyer, Ann's List	BW	Dyer, Thomas	-	1	150 acres
Dyson, Benjamin's List	BW	Hamlett, Morriss	4	5	156 acres
Eastridge, Moses	CF	-	-	1	
Eastridge, William	CF	-	-	1	
Edmondson, Benjamin	TW	-	2	3	
Eggleston, Richard	CF	Carr, William	6	7	Eggleston exempt?
Elam, John	BW	-	-	1	-
Eldridge, Bolling	JT	Burkes, Thomas	3	5	
Ellington, Jno.	BW				see Ben Ward
Ellington, John	BW				see Robert Marshall's estate
Ellis, Thomas	CF	-	1	2	
Eudaly, James	CF				see William Wood
Farley, George	BW	-	5	6	268 acres
Farley, Jeremiah	BW				see Mary Farley's List
Farley, Jno. James	BW				see John Town's List
Farley, John	CF				see Sarah Farley
Farley, John James	BW	-	1	2	-
Farley, Joseph	BW	-	7	8	689 acres
Farley, Mary's List	BW	Farley, Jeremiah	3	4	200 acres
Farley, Matthew	BW	-	3	4	250 acres
Farley, Natt	BW				see Stewart Farley
Farley, Sarah	CF	Farley, John, "her son"	0	1	
Farley, Stephen	CF	Gears, Robert	-	2	
Farley, Stewart	BW	Farley, Natt	-	2	258 acres
Farley, William	CF	-	5	6	
Farrar, Peter	BW	Cock, Stephen Roberts, Steph.	23	26	2382 acres
Fennell, Eckles	TW	-	1	2	
Fennell, Laughlin	TW	-	1	2	
Finney, John	CF	Clardy, John	9	12	

		Ca_idlomer?, John C.			
Finney, Mary	CF	-	6	6	one riding chair
Ford, Christopher	CF	Asselin, Laurence Booker, George S__iner, William	9	12	one riding chair
Ford, Culveraine	JT	-	4	5	
Ford, George	TW	-	1	2	
Ford, Hezikiah	CF				see John Ford Jr.
Ford, John	BW	-	8	9	402 acres
Ford, John Jr.	CF	Ford, Hezikiah	4	6	
Ford, William Jr.	CF	-	2	3	
Ford, William Sr.	CF	-	4	5	
Ford, William*	JT	-	-	1	"Son of Culv."
Foster, Booker	CF				Lockitt,Benjamin
Foster, George Pollard	JT				see George Foster
Foster, George*	JT	Foster, George Pollard Foster, Joseph	-	3	"(Jandy Creek)"
Foster, John	BW	-	2	3	200 acres
Foster, John	CF				see William Pillar
Foster, Joseph	JT				see George Foster
Foster, Robert	CF				see Thomas Foster Sr.
Foster, Robert	CF				see Isaac Hill
Foster, Thomas Jr.	CF	-	-	1	
Foster, Thomas Sr.	CF	Foster, Robert Foster, William	8	11	
Foster, William	CF				see Thomas Foster Sr.
Foster, William*	CF	-	-	1	"of Hock's Creek"
Frazier, Joel	CF				see Alexander Kelley
Garrett, Henry	CF				see Thomas Mumford
Garrett, James	CF				see Thomas Mumford
Gears, Robert	CF				see Stephen Farley
Gears, Thomas	CF	-	-	1	
Gibbs, Mary's List	BW	Gibbs, William Gibbs, Matthew	4	6	200 acres
Gibbs, Matthew	BW				see Mary Gibbs' List
Gibbs, Matthew's List	BW	Purdue, Ezekiel	2	3	200 acres
Gibbs, William	BW				see Mary Gibbs' List
Gill, Daniel	BW	-	-	1	-
Gill, John	BW	-	-	1	-
Gillis, Thomas	BW				see Peter Webster Jr.
Gooch, Joseph	CF	-	3	4	
Gooding, David	BW				see Daniel Worsham
Gray, John	BW	-	3	4	100 acres
Green, John	CF	-	-	1	
Green, Thomas	CF	-	-	1	
Greenwood, William	JT				see John Tabb
Hall, Thomas	BW	Blanchett, Henry	4	6	-
Hall, William Jr.	BW	-	6	7	275 acres

Ham, William	CF	-	-	1	
Hames, Edmund	TW	-	-	1	
Hames, William	TW	-	-	1	
Hamlett, Morriss	BW				see Benjamin Dyson's List
Hamlin, William	TW	-	2	3	
Hamm, George Sr.	JT	-	2	3	
Hamm, Thomas	JT				see John Tabb
Hancock, Edward	JT				see George Hancock
Hancock, George	JT	Hancock, Edw.	8	10	
Hardaway, Joseph's List	BW	Smith, Henry	3	4	290 acres
Harding, Erasmus' List	BW	Hastings, John	3	4	150 acres
Harper, Henry	CF	-	-	1	
Harrison, Nathaniel	CF	Launder, John Purkason	13	15	
Harriss, James	CF				see John Harriss
Harriss, John	CF	Harriss, James	-	2	
Harriss, William	CF	-	-	1	
Hart, William	CF	Walker, Thomas	2	4	
Hastings, John	BW				see Erasmus Harding's List
Hastings, John list of land	BW	-	0	0	200 acres
Hatchett, Abraham	BW				see William Hatchett
Hatchett, John	BW	Truly, Jno. Wilkinson, John	2	5	50 acres
Hatchett, William	BW	Hatchett, Abraham	4	6	150 acres
Hawkens, Joseph	JT				see John Tabb
Hawkins, Zachariah	BW	-	-	1	-
Hayes, Richard	BW	Hayes, Wm. Balie?, Anvil?	11	14	797 acres
Hayes, Wm.	BW				see Richard Hayes
Hendrick, Benjamin	JT	Hendrick, Bernard	8	10	
Hendrick, Benjamin Jr.	CF	-	1	2	
Hendrick, Bernard	JT				see Benjamin Hendrick
Hendrick, Hans	CF	-	6	7	
Hendrick, John*	CF	-	-	1	"Carpenter"
Hendrick, Obediah	JT	-	-	1	
Hill, Isaac	CF	Foster, Robert	-	2	
Hill, Joel	CF				see Richard Anderson
Hill, John Jr.	CF	-	-	1	
Hill, John Sr.	CF	-	1	2	
Hillsman, Willam	CF	-	2	3	
Hopkins, Francis	CF	-	3	4	
Howlett, William	BW	-	3	4	148 acres
Hubbard, John	CF	-	-	1	
Hubbard, Joseph	JT	-	2	3	
Hudson, Christopher	JT	Bell, George	17	19	
Hudson, Robert	CF				see John Burton
Hughs, John	CF	Jesse, Thomas Dowdee, John	13	16	

Hurt, Abram	CF	Hurt, William	-	2	
Hurt, James*	CF	-	-	1	"son of John"
Hurt, James*	CF	-	-	1	"son of Abram"
Hurt, William	CF				see Abram Hurt
Hurt, William (Caroline)	CF	Smith, James	5	7	
Hurt, William*	CF	-	-	1	"son of John"
Hutchason, Elkanah	JT				see William Hutchason
Hutchason, William	JT	Hutchason, Elkanah	1	3	
Hutcheson, Charles	CF	Hutcheson, Drury	-	2	
Hutcheson, Drury	CF				see Charles Hutcheson
Jackson, Benjamin	BW				see Francis Jackson
Jackson, Burwell	BW				see Francis Jackson
Jackson, Francis	CF	-	1	2	
Jackson, Francis (N)	BW	Jackson, Burwell Jackson, Benjamin	1	4	200 acres
Jackson, Irl	BW	-	4	5	250 acres
Jackson, Joseph	CF	-	1	2	
Jackson, Josiah	CF	-	-	1	
Jackson, Matthew	BW	-	3	4	200 acres
Jackson, Matthew	BW				see Joseph Wilkinson's Est.
Jackson, Rowland	CF	-	-	1	
Jackson, Samuel	CF	-	-	1	
Jackson, William	CF	-	2	3	
Jackson, Wm.	BW	-	-	1	-
Jacobs, Jeremiah	TW				see Nelson Jones
James, Thomas Sr.	CF	James, Thomas Jr.	3	5	
James, William	TW	-	1	2	
Jams, Mrs. Dorotha's List	BW	Verser, William	8	9	547 acres, 1 riding chair
Jenkins, James	CF	Southall, James White, David White, John	5	9	
Jesse, Thomas	CF				see John Hughs
Jeter, Henry	BW				see Thomas Worsham's List
Johnson, Isham	CF	-	-	1	
Johnson, Jeremiah	BW				see William Walthall (W.C.)
Johnson, Nicholas	JT				see John Tabb
Johnson, William	JT	-	3	4	
Jones, Branch	TW	-	7	8	
Jones, Col. Richard's List	BW	Oliver, Ben	6	7	-
Jones, John	BW	-	3	4	1000 acres
Jones, Mrs. Agnes' List	BW	-	6	6	1195 acres
Jones, Nelson	TW	Jacobs, Jeremiah	8	10	1 riding chair
Jones, Peter (Sheriff)	BW	-	3	4	-
Jones, Peter Sr.	BW	Jones, Batt	12	14	3700 acres
Jones, Richard	JT				see John Tabb
Jones, Uriah	JT				see John Tabb
Jones, William	CF	-	1	2	
Jordan Samuel (Jr.?)	TW				see Samuel Jordan's Estate
Jordan, Jonas	CF	-	2	3	

Jordan, Samuel's Estate	TW	Jordan, Samuel Phillips, Joseph	9	11	
Kelley, Alexander	CF	Frazier, Joel Butler, Calup	-	3	
Lamb, Anthony	JT	-	2	3	
Lanston, Thomas	JT	-	5	6	
Launder, John Purkason	CF				see Nathaniel Harrison
League, Bartholomew	CF	-	1	2	
League, James	CF				see John White
Leath, Arthur	TW	Waller, William	8	10	
Leonard, Joseph	TW	-	-	1	
Liggon, Thomas	CF	-	1	2	
Liggon, William	CF	Williams, Samuel	6	8	
Liggon, William Jr.	CF	-	2	3	
Lockit, William	CF				Lockitt,Benjamin
Lockitt,Benjamin	CF	Drinkwater, Josiah Foster, Booker Lockit, William	3	7	
Longan, John	JT	-	-	1	
Lorton, John	JT				See J__ Scott
Loving, Moses	CF	-	-	1	
Loving, William	CF	-	-	1	
Low, William	JT	-	-	1	
Major, George	CF	-	-	1	
Major, Phillip	CF	-	1	2	
Mann, Cain	BW				see Branch Tanner's List
Mann, Cain (list of land)	BW	-	-	-	200 acres
Mann, Field	BW				see Robert Mann
Mann, Robert	BW	Mann, Field Mann, Robert Jr.	2	5	150 acres
Mann, Samuel	BW	Mann, James	-	2	150 acres
Mann, Samuel Jr.	BW	-	-	1	-
Marshall, John	BW				see Robert Marshall's estate
Marshall, Robert's Estate	BW	Marshall, Wm. Marshall, John Ellington, John	13	16	793 acres
Marshall, William Jr.	BW	-	3	4	400 acres
Marshall, William Sr.	BW	-	5	6	400 acres
Marshall, Wm.	BW				see Robert Marshall's estate
Mayes, Daniel	BW	-	1	2	100 acres
McCutchion, John	TW				see Walter Boyd's List
McNabb, Alexander	JT				see John Tabb
Mead, Edward	JT	Deaton, Levi	17	19	
Meadors, Henry	CF	-	-	1	
Meadors, James	CF	-	1	2	
Meadors, James	CF				see Joel Meadors
Meadors, Joel	CF	Meadors, James	-	2	
Meadow, Benjamin	JT				see John Tabb
Miller?, Thos.	BW				see Ben Ward

Moody, Blanks*	BW				"tailor"; see Nicholas Vaughn
Moody, Thomas	BW	-	1	2	-
Moore, William	TW				see Walter Boyd's List
Morgan, Samuel	BW	Morgan, Wm. Morgan, Simon	4	7	438 acres
Morgan, Samuel	TW	-	-	1	
Morgan, Simon	BW				see Samuel Morgan
Morgan, William	BW				see Samuel Morgan
Morgin, John's List	BW	Coleman, Peter	2	3	250 acres
Morris, Moses "Patroller"	CF	-	4	4	evidently exempt
Morriss, Mary	CF	-	1	1	
Morriss, Syranus	CF	-	-	1	
Mumford, Edward	CF				see Thomas Mumford
Mumford, Thomas	CF	Mumford, Edwd Garrett, James Garrett, Henry	14	18	one riding chair
Murray, James' Tithes	JT	Worsham, Henry	12	13	
Murry, Daniel	BW	Murry, Wm.	-	2	-
Murry, Wm.	BW				see Daniel Murry
Naughn, Nicholas*	BW	Moody, Blanks	-	2	"tailor"
Neal, Roger	BW	-	2	3	100 acres
Neal, Stephen	BW	-	3	4	100 acres
Neal, William Jr.'s List *	BW	Cole, John	4	5	"Son of (D.)"; 100 acres
Neale, Joel	BW				see William Neale Sr.
Neale, Thomas's Estate	BW	-	-	-	261 acres
Neale, William Sr.	BW	Neale, Joel	5	3	351 acres
North?, Thomas	TW				see ___ (name smudged)
Nunnally, Joseph	BW				see William Thompson
Oliver, Ben	BW				see Col. Richard Jones's List
Oliver, John	CF				see Francis Anderson Jr.
Osborn, Abner					see William Osborn
Osborn, Branch					see William Osborn
Osborn, Joseph	BW	-	9	10	650 acres
Osborn, William	BW	Osborn, Branch Osborn, Abner	15	18	1570 acres
Ousley, Thomas	CF	-	-	1	
Philips, Richard	CF	-	3	4	
Phillips, Joseph	TW				see Samuel Jordan's Estate
Phillips, Joseph's List	TW	Dixon?, William	4	5	
Piles, Williamson	JT	-	-	1	
Pillar, William	CF	Foster, John	-	2	
Pollard, Joseph	CF	-	2	3	
Pollard, Thomas	CF	Pollard, Thos. Jr.	2	4	
Porter, James	CF	-	-	1	
Pride, John Jr.	CF	Walker, Asaph	13	15	one riding chair
Pringle, Richard	JT				see John Tabb
Puckett, Thos	BW				see Daniel Wilson
Purdue, Ezekiel	BW				see Matthew Gibbs' List
Raiborn, George	BW				see George Cox of Henrico's

					List
Randolph, Henry's List	BW	Randolph, Wm.	10	11	1158 acres
Randolph, William	BW				see Henry Randolph's List
Rhodes, John	JT				see Thomas Brackett
Roberts, Stephen	BW				see Peter Farrar
Robison, James	TW	-	5	6	
Rucker, James	CF	-	-	1	
Rucker, Joshua	CF	-	-	1	
Rucker, Mordecai	CF				see William Rucker
Rucker, William	CF	Rucker, Mordecai	3	5	
Rucker, Wyatt	JT				see William Ware
S__iner, William	CF				see Christopher Ford
Scott, J__	JT	Daniel, Benjamin Lorton, John	10	13	(given name smudged, illegible)
Scott, Roger	BW	-	2	3	951 acres
Seay, Gideon	CF	-	-	1	
Seay, Jacob	CF	-	5	6	
Seay, James	CF	-	2	3	
Seay, Jessee	CF	Seay, Sarjus	4	6	
Seay, Josiah	CF	-	-	1	
Seay, Moses	CF	-	1	2	
Seay, Sarjus	CF				see Jessee Seay
Smith, Henry	BW				see Joseph Hardaway's List
Smith, James	CF				see William Hurt (Caroline)
Southall, James	CF	-	-	1	
Southall, James	CF				see James Jenkins
Southall, John	JT				see John Tabb
Southall, William	CF	-	3	3	
Spain, Frederick	BW	-	1	2	100
Spain, John	BW	-	-	1	-
Spain, William	BW	-	1	2	50 acres
Stanley, Jno.	BW				see James Chappell
Stern, Ann	CF	-	7	7	
Sturdivant, James (L.M.)	BW	-	2	3	200 acres
Tabb, Edward	CF	-	3	4	
Tabb, John	JT	Tabb, Philip Pringle, Richard Southall, John Hamm, Thomas Thackston, Wm. Jones, Richard Greenwood, Wm Meadow, Benj. Cumpton, Zachariah Jones, Uriah Hawkens, Joseph Cheatam, Archer Archer, John Chappell, Wm	130	147	one chariot and one riding chair

		McNabb, Alex. Johnson, Nicholas			
Tabb, Philip	JT				see John Tabb
Tanner, Branch's List	BW	Mann, Cain	10	11	780 acres
Tanner, Lodwick	BW	-	11	12	572 acres; 1 riding chair
Tanner, Mrs. Ann's List	BW	-	6	6	-
Thackston, William	JT				see John Tabb
Thomas, Anthanasius	TW				see Lewellen Williamson
Thomas, Mark (Patroler)	BW	-	-	-	-
Thompson, Drury	BW	-	11	12	600 acres
Thompson, Peter	BW	-	8	9	532 acres
Thompson, William	BW	Nunnally, Joseph	11	13	1770 acres
Thorp, John	CF	-	2	3	
Thorp, Theothe?	BW				see William Thorp, Patroler
Thorp, William (Patroller)	BW	Thorp, Theothe?	0	1	150 acres
Tinsley, Isaac	CF	-	6	7	
Tinsley, Thomas	CF	-	3	4	
Town, John's List (land)	BW	"(Farley, Jno. James, tenant)"	0	0	674 acres
Town, Miss Mary's List	BW	Westbrook, Wm.	6	7	1200 acres
Towns, James	BW	-	7	8	545 acres
Towns, William	BW	-	6	7	150 acres
Truly, Jno.	BW				see John Hatchett
Tucker, John	TW	-	1	2	
Vaden, Henry	BW	-	3	4	356 acres
Varser, George	BW				see Richard Varser
Varser, Jno.	BW				see Richard Varser
Varser, Richard	BW	Varser, Jno. Varser, George	3	6	360 acres
Vassar, Abram	CF	-	-	1	
Vaughn, Jesse	CF				see Lewis Vaughn
Vaughn, Lewis	CF	Vaughn, Jesse	3	5	
Vaughn, Nicholas *	BW	-	-	1	"Son of Robt."
Verser, William	BW				see Mrs. Dorotha Jams' List
Waldin, John	CF				see Francis Anderson Sr.
Walker, Alexander	CF	-	3	4	
Walker, Asaph	CF				see John Pride Jr.
Walker, Thomas	CF				see William Hart
Walker, Thomas	TW				see Thomas Williams Jr's list
Waller, William	TW				see Arthur Leath
Walters, Benjamin	CF	-	-	1	
Walters, Daniel	CF	-	1	2	
Walthall, Christopher	BW	-	6	7	400 acres
Walthall, Christopher Jr.	BW	-	2	3	140 acres
Walthall, Henry	BW	-	5	6	600 acres
Walthall, Thomas	BW	Whiley, Wm Brintle, Jacob	14	17	803 acres
Walthall, Thomas	JT				see George Chr. White
Walthall, William (W.C.)	BW	Johnson, Jeremiah	8	10	385 acres
Ward, Ben	BW	?Miller, Thos.	16	20	1 riding chair

		Watkins, Jno. Ellington, Jno.			
Ward, Rowland	BW	Ward, Rowland Jr.	15	17	859 acres
Ware, William	JT	Rucker, Wyatt	1	3	
Watkins, Jno.	BW				see Ben Ward
Webster, John	BW	-	-	1	-
Webster, Peter	BW	Webster, William	4	6	780 acres
Webster, Peter Jr.	BW	Gillis, Thomas	2	4	-
Webster, Thomas	BW	Webster, Thos. Jr.	4	6	450 acres
Webster, William	BW				see Peter Webster
Westbrook, James	BW	-	-	1	-
Westbrook, William	BW				see Miss Mary Town's List
Whiley, Wm.	BW				see Thomas Walthall
White, David	CF				see James Jenkins
White, George Chr.	JT	Walthall, Thomas	7	9	
White, John	CF	League, James	3	5	
White, John	CF				see James Jenkins
Whitworth, Abram	CF	Whitworth, Claiborne	4	6	
Whitworth, Claiborne	CF				see Abram Whitworth
Whitworth, Erasmus	CF				see Samuel Whitworth
Whitworth, John	CF				see John Booker
Whitworth, Samuel	CF	Whitworth, Erasmus	-	2	
Whitworth, Thomas Sr.	CF	Whitworth, Thomas Jr.	-	2	
Wilkins, John	TW	-	2	3	
Wilkinson, Edward's List	BW	Wilkinson, Martin	7	8	553 acres
Wilkinson, James	BW				see John Drinkard
Wilkinson, John	BW				see John Hatchett
Wilkinson, Joseph's Est.	BW	Jackson, Matthew	7	8	300 acres
Wilkinson, Martin	BW				see Ewd. Wilkinson's list
Wilkinson, Wm's Estate*	BW	Drinkhard, Jno.	-	-	"apply to Jno. Drinkhard"
Williams, Samuel	CF				see William Liggon
Williams, Thomas Jr.'s List	TW	Walker, Thomas	33	34	1 riding chair
Williamson, Lewellen	TW	Thomas, Anthanasius	4	6	
Wilson, Daniel	BW	Anderson, Chas. Puckett, Thos.	8	11	689 acres
Wilson, George	BW	-	1	2	266 acres
Wilson, Thomas B.	BW	-	18	19	1160 acres, 1 riding chair
Wingo, James Sr.	CF	Wingo, James Jr.	-	2	
Wingo, John*	CF	-	-	1	"Son of James"
Wingo, John*	CF	-	-	1	"son of Thomas"
Wingo, Thomas	CF	-	-	1	
Winston, William	CF	-	3	4	
Wood, Elizabeth	CF	Wood, John	1	2	
Wood, John	CF				see Elizabeth Wood
Wood, William	CF	-	4	5	

Wood, William*	CF	Eudaly, James	-	2	"Carpenter"
Worsham, Daniel	BW	Gooding, David	11	13	819 acres
Worsham, Henry	JT				see James Murray's Tithes
Worsham, John's Estate	BW	Worsham, John Jr	10	11	940 acres, 1 riding chair
Worsham, Kennon	BW	-	3	4	150 acres
Worsham, Thomas* List	BW	Jeter, Henry	5	6	"of Chesterfield"; 646 acres
Worsham, William	BW	-	2	3	100 acres
Wright, John	CF	Wright, William Wright, Thomas	3	6	
Wright, John	CF				see Thomas Wright
Wright, Thomas	CF				see John Wright
Wright, Thomas	CF	Bell, John Wright, John	11	14	
Wright, William	CF				see John Wright
Young, Ellison	BW				see Samuel Young
Young, Saml.	BW				see Peter Besseley
Young, Samuel	BW	Young, Samuel Jr. Young, Ellison	-	3	77 acres

The 1771 AMELIA COUNTY TITHE LISTS - INCOMPLETE

Below is a indexed transcription of the extant Personal Property Tithe Lists for Amelia County for the year 1771, transcribed from LDS FHL #1902616.

The microfilm contains ***only one list for this particular year***, the list from Nottoway parish (designated below as N). We know from prior years that there should be several different lists, each from a specific area and part of a parish within Amelia County. Thus the other lists for 1771 must have been lost, and not finding an individual on this year's PPTL does NOT mean that they weren't present (unless they resided in Nottoway Parish.

The name of the commissioner that compiled this one list was not recorded.

This list is VERY dark, and difficult to read, despite their use of negative (white writing against a black background) photography, and imaging each page with several camera settings. I've done my best to make out the names, and have marked questionable names with question marks [?].

On this list, the slaves are listed by name. I have not listed them here, but it may be possible, by comparing with lists prior to and following this one, to identify men whose names are uncertain on this list, and using slaves + acres to match these men to their entries on other lists.

EXPLANATION OF COLUMN HEADINGS
NAME: the name of the person paying the Tithe
LIST: the parish where these individuals lived; this list is only for Nottoway Parish, that part of Amelia which later would become Nottoway Co. (Evidently, the other Parish Tithe Lists did not survive.)
OTHER WHITE MALE TITHES: The names of other men above the age of 16, whose tithe was paid by the taxpayer. When of the same surname, these were usually sons of the taxpayer. Otherwise, they were guests, overseers or other employees.
COMMENTS

Land = individual taxed only for land, not for self; exempt for some reason.
List = individual named not taxed for self; exempt, or taxed personally elsewhere.
List? = number of individuals named is one more than number taxed; List implied but not stated.

NAME	LIST	Other white male tithes	Slaves	Acres	COMMENTS
Allgood, Edwd?	N	0	0	0	
Anderson, John	N	0	1	100	
Bailey, John	N	0	3	270	
Ball, Thomas Sr.	N	0	3	0	
Batte, Thomas	N	0	3	450	
Bentley, John	N				See Joshua Harper's List
Bentley, Saml. Jr.	N	0	0	0	
Bentley, Samuel	N	0	0	0	
Bolling, Col. Alex EST.	N	Gunn, James	5	162	
Borum, James	N				See Cousons, William
Boyd, Elizabeth	N	Moss?, Wm	6	0	
Byrd, Bob	N				see Thomas Walker Sr.
Chappel, Est. ?Martha?	N	0	0	430	

NAME	LIST	Other white male tithes	Slaves	Acres	COMMENTS
Claibourne?, Philip	N	Goban, William	13	0	
Clark, Henry	N	Clark, Henry Jr. Clark, Alex.	2	0	
Clark, John	N	Clark, Lee??	3	0	
Clark, Lee?					see Clark, John
Clark, Peter	N	Clark, Peter Jr.	0	0	
Cocke, H. Jr.	N	0	8	1050	
Cocke, Jno.	N				See Cocke, William
Cocke, John Sen.	N	Maynard, Edw.	4	0	
Cocke, Thos	N	0	1	0	
Cocke, William	N	Cocke, Jno.	5	0	
Connally, Charles	N	Connally, Geo.	4	0	
Connally, George	N				See Charles Connally
Cousons, William	N	Borum?, James	4	0	
Creel, Absolom	N				see Ellis, Capt. Richard
Cross, Chas.	N				See William Cross?
Cross, Richard	N	0	6	480	
Cross, William	N	Cross, Chas	8	56	
Cryer, William Jr.	N	0	7	800	
Davis, Jacob	N	Davis, Thomas	5	260	
Davis, Thomas	N				See Jacob Davis
Davis, William	N				See Charles Hamlin
Dennis?, Richard Jr.	N		5	400	
Draper, James	N	Thos. Draper	0	0	
Draper, Thos.	N				See James Draper
Dunham, Charles?	N				see Echles?, Robt.
Dunham, Charnel	N				See Echles?, Robt.
Dunham, Joshua	N		0	0	
Echles?, Robt.	N	Dunham, Charnel	0	0	
Edmondson, Benj.	N		2	412	
Elder, William	N				See Nathaniel Hobbs' list
Ellington, Jeremiah	N		1	204	
Ellis, Capt. Richard	N	Creel, Absolom Holt, William	30	1952?	
Elmore, Jno.	N				see Ambrose Lipscomb
Fallen, Charles	N	Maynard, Daniel Richd.	1	0	
Fannin, Achilas	N		0	0	
Fannin?, Laughlin	N	___good, Jno.	1	0	
Farris, Abraham Jr.	N		2	200	
Ford, Albery?	N		0	100	
Ford, Frederick	N		1	0	
Ford, John	N		0	0	
Ford?, Tady?	N		0	0	

NAME	LIST	Other white male tithes	Slaves	Acres	COMMENTS
Glasby, Wm.	N				see Jacob Morgan
Goban, William	N				see Claibourne?, Philip
Green, Henry	N	Green, Jno.	4	0	
Green, Jno.	N				See Henry Green
Grigg, James	N		6	600	
Gunn, James	N				See Bolling, Col. Alex EST.
Gunn, James' List	N	Vaughan, David	6	200	
Hames, Edmond	N	Winter, Henry	0	0	
Hames, John	N	Hames, W?	3	0	
Hames, W.?	N				See John Hames
Hames, William Jr.	N		1	0	
Hamlin, Charles Jr.	N	Davis, William	4	0	
Hammock, Robt.	N		0	81	
Hammond, Lewis	N	Hammond, William Hammond, Lewis Jr.	1	0	
Hammond, William	N				see Lewis Hammond
Harper, Joshua's List	N	Bentley, John	1	0	"of Dinwiddie"
Hightower, Charnel	N				see Hightower, George
Hightower, Charnel	N				See Joshua Hightower Sr.
Hightower, George	N	Hightower, Richard Hightower, Charnel	6	895	
Hightower, Joshua Jr.	N		5	0	
Hightower, Joshua Sr.	N	Hightower, Charnel	6	0	
Hightower, Richard	N				aee Hightower, George
Hightower, William	N				see Moses Hurt, Jr.
Hobbs, Nathaniel's List	N	Elder, William	5	0	
Holloway, John	N				See Maj. Poythress
Holt, David	N				see Holt, Dibdah??
Holt, Dibdah??	N	Holt, David	2	0	
Holt, William	N				see Ellis, Capt. Richard
Hood, John	N				see Francis Lewis
Hook, Hannah	N	_, Thomas	1	0	
Hooper, Zacheriah	N		1	0	
Hurt, Absolom	N				see Hurt, Moses
Hurt, Moses Jr.	N	Hightower, William	1	160	surname could be HUNT
Hurt, Moses Sr.	N	Hurt, Zacheus Hurt, Absolom	8	300	(Surname COULD be HUNT)
Hurt, Zacheus	N				see Hurt, Moses

NAME	LIST	Other white male tithes	Slaves	Acres	COMMENTS
Jackson, Amey's List	N		1	0	
Jackson, Charles	N	Jackson, Philip	1	0	
Jackson, Daniel	N				see William Jackson
Jackson, Daniel	N		0	150	
Jackson, Edw.	N	Jackson, Wm. P	2	0	
Jackson, Isaac	N				see William Jackson
Jackson, Philip	N				see Charles Jackson
Jackson, Thos.	N		0	0	
Jackson, William	N	Jackson, Daniel Jackson, Isaac	3	0	
Jackson, William Jr.	N		2	0	
Jackson, Wm. P	N				see Edw. Jackson
James, George	N				see William James
James, John	N		2	0	
James, William	N	James, George	1	0	
Jones, ___ Sr.	N		1	0	
Jones, Adam	N		7	300	
Jones, Henry	N		2	0	
Jones, William	N		5	393	
Kirkland, Hugh	N				See Maj. Poythress
Kirkland, John	N		0	0	
Leeth, Arthur	N	Wills, Jno. Waller, William	9	0	
Levisie??, Richard	N	Levisie??, Bolling	2	168	
Lewis, Francis	N	Hood, John	3	0	
Lewis, Griffin "Patroler"	N	Minor, Daniel	3	295	
Lipscomb, Ambrose	N	Elmore, Jno.	3	104	
Loafman, Jno.	N				see Richard Walthall
Long, George	N		3	370	
Love, Charles	N		3	0	
Malone, Isham	N		3	0	
Manire, John	N		0	0	
Manire, William	N		0	0	
Mayes, Daniel	N	Daniel Mayes Jr	2	0	
Mayes, Matthew	N		10	0	
Maynard, Daniel Richd.	N				see Fallen, Charles
Maynard, Edw.	N				See Cock, John Sen.?
Maynard?, Edward?	N		0	0	
McKinney, Travis	N		0	125	
Mills, John	N		0	171	"overseer for Wm Leeth"
Minor, Daniel	N				see Griffin Lewis
Moor, Robt.	N				see Thomas, Athanaleus
Moore, James	N		5	0	

NAME	LIST	Other white male tithes	Slaves	Acres	COMMENTS
Morgan, Jacob	N	Morgan, Saml. Glasby, Wm.	19	0	
Morgan, John	N	Morgan, Thos.	0	0	
Morgan, Saml.	N				see Jacob Morgan
Morgan, Samuel	N		0	0	
Morgan, Thos.	N				see John Morgan
Moss?, William	N				see Boyd, Elizabeth
Porte, Jno.	N				see Isham Vaughn
Powell, John	N		0	0	
Powell,Marlin	N		0	0	
Poythress, Maj. Peter (Prince George Co.)	N	Holloway, John Kirkland, Hugh	6	0	
Pryor, Alex	N				see Pryor, John Jr.
Pryor, John Jr.	N	Pryor, Alex	9	624	(in Js on this list!)
Redford, Andrew	N		9	0	
Rogers, John	N		2	0	
Sallard, Charles	N		8	0	
Simmons, Benjamin's List	N	Simmons, Thomas	1	196	
Simmons, Thomas	N				see Benj. Simmons' List
Stanley, Thos.	N				see Joseph White
Stokes, Mathew	N		0	280	
Stokes, Robert Sr.	N		2	0	
Stokes, Robt. Jr.	N		2	200	
Thomas, ?Athanalius?	N		0	0	
Thomas, Athanaleus	N	Moor, Robt	0	0	
Thomas, David	N		0	0	
Thomas, T___	N		6	942	
Thomas, William Jr.	N		0	0	
Thomas, William Sr.	N		1	0	
Tucker, John	N				see William Tucker
Tucker, William	N	Tucker, John	1	0	
Vaughan, David	N				see Gunn, James
Vaughn, Isham	N	Vaughan, Randolph Porte, Jno.	0	0	
Vaughn, Randolph	N				see Isham Vaughn
Walker, Jno.	N				see Thomas Walker Sr.
Walker, Thomas Sr.	N	Walker, Jno. Byrd, Bob	4	400	
Waller, William	N				see Arthur Leeth
Walthall, Richard	N	Loafman, Jno.	3	276	
White, Joseph	N	Stanley, Thos.	1	100	
Williams, Ben	N				see Charles Williams

NAME	LIST	Other white male tithes	Slaves	Acres	COMMENTS
Williams, Charles	N	Williams, Ben	1	0	
Wills, Jno.	N				see Arthur Leeth
Winter, Henry	N				see Henry Hames

The 1778 AMELIA COUNTY TITHE LISTS

No tithe lists exist for the years 1772-1777. In 1777, the newly formed Virginia State Assembly changed the age at which white males became tithables from sixteen to twenty-one years of age. The age at which slaves became tithable was unchanged, remaining sixteen years or older.

The 1778 PPTLs are the first to use this new age criterion for white male tithes.

The microfilm containing the PPTLs for 1778 contains 13 individual commissioner's lists, as follows:
HA = Henry Anderson's lists (2), Raleigh Parish (5 pages)
EB = Edmond Booker's list, Raleigh Parish (3 pages) (**faded**, faint images)
VB = Vivion Brookings' list, lower end of Raleigh Parish (6 pages)
CH = Christopher Hudson's list, Raleigh Parish (4 pages)
TM = Thomas Mumford's list, Raleigh Parish (3 pages)
JT = John Tabb's lists (2), Raleigh Parish (7 pages)
LW = Lau. Wills' list, Raleigh Parish (2 pages)
PRB = Peter Randolph Bland's list, Nottoway Parish (3 pages)
SB = Stephen Bolling's list, Nottoway Parish (14 pages)
EBj = Edmund Booker, Jr.'s list, Nottoway Parish (2 pages) – EXTREMELY FADED
SC = Stephen Cocke's list, Nottoway Parish (2 pages)
PL = Peter Lamkin's list, Nottoway Parish (8 pages)
TBM = Thomas B. Munford's lists (2), Nottoway Parish (7 pages)

Summary of lists, Raleigh and Nottoway Parishes (2 pages)

I have transcribed these names as accurately as possible, given the marked variations in handwriting, spelling, etc. of the various commissioners, the faded or blurred images for some of the pages, and other factors that made deciphering the names difficult. The list of Edmund Booker is particularly faded in some areas, but not others. When unsure, I've noted such by following the name with a question mark (?). Unfortunately, the ink for many of the entries has faded so much over time that they are on longer readable; thus for this particular year's Tithe Lists, not finding a name on this transcription does NOT mean that person's name is not on the list. It could be one of those that has faded. This is especially true if that particular name appears on the 1779 Tithe List.

I've spelled the names just as the tax commissioner did, not imposing my impression of what the commissioner intended; for this reason, users *should* look for spelling variations of the names they are searching for.

EXPLANATION OF COLUMN HEADINGS
TAXPAYER: the name of the person paying the Tithe
LIST: The initials of the person who compiled the tithe list on which the individual appears (an indication of the geographic area and the parish where these individuals lived.
OTHER WHITE MALE TITHES: The names of other men **above the age of 21**, whose tithe was paid by the taxpayer. When of the same surname, these were usually sons of the taxpayer. Otherwise, they were guests, overseers or other employees.
SLAVES: slaves over the age of 16, for whom a tithe was due (doesn't include ALL slaves).
TITHES = Total tithes (WMT 21 and over, plus slave tithes). As before the number of white male tithes plus slave tithes should equal the total tithes; when it doesn't, the reason is usually that the taxpayer paid his tithe elsewhere, or was for some reason exempt.

ACRES – unlike prior years, very few entries in 1778 recorded the acres owned by the taxpayer. The reason for this isn't apparent.

COMMENTS

Land = individual taxed only for land, not for self; exempt for some reason.

List = individual named not taxed for self; exempt, or taxed personally elsewhere.

List? = number of individuals named is one more than number taxed; List implied but not stated.

TAXPAYER	List	Other WMTs	Slaves	Tithes	Acres	COMMENTS
___, Thos.	EB					see William Clemons' estate
Adams, Dancey?	VB					see David Adams
Adams, David	VB	Adams, Dancey?	2	4		
Adams, William	VB					see Claiborne Anderson Estate
Alfriend, Benj.	PL	-	1	2		
Alkerson, Ellis	EB					see John Alkerson
Alkerson, John	EB	Alkerson, Ellis	-	2	-	
Allen, Daniel	VB	Allen, Richard Neal, John	6	3		
Allen, David	TM					see Mary Molson's tithes
Allen, Richard	VB					see Daniel Allen
Allin, ___?	TM	-	-	1		stained page edge obscures name
Allin, Isack	TM					see Thomas Foster
Anderson, __lin?	TM		8	9		stained page edge obscures name
Anderson, Allen	SC					see John Anderson
Anderson, Charles	PRB	-	8	9		
Anderson, Charles	TBM	Anderson, Jas.	3	5		
Anderson, Claiborne Est.	VB	Austin, Absolom Adams, William	16	18		
Anderson, Francis	TM	Anderson, Francis Jr. Walding, John	16	19		
Anderson, Frank	EB	Dunkin, Josiah	14	16	-	
Anderson, Henry	HA	Johnson, Richd. Johnson, Isham	53	56	-	1 riding chair
Anderson, Henry	TBM	-	4	5		
Anderson, James	SB	Anderson, Worsham	3	5		
Anderson, Jas.	TBM					see Charles Anderson
Anderson, John	SC	Anderson, Allen	1	3		
Anderson, John	TBM	-	5	6		
Anderson, Richard	TM	Foster, William	7	9		
Anderson, Worsham	SB					see James Anderson
Anian, John	SB	Anion, Ruben	-	2		

TAXPAYER	List	Other WMTs	Slaves	Tithes	Acres	COMMENTS
Anion, Ruben	SB					see John Anion
Archer, John's List	EB	Hatton, Thos.	8	9	-	
Asque, __ah (Sarah?)	TM	-	2	2		'Askew' intended? stained page edge
Asslin, David	TM	Asslin, David Jr.	4	6		
Atkinson, Joshua	EBj					see Thomas Atkinson
Atkinson, Musco	EBj	-	3	4		
Atkinson, Thomas	EBj	Atkinson, Joshua	9	11		
Austin, Absolom	VB					see Claiborne Anderson Estate
Avory, Wm.	HA	-	1	2	202?	
Bagley, George	SB	-	3	4		surname could be "Bogley"
Bagley, James	TBM	-	6	7		
Bagley, Jas.	JT					see Chasteen Cocke
Bailey, Charles	PL	-	1	2		
Bailey, John	PL	-	3	4		
Bailey, Thomas	JT	-	-	1		
Baldwin, William	TBM	-	3	4		
Ball, David	PL					see Thomas Ball
Ball, Thomas	PL	Ball, David	6	8		
Barker, Charles	PRB	-	2	3		
Barnes, Francis	JT					see Sarah Scott's tithes
Barnes, Francis	JT	-	-	1		
Barry, Peter	EB	-	3	4	-	
Bass, Christopher	JT					see William Bass, Jr.
Bass, Col. Joseph*	TBM	Butright?, Zachary	8	9		"Chesterfield" (Co.)
Bass, Edward	JT	Burton, Saml.	15	17		
Bass, John	TBM	-	5	6		
Bass, Mary's tithes	JT	-	5	5		
Bass, William Jr.	JT	-	4	5		
Bass, William Jr.	JT	Bass, Christopher	5	7		
Bates, Abner	PL	Bates, Wm.	4	6		
Bates, Wm.	PL					see Abner Bates
Beadle, Abraham	EBj	Beadle, Thomas	1	3		
Beadle, Augustine	EBj	-	2	3		
Beadle, John	EBj	-	3	4		
Beadle, Thomas	EBj					see Abraham Beadle
Beasley, Ambros	TBM	-	4	5		
Beasley, John	TBM	Beasley, Wm.	4	6		
Beasley, Richard	TBM	-	6	7		
Beasley, Robert	TBM	-	-	1		
Beasley, William	TBM	-	3	4		
Beasley, Wm.	TBM					see John Beasley
Bell, John	TM					see Thomas Mumford
Bell, William	TBM	Mays, Gardner	10	10		10 tithes and 10 named

TAXPAYER	List	Other WMTs	Slaves	Tithes	Acres	COMMENTS
						slaves
Belsher, ___as	TM	-	-	1		stained page edge obscures name
Belsher, Jacob??	TM	-	2	3		stained page edge obscures name
Bennet, John	SB					see Richard Bennet's List
Bennet, Richd's List	SB	Johnson, Ben Bennet, John	8	10		
Bennett, Benjamin	VB	-	-	1		
Bennett, William	VB	-	-	1		
Bennit, Walther	TM	Wish, John	1	3		
Bentley, Efford	JT					see Samuell Bentley
Bentley, Samuell	JT	Bentley, Efford	9	11		
Bevill, Archer	LW	-	-	1		
Bevill, Arther (sic)	EB	-	-	1	-	
Bevill, Carter	TBM					see Peter Jones Sr. (Rawleigh)
Bevill, Charles	HA					see Wm. Booth
Bevill, James Sr.	VB	Bevill, James Jr.	4	6		
Bevill, Joseph	LW	-	1	2		
Bevill, Joseph Jr.	LW	-	-	1		
Bevill, Robert	VB	-	1	2		
Bevill, Robert Sr.	VB		0	1		
Bevill, Thos. Estate	VB	Spinner, John	1	2		"deceased"
Blackley, William Jr.	PL	-	2	3		
Blackly, William Jr.	SB	-	-	1		
Bland, Benj. Sr.	EB	Bland, Benj Jr.	9	11		extremely faint
Bland, Col. Thomas	PRB	Lamb, William	23	24		no tithe for Col. Bland
Bland, Col. Thos. Jr.	PRB	-	5	5		no tithe for himself
Bland, Peter R.	PRB	-	30	31		
Blankenship, Jeremiah	HA					see Jos. Hardaway's List
Bolling, Mary	VB	Dunnavant, Wm. Dunnivant, Norvel	16 28	17 29		"For Mrs. Mary Bolling"
Bolling, Stith	SB	Gunn, Daniel Bruce, John	13	16		1 riding chair
Bolton, John	VB	-	-	1		
Bonner, Thos.	LW	-	-	1		
Booker, Edmd.	HA	Forster, Richd.	12	14	-	
Booker, Edmond	EB	Booker, Saml.	19	21	-	
Booker, Edmund	EBj	Flemming, Wm	6	7		no tithe for Edmund Booker
Booker, Edmund Jr.	EBj	Brumfield, Joseph	4	6		
Booker, Edward	TM	-	2	3		

TAXPAYER	List	Other WMTs	Slaves	Tithes	Acres	COMMENTS
Booker, Efford	TM					see George Booker
Booker, George	TM	Booker, Efford Booker, Warshal	13	16		1 riding chair
Booker, John	JT	Jolly, Dudley	16	18		1 riding chair
Booker, John Jr.	HA	Wilkerson, Towns	9	11	-	
Booker, Mrs. Ann	HA	-	12	12	-	
Booker, Saml.	EB					see Edmond Booker
Booker, Warshal	TM					see George Booker
Booth, John	EB	-	5	6	-	
Booth, Will	HA					see Wm. Booth
Booth, William	HA	Bevill, Charles Booth, Will	4	7	-	
Boothe, William	LW	Howell, John	5	7		
Borum, Edmond	TBM	-	3	4		
Borum, James	TBM	-	-	1		
Borum, Richd. Sr.	TBM	-	1	2		
Bott, James	EB					see Miles Bott
Bott, Joel?	EB					see Miles Bott
Bott, Miles	EB	Bott, James Bott, Joel?	11	14	-	
Bott, Robt.	EB					see William Bott
Bott, Thos.	EB					see William Bott
Bott, William	EB	Bott, Thos. Bott, Robt.	3	6	-	
Bottom, Thomas	SB	-	3	4		
Brackett, Benjamin	CH		4	5		
Brackett, Boyel?	CH					see Thomas Brackett
Brackett, Thomas	CH	Brackett, Boyel?	9	11		
Bradbury, Wm.	HA					see Richard Vasser
Bradshaw, Richard	TBM	Ferguson, Abner	-	2		
Bridgeforth, James	PL					see Benjamin Bridgforth
Bridgforth, Benj.	PL	Bridgforth, John Bridgforth, James	11	14	2800	
Bridgforth, John	PL					see Benjamin Bridgforth
Brodnax, Sarah's tithes	JT	-	2	2		
Brooking, Robt. E.	VB					see Vivion Brooking
Brooking, Vivion	VB	Brooking, Robt E. King, Henry	41	44		2 riding chairs
Brooks, William	EBj	-	-	1		
Brooks, Wm.	EB	Hassell?, John	5	7	-	
Brown, Thomas	PRB	-	1	2		
Bruce, Alexander	EBj	-	8	9		
Bruce, John	PL	-	1	2		
Bruce, John	SB					see Stith Bolling

TAXPAYER	List	Other WMTs	Slaves	Tithes	Acres	COMMENTS
Brumfield, Joseph	EBj					see Edmund Booker Jr.
Brumfield, Major	EBj	-	-	1		
Brummell, William	TBM					see Drury Thompson's List
Bryan, John	TBM	-	1	2		
Buford, Henry's List	PL	Maynard, John	6	7		no tithe for Buford
Buford, William	PL	-	6	7		
Bullington, Wm.	LW					see John Clardy
Bullock, Henry	SB	-	2	3		
Burrow, Peter	TBM	-	4	5		
Burton, Saml.	JT					see Edward Bass
Burton, Sarah's List	EB	Hudson, Burton	12	13	-	
Busley(?), Benj.	PRB	Clardy, John	6	7		no tithe for Benj. Busley
Butler, William	JT	-	2	3		could be "Butters"
Butright?, Zachary	TBM					see Col. Jos. Bass (Chesterfield)
Cabaness, George	TBM	Cabaness, Wm.	9	11		
Cabaness, Henry	TBM					see Matthew Cabiness Sr.
Cabaness, Mathew Jr.	TBM	-	2	3		
Cabaness, Mathew Sr.	TBM	Cabiness, Henry	2	4		
Cabaness, Wm.	TBM					see George Cabaness
Cambell, William	TM					see Shadrick Holt's Tithes
Campbell, William	EBj	-	-	1		
Candleman?, John Christopher	JT					see Mary Finney's tithes
Cannon, John	EBj					see William Cannon
Cannon, William	EBj	Cannon, John Cannon, Wm Sr.	-	3		
Cardwell, Richard	VB					see Robert Kennon's Estate
Carter, Rawleigh	PL	-	5	6		
Cavand__, Hugh	EB	-	2	3		extremely faded ink
Caviness, Charles' List	SB	-	2	2		
Chambers, Mary Est.	PL	Nash, Thomas	3	4		"Mary Chambers Estate List"
Chambrus?, John	PL					see Charles Irby
Chandler, Martin	VB	-	2	3		
Chappell, James	LW	-	3	4		
Chappell, John	LW	-	2	3		
Chappell, Robert	LW	Chappell, Samuel	4	6		
Chappell, Samuel	LW					see Robert Chappell
Chappell?, John	EB	-	3	4	-	extremely faded ink
Cheatham, Archer	JT	Hatchett, Wm.	-	2		
Chisam, Absolum	TM					see John Chisam (Chism)
Chisam, John	TM	Chisam, Absolum	1	3		
Chumley, John	EB	-	1	2	-	

TAXPAYER	List	Other WMTs	Slaves	Tithes	Acres	COMMENTS
Claiborne, Barbur	PRB	-	2	3		
Clardy, (smudged)	LW					see Benj. Clardy
Clardy, Benjamin	LW	Clardy, Henry Clardy, (smudge)	7	10		
Clardy, Henry	LW					see Benj. Clardy
Clardy, John	LW	Bullington, Wm.	4	3		
Clark, Lew	TBM	-	1	2		
Clark, Peter	PRB	-	-	1		
Clarke, John	PRB	Clarke, William	5	7		
Clarke, William	PRB					see John Clarke
Clay, Caleb	TBM					see James Oliver
Clay, Charles	LW	-	3	4		
Clay, John Jr.	LW	-	3	4		
Clay, John Sr.	LW	-	6	7		unsure of this name – FAINT
Clay, Thos. Sr.	LW	Clay, Thos. Jr.	-	2		
Claybrook, Peter	EB	-	1	2	-	
Clement, Isham	TM	Duglis, John Chapman, George	3	6		
Clements, William	TM	-	-	1		
Clemons, Wm's Est.	EB	__?, Thos	7	8	-	extremely faded ink
Clough, Richd.'s Est.	EB	-	9	9	-	
Co____, Jehu?	JT					see John Tabb
Cobbs, __ill	TM	Pollard, James	6	8		stained page edge obscures name
Cobbs, Theodosha	TM	-	1	1		"her tithes"; 1 riding chair
Cocke, Chasteen?	JT	Bagley, Jas. Ingram, Jos.	12	15		
Cocke, Col. John*	TBM	Ramsay, Richard	14	15		"Surry" (Co.)
Cocke, John	PL	Young, Wm.	7	9		
Cocke, John	SC	Young, William	6	8		
Cocke, Stephen	HA	Pitchford, Wm.	38	40	-	
Cocke, Stephen	SC	Elmore, Jno.	9	11		
Cocke, Thomas	SC	-	7	8		
Coleman, Abraham	VB	Coleman, Burwell	2	4		
Coleman, Burwell	VB					see Abraham Coleman
Coleman, Daniel Jr.	VB	Coleman, Obediah	2	4		
Coleman, Daniel Sr.	VB	Coleman, Jesse	5	7		
Coleman, Isaac	VB					see Peter Coleman
Coleman, Jesse	VB					see Daniel Coleman Sr.
Coleman, John	LW	-	-	1		
Coleman, Joseph	LW	-	-	1		
Coleman, Obediah	VB					see Daniel Coleman Jr.
Coleman, Page	LW	Murray, Wm.	2	4		
Coleman, Peter	VB	Coleman, Isaac	-	3		

TAXPAYER	List	Other WMTs	Slaves	Tithes	Acres	COMMENTS
		Coleman, Sol.				
Coleman, Sol(omon)	VB					see Peter Coleman
Coleman, Sutten	LW					see William Crawley
Collinson?, James	JT	-	7	8		
COLUMN 3	EB					
Column 4	EB					
Compton, Caleb	EBj	-	1	2		
Compton, Jeremiah	JT					see John Compton
Compton, Joel	JT					see John Compton
Compton, John	JT	Compton, Joel Compton, Ruben Compton, Jeremiah	7	11		
Compton, Micajah	JT					see John Tabb
Compton, Ruben	JT					see John Compton
Compton, Zachariah	EBj	-	3	4		
Cone?, George's tithes	JT	Raibun?, George	14	15		
Cook, James	TBM	Cook, Thos.	2	4		
Cook, James	TM	-	1	2		
Cook, Thos.	TBM					see James Cook
Cordle, Richd.	JT					see Thos. Griffin Peachey
Cousens, John	VB	-	6	7		
Cousens, Rosamond's Est.	VB	-	2	2		
Cousens, William	VB	-	2	3		
Cousings, George *	LW	Franklin, James	4	5		"To George Cousings of Chesterfield"
Cousons, Robert	VB	Dyson, Danl.	9	11		
Cousons, Thomas	VB	-	-	1		
Cox, Henry's tithes	TM	Johns, Stephen	4	5		"Henry Cox Tithes"
Craddock, John	EBj	Craddock, Wm	2	4		
Craddock, Moses	TBM	-	1	2		
Craddock, William	EBj	-	4	5		
Craddock, William	EBj					see John Craddock
Craddock, William Sr.	TBM	-	2	3		
Craddock?, Charles	EB	-	1	2		extremely faded ink
Crawley, John	LW					see William Crawley
Crawley, William	LW	Crawley, Wm. Jr. Crawley, John Coleman, Sutten Shepherson, Nathan Roach, William Farrel, George	51	58		

TAXPAYER	List	Other WMTs	Slaves	Tithes	Acres	COMMENTS
Crenshaw, David	JT	-	3	4		
Crenshaw, David	PL					see Wm. Crenshaw Sr.
Crenshaw, James	PL	-	2	3		
Crenshaw, Mary's tithes	JT	Street, William	5	6		
Crenshaw, William Jr.	PL	-	6	7		
Crenshaw, Wm. Sr.	PL	Crenshaw, David	7	9		
Crittindon?, Pryor	JT	-	-	1		
Cro___, Joshua	EB	-	5	6	-	extremely faded ink
Cross, William	SC	-	11	12		
Crowder, William	EB	-	6	7	-	
Crute?, Hannah's list	PL	Crute?, Robert	1	2		
Crute?, Robert	PL					see Hannah Crute's List
Cumton, Joshua	TM					see William Hurt
Dalby, John	TBM	Waddel, Thos.	4	6		
Davis, Asa	TBM					see William Davis
Davis, Christopher	PL					see Jacob Davis
Davis, Jacob	PL	Davis, Christopher Davis, Matthew Davis, Jacob (Jr.)	3	7		
Davis, James	SB	-	2	3		
Davis, James	SB	Davis, Judah	-	2		
Davis, Joshua	PL	-	-	1		
Davis, Judah	SB					see James Davis
Davis, Matthew	PL					see Jacob Davis
Davis, Robert	PL	Waller, Matthew	-	2		
Davis, Thos	PL	-	2	2		(no tithe for himself?)
Davis, William	TBM	Davis, Asa	1	3		
Dawson, Christopher	PL	Dawson, Johnathan Brooks	6	8		
Dawson, Johnathan Brooks	PL					see Christopher Dawson
Dearen, John	EBj	-	-	1		
Dearen, Richard	EBj	-	1	2		
Dearen, William	EBj	-	-	1		
Deaton, Geage?	EBj					see Levy Deaton
Deaton, Levy	EBj	Deaton, Geage?	1	2		given name NOT George
Dennis, Henry	PRB	Hall, John	9	11		
Dennis, John	PRB	-	4	5		
Dennis, Richard	PRB	Mills, James	7	9		
Dickinson, Barnet	TBM	-	2	3		
Dilling, John	TM	-	-	1		
Dixen, Wm.	SB					see John Pace
Dobson, Thomas Sr.	TBM	-	1	2		

TAXPAYER	List	Other WMTs	Slaves	Tithes	Acres	COMMENTS
Docwell?, William	PL	-	3	4		surname smudged, illegible
Dodson, John	VB	-	3	4		
Doss, James	EB	-	-	1	-	
Dowdy, Richard	TM					see John Hughes
Drake, Thomas	JT					see John Tabb
Drake, Thos. Jr.	VB	-	-	1		"for Thos. Drake Sr."
Drinkard, John	TBM	Drinkard, Wm. Drinkard, John Jr.	2	5		
Drinkard, Wm.	TBM					see John Drinkard
Dudley, Edward	LW	Dudley, James	8	10		
Dudley, James	LW					see Edward Dudley
Dudley, Thos	SB	Dudley, Wm.	5	7		
Dudley, William	SB					see Thomas Dudley
Duglis, John	TM					see Isham Clement; ?Douglas intended??
Dunkin, Josiah	EB					see Frank Anderson
Dunn, John	LW	-	-	1		
Dunnavant, Abraham	JT	Hood, Tucker	15	17		
Dunnavant, Hodge	JT	Dunnavant, Joel Dunnavant, Frederick	6	9		
Dunnavant, Joel	JT					see Hodge Dunnavant
Dunnavant, Phill	HA	Dunnavant, Wm	2	4	250	
Dunnavant, Thos.	CH					see Joseph Royall
Dunnavant, William	JT	Dunnivant, John Dunnivant, Abner Dunnivant, Danl.	2	6		
Dunnavant, William	VB					see Mary Bolling
Dunnavant, Wm.	CH					see Peter Jones
Dunnavant, Wm.	HA					see Phill Dunnavant
Dunnivant, Abner	JT					see William Dunnavant
Dunnivant, Clement	LW	-	1	2		
Dunnivant, Danl	JT					see William Dunnavant
Dunnivant, Frederick	JT					see Hodge Dunnavant
Dunnivant, John	JT					see William Dunnavant
Dunnivant, Norvel	VB					see Mary Bolling
Dupey, Peter	SB	-	4	5		
Dupuy, Bartholemew	TBM	Dupuy, James	7	9		
Dupuy, James	TBM					see Bartholemew Dupuy
Dupuy, Jno. Bartholomew	PL	Dupuy, Peter Maddox, Robert	10	13		
Dupuy, Peter	PL					see Jno. Bartholomew Dupuy
Dyson, Dan(iel)	VB					see Robert Cousons
Dyson, Francis	JT					see Capt. Edmond Walker

TAXPAYER	List	Other WMTs	Slaves	Tithes	Acres	COMMENTS
Dyson, William	EBj					see Griffin Peachy
Eggleston, Edward	TM					see William Eggleston
Eggleston, Jos.	HA	-	26	27	-	1 riding chair
Eggleston, Joseph	EBj	Johnson, Stephen	5	6		no tithe for Joseph Eggleston
Eggleston, Richard	TM	Porter, Nathaniel	6	7		"Richard Eggleston's Tithes"
Eggleston, William	TM	Eggleston, Edw.	?	?		stain obscures numbers
Ellett?, John	TBM	-	6	7		
Ellington, Jesse	LW					see Rice Newman
Ellington, John	VB	Ellington, Reser?	9	11		
Ellington, Reser?	VB					see John Ellington
Ellis, Ambrose	PL	-	3	4		
Ellis, Thomas	PL	Ellis, Thomas Jr.	2	4		
Ellis, Thomas's Est.	TM	-	2	2		
Ellis, Wm.	SB	-	-	1		
Elmore, John	SC					see Stephen Cocke
Elmore, Thomas	EBj	-	2	3		
Eppes, Peter's List	PRB	Sadler, Thomas	12	13		no tithe for Peter Eppes
Erving, William	TM					see Thomas Mumford
Ewing, Saml.	EB	-	-	1	-	
Farguson, Peleg	SC	Farguson, Robt.	4	6		
Farguson, Robt.	SC					see Peleg Farguson
Fargusson, John	EB	-	8	9	-	
Farley, Daniel Stewart	EB					see Stewart Farley
Farley, Gates	EBj					see William Farley
Farley, Henry	TBM	-	-	1		
Farley, James	PRB	-	4	5		
Farley, John	EB	-	-	1	-	-
Farley, John	EB	-	2	3	-	
Farley, Joseph	VB	-	7	8		
Farley, M___?	EB	-	4	5	-	extremely faded ink
Farley, M__'s List	EB	-	5	5		extremely faded ink
Farley, Nathan	EB	-	1	1	-	extremely faded ink
Farley, Stephen	EB	-	2	3	-	
Farley, Stewart	EB	Farley, Daniel Stewart	6	8	-	
Farley, William	EBj	Farley, Gates	4	6		
Farley, William Jr.	EB	-	-	1	-	
Farley, William Sr.	EB	?	5?	6	-	
Farrel, George	LW					see William Crawley
Featherstone, Burwell	PRB					see William G. Featherstone
Featherstone, Wm G.	PRB	Featherstone, Burwell	5	7		
Ferguson, Abner	TBM					see Richard Bradshaw

TAXPAYER	List	Other WMTs	Slaves	Tithes	Acres	COMMENTS
Ferguson, Henry	TBM	-	5	6		
Ferguson, William	TBM	-	-	1		
Finney, John	JT					see Mary Finney's tithes
Finney, Mary's tythes	JT	Finney, John Candleman?, John Christopher	13	15		
Finney, William	CH	Stephen, Wm.	18	20		
FitzGerrald, William	PRB	Hudson?, Drury	14	16		
FitzGerrald, William's Estate	PRB	Riggon, Moses	6	7		
Flemming, Beverley	EBj	Flemming, John	1	3		
Fletcher, Nathan	TBM	-	8	9		
Flin, John	TBM	Flin, Wm.	-	1		only 1 tithe despite 2 WM
Flin, Wm.	TBM					see John Flin
Flood, John	EBj	-	-	1		
Folks, Gabriel Sr.	TBM	Folks, Gab. Jr. Folks, Nathan	10	13		see also Fowlkes, etc.
Folks, Jennings	TBM	-	3	4		
Folks, Nathan	TBM					see Gabriel Folks Sr.
Ford, Abraham	PRB	Ford, Daniel	-	2		
Ford, Christopher	TM	Smith, James Ford, Milton Ford, Samuel Jones, John	11	16		
Ford, Daniel	PRB					see Abraham Ford
Ford, Frederick	PRB	-	-	1		
Ford, Frederick	VB	-	3	4		
Ford, George	PRB	-	1	2		
Ford, Isaac	EB					see William Ford
Ford, John	JT	Yeodaley?, Moses	6	8		
Ford, Lewis	TM	Stewart, John	-	2		
Ford, Milton	TM					see Christopher Ford
Ford, Samuel	TM					see Christopher Ford
Ford, Tady	PRB	-	1	2		
Ford, William	EB	Ford, Isaac	9	11	-	
Ford, Wm.	JT	-	5	6		
Forest, Abraham Jr.	TBM	-	1	2		
Forest, Josiah	TBM					see Abraham Forest Sr.
Forrest, Abraham Sr.	TBM	Forrest, Josiah	4	6		
Forrest, John	EBj	-	-	1		
Forster, Richd	HA					see Edmd. Booker
Foster, Ann's List	EB	-	2	2	-	
Foster, Booker	EBj	-	3	4		
Foster, George's Est.	TBM	Foster, John	8	9		"deceased"
Foster, James	TBM	-	3	4		

TAXPAYER	List	Other WMTs	Slaves	Tithes	Acres	COMMENTS
Foster, John	EB	-	2	3	-	
Foster, John	EBj	-	-	1		
Foster, John	TBM					see George Foster, Estate
Foster, John	TM	Foster, Thos.	1	3		
Foster, John	TM	-	-	-		"Son of Wm."
Foster, Richard	EB	-	1	2	-	
Foster, Robert	TM	-	2	3		
Foster, Thomas	TM	Allin, Isack Udaly?, David	6	9		
Foster, Thos.	TM					see John Foster
Foster, William	EB	-	-	1	-	
Foster, William	EBj	-	-	1		
Foster, William	TM					see Richard Anderson
Fowlkes, James	SB					see John Fowlkes
Fowlkes, John	SB	-	4	5		
Fowlkes, John	SB	Fowlkes, James	8	10		
Fowlkes, John	SB					see Joseph Fowlkes
Fowlkes, Joseph	SB	Fowlkes, John	5	7		
Franklin, James	LW					see George Cousings
French, Robert	LW	-	-	1		
Fulk, Henry	PL	-	2	3		
Fulk, Wm.	PL	-	2	3		
Furman?, Gideon	JT	-	3	4		
Gallimore?, George	EBj	-	4	5		could be 'Gablemore'
Gibbs, Matt	JT					see William Gibbs
Gibbs, William	JT	-	6	7		
Gibbs, William*'s tithes	JT	Gibbs, Matt.	3	4		"William Gibbs, Chesterfield Tythes"
Gil__, John	JT	Weeks, William	1	3		
Giles, John H.	JT					see William Giles
Giles, William	JT	Giles, John H. Sadler, John	14	17		
Gilliam, John*	TBM	S_ott?, James	21	22		"(Prince George)" (Co.)
Gilliam, John's Est.	TBM	Hastings, Zachary	7	8		"deceased"
Gilliam, Mrs.	LW	Clardy, ___	5	6		"To Mrs. Gilliam"
Gooch, John	EBj	-	3	4		
Goode, Mack	TM	-	4	5		
Granger, Benjamin	JT	-	1	2		
Graves, Edmd.	LW					see Wood Jones
Gray, Alexander Jr.	TBM	-	4	5		
Gray, John	TBM					see Joseph Gray
Gray, John	TBM	Gray, Thos.	2	4		
Gray, Jos.	TBM					see John Hall
Gray, Joseph	TBM	Gray, John	3	5		
Gray, Joseph Jr.	TBM	-	1	2		

TAXPAYER	List	Other WMTs	Slaves	Tithes	Acres	COMMENTS
Gray, Thos.	TBM					see John Gray
Green, Abraham Sr.	VB	-	11	12		1 (riding) chair
Green, John	TBM	-	3	4		
Green, Marston	SB	Lea, John	7	9		
Green, Thomas	LW	-	3	4		
Green, William	VB	-	2	3		
Greenhill, David Jr., for the Est. of	VB	Greenhill, Saml. Willkerson, Thos.	16 7	17 8		"For the estate of David Greenhill Jr."
Greenhill, John's tithables	JT	-	8	8		appears he is another of John Tabb's overseers or employees
Greenhill, Samuel	VB					see David Greenhill Jr.'s Est.
Greenhill, William	VB	Mayton?, Jno.	7	9		
Grigg, James	SC	Grigg, Peter Grigg, William Grigg, Josiah	6	10		
Grigg, Josiah	SC					see James Grigg
Grigg, Peter	SC					see James Grigg
Grigg, William	SC					see James Grigg
Gunn, Daniel	SB					see Stith Bolling
Gunn, Elisha	PL					see Thomas Gunn Jr.
Gunn, Elisha	SC					see James Gunn
Gunn, James	SC	Gunn, Elisha	7	9		
Gunn, Thomas Jr.	PL	Gunn, Thos. Sr. Gunn, Elisha	4	7		
Hall, Ambros	TBM	-	-	1		
Hall, Bowler	TBM	-	3	4		
Hall, John	PRB					see Henry Dennis
Hall, John	TBM	Gray, Jos.	8	10		
Hall, William	EB	-	6	7	-	
Ham, George Jr.	TM	-	1	2		
Ham, George Sr.	TM	-	2	3		
Ham, Thomas	TM	-	3	4		
Ham, William	TM	-	-	1		
Hamblin, Stephen	VB	Jackson, Abner	9	10		"For Stephen Hamblin"
Hamlett, Morris	LW	-	-	1		
Hanson, John	TBM	-	7	8		
Hardaway, Daniel	VB	-	15	16		
Hardaway, Jos. List	HA	Blannkenship, Jeremiah	2	3	-	
Hardaway, Purify's L	JT	-	2	2		"(her) List"
Hardaway, Stith	PRB	Moore, Mark	13	15		
Harper, Henry	TM	-	1	2		
Harris, James	EB	-	-	1	-	extremely faded ink

TAXPAYER	List	Other WMTs	Slaves	Tithes	Acres	COMMENTS
Harris, Wm.	EB	-	-	1	-	
Harrison, Christopher	TBM	-	1	2		
Harrison, Moses	TBM	-	2	3		
Harrison, Nathl's List	EB	Johnson, William	16	17	-	
Harriss, William*	TBM	Hudgings, Thos.	8	9		"(Surry)" (Co.)
Harrisson, Richard	PL	-	2	3		
Hassell?, John	EB					see Wm. Brooks
Hastings, Sutton	VB					see William Hastings Sr.
Hastings, William	TBM	-	-	1		
Hastings, William Sr.	VB	Hastings, Sutton	1	3		
Hatcher, Abram	TBM					see William Hatcher
Hatcher, William	TBM	Hatcher, Abram	3	5		
Hatchett, Josiah	EB	-	-	1	-	
Hatchett, Wm.	JT					see Archer Cheatham; ?Hatchell?
Hatchett?, Archer	HA	Wesbrook, Amos	-	2	-	
Hatton, Thos.	EB					see John Archer's List
Hawkes, Angelica Mrs.	LW	Hawkes, John	6	7		"To Mrs. Angelica Hawkes"
Hawkes, George	LW	-	-	1		
Hawkes, John	LW					see Mrs. Angelica Hawkes
Hawkes, Richd.	LW	-	1	2		
Hawkins, David	LW	-	3	4		
Hawkins, John	PL					see William Theart?
Hawkins, William	LW	-	1	2		
Hawkins?, Zachary	EB	____, William	-	2		extremely faded ink
Hayes, Richard	LW	Hayes, Richard Jr.	15	17		
Henderson, James	PL	Stewart, Wm	9	11		
Hendrick, Barnard	EB	Hendrick, Danl.	4	6	-	
Hendrick, Benj.??	EB	Hendrick, Zach.?	4	6	-	
Hendrick, Danl.	EB					see Barnard Hendrick
Hendrick, John	EB	-	3	4	-	
Hendrick, Obediah	EB	-	6	7	-	
Hendrick, Zach.?	EB					See Benj. Hendrick
Hill, Eliza's List	EB	-	5	5	-	
Hill, James	EB					see James Hill's estate
Hill, James Est, dec'd	EB	Hill, James Mayes, Daniel	6	8	-	
Hill, Joel	TM	-	1	2		
Hill, John	EB	-	2	3	-	
Hill, John Sr.	TM	-	1	2		
Hilsman, Joseph	TM					see Mathew Hilsman
Hilsman, Mathew	TM	Hilsman, Joseph	1	3		
Holt, Jesse	EBj					see Thomas Holt

TAXPAYER	List	Other WMTs	Slaves	Tithes	Acres	COMMENTS
Holt, Richard	JT					see John Tabb
Holt, Shadrick	EBj	-	1	1		no tithe for Shadrick Holt
Holt, Shadrick	JT					see John Tabb
Holt, Shadrick	TM	Cambell, William	1	2		"His Tythes"
Holt, Thomas	EBj	Holt, Jesse	2	4		
Holte, David	PL					see William Watson
Holton, Zachariah	PL					see Medrap? Thompson
Hood, (smudged)	LW	-	-	1		
Hood, Abraham	VB	Hood, Joshua Hood, John	-	3		
Hood, Charles	LW					see John Hood
Hood, Joel	VB					see Robert Hood
Hood, John	LW	Hood, Charles	4	6		
Hood, John	VB					see Abraham Hood
Hood, John Jr.	LW	-	-	1		
Hood, Joshua	VB					see Abraham Hood
Hood, Robert	VB	Hood, Joel	2	4		
Hood, Solomon	VB	-	-	1		
Hood, Tucker	JT					see Abraham Dunnavant
Hood, Tucker	VB	Wells, Richard	1	2		"For Tucker Hood"
Howell, John	LW					see William Boothe
Howell, M__er	EBj	-	-	1		
Howlett, William	LW	-	4	5		
Hubbert, John	TM	Hubbert, Joseph	-	2		
Hubbert, Joseph	TM					see John Hubbert
Hubbert, Joseph	TM	Hubbert, Samuel Davis	3	5		
Hubbert, Samuel D.	TM					see Joseph Hubbert
Huddleston, Robt.	LW					see Thos. Huddleston
Huddleston, Thos.	LW	Huddleston, Robt.	-	2		
Hudgings, Thos.	SB					see Samuel Sherwin
Hudgings, Thos.	TBM					see William Harris (Surry)
Hudson, Burton	EB					see Sarah Burton's List
Hudson, Burton's List	EB	Cooper, Peter	3	3	-	extremely faded ink
Hudson, Christopher	CH	Fosset(?), Raleigh	21	22		
Hudson, Drury	PRB					see William FitzGerrald
Hudson, Edward	EBj	-	-	1		
Hudson, John	EBj	-	1	2		
Hudson, Peter	TBM	-	2	3		
Hudson, Robert	EB		7	8	-	extremely faded ink
Hudson, Thomas	TBM	-	1	2		
Hudson, William	PL	-	4	5		
Hughes, Anderson	TM					see John Hughes
Hughes, John	TM	Hughes, Anderson	17	20		

TAXPAYER	List	Other WMTs	Slaves	Tithes	Acres	COMMENTS
		Dowdy, Richard				
Hundley, Charles Est.	TBM	Hundley, Josiah	5	6		"deceased"
Hundley, Geo.	TBM					see Josiah Hundley
Hundley, Joel	TBM	-	3	4		
Hundley, John	TBM	-	3	4		
Hundley, Josiah	TBM	Hundley, Geo.	8	10		
Hundley, Josiah	TBM					see Charles Hundley's Estate
Hurt, James	TM	-	-	1		
Hurt, Moses Sr.	SC	-	12	13		
Hurt, Mosses (sic) Jr.	PL	-	1	2		
Hurt, William	TM	Cumton, Joshua	4	6		
Hurt, William	TM	-	-	1		
Hurt, Zachariah	SC	-	3	4		
Huse, Benj.	TBM					see David Zachary Sr.
Hutcharson, William	JT	-	1	2		
Hutcherson, Caner?	TM					see John White
Hutcherson, Charles	TM	Hutcherson, Wm Southall Hutcherson, Jas.	-	3		
Hutcherson, James	TM					see Charles Hutcherson
Hutcherson, William Souhall	TM					see Charles Hutcherson
Hutcheson, Wm.	VB					see Benjamin Wiley
Ingram, Jos.	JT					see Chasteen Cocke
Irby, Charles	PL	Chambrus?, John	12	14		
Irby, Charles' Estate	PL	Irby, John Irby, Wm	8	10		
Irby, John	PL					see Charles Irby's estate
Irby, William	PL					see Charles Irby's estate
J_tine?, Jno. W.	PL					see John Winn Sr.
Jackson, Able	PL					see Samuel Jordan
Jackson, Abner	VB					see Stephen Hamblin
Jackson, Arthur	SB	-	-	1		
Jackson, Burwell	JT					see Matt Jackson
Jackson, Francis	EB	-	3	4	-	
Jackson, Francis "Long"	EB	Jackson, Joel	3	5	-	
Jackson, Henry	EBj					see John Jackson
Jackson, Isaiah	TBM					see Moses Overton
Jackson, Joel	EB					see Francis "Long" Jackson
Jackson, John	EB	-	1	2		"son (of?) Wm"
Jackson, John	EBj	Jackson, Henry	2	4		
Jackson, Josiah	EB	-	1	2	-	"Constable"
Jackson, Mark Jr.	TBM	-	-	1		

TAXPAYER	List	Other WMTs	Slaves	Tithes	Acres	COMMENTS
Jackson, Mark Sr.	TBM	-	-	1		
Jackson, Matt	JT	Jackson, Burwell	3	5		
Jackson, Stewart	EB					see Roland Ward
Jackson, William	EBj	-	-	1		
Jackson, William	JT					see John Tabb
Jackson, Wm.	EB	-	2	3	-	
Jackson, Wm.	SB	-	-	1		
James, John	TM					see Thomas James
James, Thomas	TM	James, John	1	3		
James, Thomas Jr.	TM	-	2	3		
Jankins, James	EB	-	5	6	-	
Jeffress, James	SB					see Thos. Jeffress
Jeffress, Thos.	SB	Jeffress, James Jeffress, Thos.	9	12		definitely JEFFRESS, not Jeffreys
Jennings, Dickerson	PL	-	2	3		
Jennings, Henry	TBM	-	2	3		
Jennings, James	PL	-	1	2		
Jennings, John Jr.	TBM	-	1	2		
Jennings, Joseph	TBM	-	6	7		
Jennings, William	PL	-	1	2		
Jennings, William Jr.	TBM	-	3	4		
Jeter, Oliver	TBM	-	2	3		
Jeter, Pansom?	SB	-	-	1		
Jeter, Presley	SB					see Winifred Jeter's List
Jeter, Winifred's List	SB	Jeter, Presley	5	6		
Jinnings, James	SB					see John Jinnings
Jinnings, John	SB	Jinnings, James	5	7		
Jinnings, Robert	SB	Chiles, William	5	7		
Jinnings, William	SB		5	6		(5 slaves named, but no tithes)
Johns, John's Estate	EBj	Johns, Stephen Johns, Nathaniel	4	6		
Johns, Nathaniel	EBj					see John Johns' Estate
Johns, Stephen	EBj					see John Johns' Estate
Johns, Stephen	TM					see Henry Cox's Tithes
Johnson, Ashley	EBj	-	2	3		
Johnson, Ben	SB					see Richard Bennet's List
Johnson, Benjamin	EBj	-	-	1		
Johnson, Christopher	EBj					see James Johnson
Johnson, Garrard	EBj	-	2	3		
Johnson, Garrard Jr.	EBj	-	-	1		
Johnson, Isham	HA					see Henry Anderson
Johnson, James	EBj					see John Johnson
Johnson, James	EBj	Johnson, Mormon Johnson,	4	7		

TAXPAYER	List	Other WMTs	Slaves	Tithes	Acres	COMMENTS
		Christopher				
Johnson, John	EBj	Johnson, James Johnson, Samuel	2	5		
Johnson, Mormon	EBj					see James Johnson
Johnson, Nahum	EBj	-	-	1		
Johnson, Nicholas	EBj	-	2	3		
Johnson, Richd.	HA					see Henry Anderson
Johnson, Samuel	EBj					see John Johnson
Johnson, Samuel	JT					see John Tabb
Johnson, Stephen	EBj					see Joseph Eggleston
Johnson, Stephen	EBj	-	2	3		
Johnson, William	EB					see Nathl. Harrison's List
Johnson, Wm.	HA					see Daniel Toms
Johnson?, James	HA					see Thos. Webster
Johnston, Archer	LW	-	8	9		
Jolly, Dudley	JT					see John Booker
Jones, Adam Jr.	PL					see Adam Jones Sr.
Jones, Adam Sr.	PL	Jones, Adam Jr.	7	9		
Jones, Aggr.'s List	EB	Jones, Edward	9	10	-	
Jones, Archer	LW					see Peter Jones Sr.
Jones, Batte	TBM	-	7	8		
Jones, Capt. Wm.	SC	Jones, Thomas	4	6		
Jones, Col. Richard	TBM	Muse, Geo. Pollard, William	18	21		
Jones, Edward	EB					see Aggr. Jones List
Jones, Edward	LW					see Peter Jones Sr.
Jones, Gabriel	EBj					see Hannah Jones
Jones, George	EB	-	-	1	-	
Jones, Hannah's list	EBj	Jones, Gabriel	3	4		
Jones, James	TBM					see Peter Jones Sr. (Rawleigh)
Jones, John	LW	-	8	9		
Jones, John	TM					see Christopher Ford
Jones, Mrs. Dorothy	LW	-	8	8		"To Mrs. Dorothy Jones"
Jones, Peter	CH	Dunnavant, Wm.	10	12		"Peter Jones' List"
Jones, Peter (Sweathouse [creek])	LW	Jones, William	10	12		
Jones, Peter Sr.	LW	Jones, Archer Jones, Robt. Jones, Edwd.	19	23		
Jones, Peter Sr.*	TBM	Bevill, Carter Jones, James	8	10		"(Rawleigh)"
Jones, Philip	LW	Meanly, Wm.	14	16		
Jones, Richard Jr.	TBM	Williams, Jno.	14	16		
Jones, Richd.	EB	-	8	9	-	

TAXPAYER	List	Other WMTs	Slaves	Tithes	Acres	COMMENTS
Jones, Riper?	SC	-	1	2		
Jones, Robt.	LW					see Peter Jones Sr.
Jones, Tho. Field	JT	-	-	1		
Jones, Thomas	SC					see Capt. Wm. Jones
Jones, Thomas	TM	-	16	17		1 riding chair
Jones, Uriah	JT					see John Tabb
Jones, William	EB	-	2	3	-	
Jones, William	LW	-	6	7		
Jones, William	LW					see Peter Jones (Sweathouse)"
Jones, Wood	LW	Jones, Wood Jr. Graves, Edmd.	12	15		
Jones?, Danl.'s Est.	HA	Willson, Richd.	9	10	-	
Jordan, Samuel	PL	Jackson, Able	14	16		
Jordan, Thomas	SC	-	4	5		
Kennon, Robert's Est.	VB	Cardwell, Richard	15	16		
Kidd, Benjamin	VB					see George Kidd
Kidd, George	VB	Kidd, Benjamin				
King, Henry	VB					see Vivion Brooking
Knight, Charles	TBM	-	4	5		
Knight, John	PL	-	5	6		
Lamb(?), Anthony	CH	-	2	3		
Lamb, William	PRB	-	1	1		no tithe for William Lamb; see Col. Thomas Bland's List
Lampkin, Peter	PL	-	14	15		1 riding chair
Lea, ___'s List	SB	-	1	1		given name blank = female
Lea, John	SB					see Marston Green
League, Aaron	EBj	League, Edmund	-	1		evidently no tithe for Aaron
League, Benjamin	SB	-	-	1		
League, Edmund	EBj					see Aaron League
League, James	EBj	League, Joab	-	2		
League, Joab	EBj					see James League
League, Joshua	EBj	-	-	1		
Lewis, Griffin	PL	Lewis, John	3	5		
Lewis, Henry	PRB	-	1	2		
Lewis, Jas	PL					see John Lewis
Lewis, John	PL					see Griffin Lewis
Lewis, John	PL	Lewis, Wm. Lewis, Jas.	4	7		
Lewis, John (Dinw.)	TBM	Pace, Newsum	3	4		evidently resident of Dinwiddie
Lewis, Wm	PL					see John Lewis
Liggon, Richard	TBM	-	2	3		

TAXPAYER	List	Other WMTs	Slaves	Tithes	Acres	COMMENTS
Ligon, John	JT	-	-	1		
Ligon, Robt.	EB	-	3	4		extremely faded ink
Ligon, Thos.	SC	-	-	1		
Ligon, William	EB	-	5	6		
Ligon, William Jr.	EB	-	3	4		
Lipscomb, Benj.	TBM					see Uriah Lipscomb
Lipscomb, Richard	TBM	-	1	2		
Lipscomb, Uriah	TBM	Lipscomb, Benj.	4	6		
Lister, Thomas	EBj	-	-	1		
Lockett, Abraham	EB	-	3	4		
Lockett, Benj.	EB	-	2	3		
Loving, Moses	TM	-	-	1		
Lumkin, Dickinson	TBM	-	-	1		
Lundon, Thomas G.	TM					see Henry Scipworth's Tythes
Lunsford, John	TBM	-	4	5		
Maddox, Robert	PL					see Jno. Bartholomew Dupuy
Malone, Ishum?	PL	-	2	3		
Mann, Cain	HA	-	3	4	200	
Mann, Catlett	TBM	Mann, Jonathan	4	6		
Mann, Field	HA	-	3	4	150	
Mann, James	EB					see Samuel Mann
Mann, James	TBM	-	-	1		
Mann, John	EB					see Samuel Mann
Mann, John	TBM	-	-	1		
Mann, Jonathan	TBM					see Catlett Mann
Mann, Saml. Jr.	HA	Ponton?, Wm	0	2	-	
Mann, Samuel	EB	Mann, James Mann, John	0	3		
Mann, William	EBj					see Anthony Webster
Marcy, Zachariah	EBj	-	-	1		
Marshall, Abraham	EB	-	5	6		
Marshall, Alex's List	EB	-	5	6		extremely faded ink
Marshall, John	EB	-	4	5		
Marshall, Judah's List	EB	-	4	4		
Marshall, Robt.	HA	-	5	6	-	
Martin, Abram	TBM					see George Martin
Martin, George	TBM	Martin, Abram	5	7		
Mayes, Daniel	EB					see James Hill's estate
Mayes, Daniel	PRB	Mayes, Daniel Jr.	3	5		
Maynard, John	PL					see Henry Buford's list
Mays, Gardner	TBM					see William Bell
Mayton?, Jno.	VB					see William Greenhill
McGahee, ___'s List	EB	-	?	?		given name smudged

TAXPAYER	List	Other WMTs	Slaves	Tithes	Acres	COMMENTS
McGukin?, Barnet G.	TBM	-	-	1		
McNabb, Alexander	VB	Perquerson, David	8	10		
Meadow, Henry's list	EB	-	2	2		
Meadow?, Micajah	EB	-	1	2		extremely faded ink
Meadows, Benjamin	EBj	-	2	3		
Meadows, James	EBj	-	2	3		
Meanly, Wm.	LW					see Philip Jones; "Manley" intended?
Medows, Joel	TM	-	-	1		
Mills, James	PRB					see Richard Dennis
Mills, James' List	PL	More, Wm overseer	6	7		no tithe for James Mills
Mills, John	SB	-	1	2		
Mitchel, James	TBM	-	2	3		
Mitchel, Thomas	TBM	-	2	3		
Mitchel?, Evan	VB	-	2	3		
Molson, Mary's tithes	TM	Allen, David	8	9		
Monday, Francis	JT					see Sarah Scott's tithes
Moore, Drury	TBM	-	-	1		
Moore, Mark	PRB					see Stith Hardaway
More, William	PL					see James Mills' List; "overseer"
Morgan, Cignon?	HA	-	6	7	219	
Morgan, Ellington	LW					see John Morgan
Morgan, John	LW	Morgan, Ellington	3	5		
Morgan, Samuel	PL	-	6	7		
Morgan, Samuel Sr.	PL	-	3	4		
Morgan, Wm.	HA	-	2	3	219	
Morris, Moses	TM	Morris, Zachariah	5	7		
Morris, Zachariah	TM					see Moses Morris
Motley, Daniel	TBM					see Joseph Motley
Motley, Joel	TBM	-	11	12		
Motley, Joseph	TBM	Motley, Daniel	8	10		
Mumford, Thomas	TM	Bell, John Erving, William	21	23		1 riding chair
Munford, Edward	LW	Munford, James	11	13		
Munford, James	LW					see Edward Munford
Munford, James	LW					see Mrs. Ann Munford
Munford, Mrs. Ann	LW	Munford, James	5	6		"To Mrs. Ann Munford"
Munford, Thomas B.	TBM	Zachary, Crawford	14	16		
Murray, Wm.	LW					see Page Coleman
Muse, Geo.	TBM					see Col. Richard Jones
Nance, Giles	PL	Nance, Wm. Nance, James	1	4		
Nance, James	PL					see Giles Nance

TAXPAYER	List	Other WMTs	Slaves	Tithes	Acres	COMMENTS
Nance, Wm.	PL					see Giles Nance
Nash, Thomas	PL					see Mary Chambers' Estate
Neal, (faded)	EB					see Roger Neal
Neal, David	EB					see Roger Neal
Neal, John	VB					see Daniel Allen
Neal, Roger	EB	Neal, David Neal, (faded)	3	6		extremely faded ink
Neale?, ___	EB		5	6		extremely faded ink
Newman, Rice	LW	Ellington, Jesse	10	12		
Noble, John	EBj					see Joseph Noble
Noble, Joseph	EBj	Noble, John	-	2		
Norris, John	TBM	-	3	4		
Nowell?, William	JT					see John Tabb
Ogilsby, William	EB	-	-	1		
Okely, Thomas	SB	-	-	1		"Oakley" phonetically???
Old, William	LW	-	2	3		
Oliver, Benj.	TBM					see Capt. Thomas Short
Oliver, Isack	SB	-	3	4		
Oliver, James	TBM	Clay, Caleb	6	8		
Orsborn, Thomas	EBj	-	2	3		
Osbo__?, William	EB	-	10	11		extremely faded ink
Osborne, Abner	JT	Pamplin?, Henry	9	11		
Osborne, Branch	TBM	-	5	6		
Osborne, George	CH					see John Robertson
Osborne, Jos.	HA	-	15	16	-	
Osborne, Wm. Jr.	HA	-	-		-	No tithes listed
Ously, Thomas	TM	-	-	1		
Overstreet, William	PL					see John Winn Sr.
Overton, Benjamin	EBj	-	-	1		
Overton, Moses	TBM	Jackson, Isaiah	4	6		
Overton, Thomas P.	TM	-	2	3		
Pace, John	SB	Pace, Montague Dixen, Wm	2	5		
Pace, Montague	SB					see John Pace
Pace, Newsum	TBM					see John Lewis (Dinw.)
Page, John	EBj	-	1	2		
Palmer, Elijah	TM	-	-	1		
Palmor?, Elisha	EB	-	1	1		extremely faded ink
Pamplin?, Henry	JT					see Abner Osborne
Pardue, John	JT					see William Pardue
Pardue, Jos.	JT					see William Pardue
Pardue, Pateman?	JT					see William Pardue
Pardue, William	JT	Pardue, Pateman? Pardue, John Pardue, Jos.	1	5		surname could be "Pardus"

TAXPAYER	List	Other WMTs	Slaves	Tithes	Acres	COMMENTS
Parham, James Jr.	TBM	-	1	2		
Parish, Abram	HA	-	1	2	-	
Parkinson?, Mathew	EB	-	2	3		extremely faded ink
Parram, Danl.	HA					see Wm. Param
Parram, James	HA	Parram, James	-	2	-	
Parram, Wm.	HA	Parram, Danl.	5	7	-	
Payne, Jos.	TBM					see Thomas Payne
Payne, Thomas	TBM	Payne, Jos.	5	7		
Peachy, Griffin*	EBj	Dyson, William	13	14		"Griffin Peachy, Nottoway"
Peachy, Thos. Griffin	JT	Cordle, Richd. Thompson, Wm Peachy, T.G. Jr.	12	16		
Pearman, William	JT					see Findal Southerland
Pearson, David	PRB	-	-	1		
Perkerson, Field	HA	Perkerson, Isham	1	3	-	
Perkerson, Isham	HA					see Field Perkerson
Perkerson, John	HA					
Perkerson, Ralph	HA	Perkerson, John	1	3	-	
Perquerson, David	VB					see Alexander McNabb
Phillips, Richard	TM	Phillips, William	3	5		
Phillips, William	TM					see Richard Phillips
Pillow, William	EBj	-	-	1		
Pitchford, John	VB	-	-	1		
Pitchford, Samuel	VB	-	1	2		
Pitchford, Wm.	HA					see Stephen Cocke
Pollard, Ambrose	EB					see Thomas Pollard
Pollard, James	TM					see ___ill Cobbs
Pollard, Thos.	EB	Pollard, Thos. Jr. Pollard, Ambrose	4	7		
Pollard, William	EB	-	1	2		
Pollard, William	TBM					see Col. Richard Jones
Pollard?, Joseph	EB	Pollard?, Wm.	2	4		extremely faded ink
Pollard?, William	EB					see Joseph Pollard?
Ponton?, Wm	HA					see Saml. Mann, Jr.
Porter, Nathaniel	TM					see Richard Eggleston's Tithes
Powell, Abner	LW	-	-	1		
Powell, Abraham	LW					see George Worsham
Powell, John	LW	Powell, John Jr.	1	3		
Powell, Mrs. Mary	LW	-	2	2		"To Mrs. Mary Powell"
Powell, Robert	LW	-	2	3		
Powell, Thomas	JT					see John Tabb
Pride, Roush	EB	Davis, P.	9	11		extremely faded ink
Prindle, Parrott	EBj	-	-	1		
Pringle, Oliver	CH					see Joseph Wilkinson's

TAXPAYER	List	Other WMTs	Slaves	Tithes	Acres	COMMENTS
						Estate
Pryor, John	PRB	Pryor, Samuel	10	12		
Pryor, Samuel	PRB					see John Pryor
Purkinson, Jeremiah	VB	-	-	1		
Ragsdale, George	HA	-	4	5	-	
Raibun?, George	JT					see George Cone?'s tithes
Ramsay, Richard	TBM					see Col. John Cocke, Surry
Ramsay, Richard's list	TBM	-	1	1		no tithe for Richard here
Randolph, Peter	HA	Riving?, Richd.	6	8	-	
Randolph, Tabitha	HA	-	6	6	-	
Rawlett, Robert	PRB	-	-	1		
Ray, James	EBj	-	-	1		
Ray, John	EBj	-	-	1		
Ray, Thomas	EBj	-	-	1		
Reams, Fed'k?	HA	-	-	1	150	
Reasons, John	TM	-	-	1		
Redford, Andrew	TBM	-	10	11		
Richardson, Ruler?	TBM	-	2	3		
Riggon, Moses	PRB					see estate of Wm Fitzgerrald, deceased
Riving?, Richd.	HA					see Peter Randolph
Roach, Jos.	VB					see William Roach
Roach, Millinton	VB	-	2	3		
Roach, William	LW					see William Crawley
Roach, William	VB	Roach, Jos.	1	3		
Roach, Wm.	TBM					see Samuel Vaughn (Dinwiddie)
Roberts, John	TBM	Roberts, Stephen	-	2		
Roberts, Pleasant	VB	-	2	3		
Roberts, Sarah's list	EB	Roberts, ___	2	3		
Roberts, Step.	TBM	-	3	4		
Roberts, Stephen	TBM					see John Roberts
Robertson, Bridge	CH					see Daniel Worsham
Robertson, Christopher	TBM	-	2	3		
Robertson, Edward (deceased) Estate	TBM	Robertson, Edward (Jr.?)	3	4		
Robertson, George	JT	-	3	3		
Robertson, Henry	TBM	Robertson, Peter	8	10		
Robertson, James	SB					see Nathaniel Robertson
Robertson, James Est	TBM	-	1	1		
Robertson, John	CH	Osborne, George	8	10		
Robertson, John	TBM	-	2	3		
Robertson, Matthew	HA	-	3	4	-	
Robertson, Nathaniel	SB	Robertson, James	7	10		

TAXPAYER	List	Other WMTs	Slaves	Tithes	Acres	COMMENTS
		Robertson, Nathaniel (Jr.)				
Robertson, Peter	TBM					see Henry Robertson
Robertson, William	JT	-	6	7		
Rowlett, George	HA	Rowlett, George Jr.	1	3	-	
Royall, John	CH	Royall, John Jr.	17	19		
Royall, Joseph	CH	Dunnavant, Thos.	12	14		
Royall, Litttlebury	TBM	-	4	5		
Rucker, Elisha	TM	-	-	1		
Rucker, Joshua	TM	-	1	2		
Rucker, Mordacai	TM	-	-	1		
Rucker, William	TM	-	3	4		
S_ott?, James	TBM					see John Gilliam (P.G.); ?Srolt?
Sadler, John	JT					see William Giles
Sadler, Thomas	PRB					see Peter Eppes
Sallard, Charles	PL	-	8	9		
Scipworth, Henry	TM	Lundon, Thomas Gunter	8	10	375	"(His) Tythes"
Scott, George	EB					see Roger Thompson
Scott, George __	EB	-	-	1		
Scott, James	LW	-	7	8		
Scott, John	EB					see Roger Scott
Scott, Roger	EB	Scott, John	1	3		
Scott, Sarah's Tithes	JT	Monday, Francis Barnes, Francis	13	15		
Sea, James	EBj	-	1	2		
Seay, Gideon	TM	-	-	1		
Seay, Jacob	JT	-	7	8		
Seay, Jacob	TM					see Moses Seay
Seay, Jesse	TM	-	8	9	196	
Seay, Moses	TM	Seay, Jacob Seay, Samuel	2	5		
Seay, Samuel	TM					see Moses Seay
Shell, Thomas	JT	-	-	1		
Shelton, James	SB	Shelton, Thos.	5	5		unclear why no white tithes pd.
Shelton, Joel	PL					see William Thomas
Shepherson, Nathan	LW					see William Crawley
Sherwin, Samuel	SB	Hudgings, Thos.	15	17		
Short, Capt. Thomas	TBM	Oliver, Benj.	11	13		
Singleton, Avis	EBj	-	1	1		no tithe for Avis
Singleton, Robert	EBj	-	-	1		
Singleton, William	EBj	-	-	1		

TAXPAYER	List	Other WMTs	Slaves	Tithes	Acres	COMMENTS
Smith, Burril	PL					see Samuel Smith
Smith, Burril	PL					see Samuel Smith
Smith, Griffin	PL	-	3	4		
Smith, James	TM					see Christopher Ford
Smith, John	LW					see William Walthall Sr.
Smith, Richard	TBM	-	1	2		
Smith, Samuel	PL	Smith, Burril	8	10		
Smith, Samuel	PL	Smith, Burril	7	9		
Smytha, Joshua	TBM					see Col. Richard Tunstall's List
Snead, Robert	PL					see William Snead
Snead, William	PL	Snead, Robert	3	5		
Snellings, Geo.	TBM					see Isham Thompson's estate
Southall, James	VB	-	2	3		
Southall, John	VB	-	1	2		
Southall, William	TM	-	1	2		
Southerland, Findal's list	JT	Pearman, William	14	15		
Spain, Joshua	LW	Spain, Newman Spain, Joshua Jr.	1	4		
Spain, Newman	LW					see Joshua Spain
Spinner, John	VB					see Thomas Bevill's Estate
Stainback, Peter	PL	-	9	10		
Stephen, Wm.	CH					See William Finney
Stern, Francis	VB	-	4	5		
Stern, Tabitha's tithes	TM	-	3	3		
Steward, Wm.	PL					see James Henderson
Stewart, Charles	TBM	-	2	3		
Stewart, Edward	TBM					see Littlebury Stewart
Stewart, John	TM					see Lewis Ford
Stewart, John Sr.	TBM	-	1	2		
Stewart, Littlebury	TBM	Stewart, Edward	-	2		
Stewart, Mary's tithes	TM	-	2	2		
Still, George	TBM	-	1	2		
Stow, Jacob	PRB	-	-	1		
Street, William	JT					see Mary Crenshaw's tithes
Sutebury?, John	JT					see Jacob Williamson
Swiney, Thomas	EBj	-	-	1		
Swinney, Elizabeth	PL	-	1	1		"her List". number of tithes obscured, only one slave named
Tabb, Edward	TM	-	4	5		
Tabb, John	JT	Tabb?, Williamson Tabb, Thomas	142	166		

TAXPAYER	List	Other WMTs	Slaves	Tithes	Acres	COMMENTS
		Jones, Uriah White, John Powell, Thomas Co____, Jehu? Johnson, Samuel Nowell?, William Holt, Shadrick Holt, Richard Jackson, William Drake, Thomas Compton, Micajah				
Tabb, Thomas	JT					see John Tabb
Tabb?, Williamson	JT					see John Tabb
Talley, Abner	VB					see Lodwick Talley
Talley, Abraham	VB					see William Talley
Talley, Frederick	VB					see Tucker Talley
Talley, Grief	VB					see William Talley
Talley, Jesse	LW	-	-	1		
Talley, John	LW	-	-	1		
Talley, Lodwick	VB	Talley, Lodwick Jr. Talley, Abner Talley, Peyton	1	5		
Talley, Peyton	VB					see Lodwick Talley
Talley, Robt.	VB					see Tucker Talley
Talley, Thos.	VB	-	1	1		"For Thos. Talley"
Talley, Tucker	VB	Talley, Robt. Talley, Frederick	2	4		
Talley, William	LW	-	-	1		
Talley, William	VB	Talley, Abraham Talley, Grief	3	6		
Tanner, Branch	JT	Tanner, Martin	23	24		
Tanner, Field	LW					see Jeremiah Tanner
Tanner, Jeremiah	LW	Tanner, Field	-	2		
Tanner, Joel	TBM	Tanner, Thomas	2	4		
Tanner, Martin	JT					see Branch Tanner
Tanner, Mrs. Ann	LW	-	8	8		
Tanner, Robert	LW	-	1	2		
Tanner, Thomas	TBM					see Joel Tanner
Tayler, John	TM	-	-	1		
Taylor, Geo.	SC					see Francis Woodward
Theart?, William	PL	Hawkins, John	1	3		
Tho__, John?	EB	-	3	4		
Thomas, Atha	SC					see Saml. Thomas
Thomas, John	TBM	-	-	1		
Thomas, Joshua	PL					see Woodleif Thomas

TAXPAYER	List	Other WMTs	Slaves	Tithes	Acres	COMMENTS
Thomas, Saml.	SC	Thomas, Atha	4	6		
Thomas, William	PRB	-	2	3		
Thomas, Woodleif	PL	Thomas, Joshua	3	5		
Thompson, David	TBM	-	4	5		
Thompson, Drury	JT	Thompson, Ro.	11	13		
Thompson, Drury's List	TBM	Brummell, William	6	7		no tithe for Drury Thompson
Thompson, Isham's Estate	TBM	Snellings, Geo.	10	11		
Thompson, Medrap?	PL	Holton, Zachariah	2	4		
Thompson, Peter	EB	(illegible)	11	13		
Thompson, Ro.	JT					see Drury Thompson
Thompson, Roger	EB	Scott, George?	5	7		
Thompson, Wm.	JT					see Thos. Griffin Peachey
Thomson, Jinnings	SB					see Samuel Thomson
Thomson, Samuel	SB	Thomson, Jinnings	5	7		
Thornton, Sterling C.	TBM	-	4	5		
Thowet, John	PL	Williams, Thos.	5	6		"(of) Prince George" (Co.)
Toms?, Dan'l	HA	Johnson, Wm.	17	19	-	1 riding chair
Townes, James??	EB	-	10	11		
Townes, John	EB	Townes, Richard Townes, John Jr.	9	12		extremely faded ink
Townes, Richard	EB					see John Townes
Tucker, Abel	LW					see William Wilson
Tucker, Absalom	LW	-	-	1		
Tucker, Daniel	LW	-	3	4		
Tucker, David	LW					see William Tucker Sr.
Tucker, Francis	LW	Tucker, Herodian?	2	4		
Tucker, Godfrey	VB	-	1	2		
Tucker, Henry	LW	-	-	1		
Tucker, Herodian?	LW					see Francis Tucker
Tucker, John *	LW	-	3	4		"John Tucker (waller)"
Tucker, John Jr.	PRB	-	3	4		
Tucker, John Sr.	LW	Tucker, John Jr. Tucker, Shadrick	1	4		
Tucker, Matthew Jr.	LW	Tucker, Paskal	1	3		
Tucker, Paskal	LW					see Matthew Tucker Jr.
Tucker, Robt.	LW					see William Tucker Sr.
Tucker, Shadrick	LW					see John Tucker Sr.
Tucker, Thos.	VB		1	2		
Tucker, William Jr.	LW	-	-	1		
Tucker, William Sr.	LW	Tucker, David Tucker, Robt.	6	9		
Tully, John	JT	-	2	3		

TAXPAYER	List	Other WMTs	Slaves	Tithes	Acres	COMMENTS
Tunstall, Col. Richard's List	TBM	Smytha, Joshua	5	6		
Udaly?, David	TM					see Thomas Foster
Vaden, Henry	LW	-	4	5		
Vasser, George	HA					see Richard Vasser
Vasser, John	HA	-	2	3	-	
Vasser, Richd.	HA	Vasser, George Bradbury, Wm.	5	8	-	
Vaughan, James	EB	-	4	5		
Vaughan, Lewis??	EB	Vaughan, Zedekiah	2	4		
Vaughan, William	EB	-	-	1		
Vaughan, Zedekiah	EB					see Lewis Vaughan
Vaughn, John	EBj					see Robert Vaughn
Vaughn, Robert	EBj	Vaughn, John	7	9		
Vaughn, Samuel (Dinwiddie)	TBM	Roach, Wm.	2	3		
Verser, Abroham	TM	-	-	1		
Verser, Nathaniel	TM	-	-	1		
Waddel, Thos.	TBM					see John Dalby
Walding, John	TM					see Francis Anderson
Walker, Capt. Edm[d].	JT	Dyson, Francis	7	9		
Walker, Elexander	TM	-	1	2		really 'Elexander'
Walker, Jerrymiah	SB	-	3	4		
Walker, Judith's tithes	JT	Walker, William Tanner	6	7		
Walker, Richard	PL					see Thomas Walker Sr.
Walker, Thomas Sr.	PL	Walker, Richard	6	8		
Walker, William	TBM	-	-	1		
Walker, Wm. Tanner	JT					see Judith Walker's tithes
Waller, Major's List	PL	Waller, William	4	6		
Waller, Matthew	PL					see Robert Davis
Waller, William	PL					see Major Waller
Wallington?, Sterling Thornton	SB	-	-	1		
Walthall, Christopher	JT	-	4	5		
Walthall, Daniel	EB	-	2	3		
Walthall, Henry	JT	-	12	13		
Walthall, Henry	LW					see William Walthall Sr.
Walthall, John	JT	-	5	6		
Walthall, Richard	JT	-	6	7		
Walthall, Thomas	JT	Wyatt, Thos.	9	11		
Walthall, William Jr.	LW	-	2	3		
Walthall, William Sr.	LW	Walthall, Henry Smith, John	6	9		

TAXPAYER	List	Other WMTs	Slaves	Tithes	Acres	COMMENTS
Walthall, Wm.	HA	-	7	8	-	
Walton, Jesse	TBM	-	4	5		
Walton, Mathew?	EB					see Sherwood Walton
Walton, Sherwood	EB	Walton, Mathew?	5	7		
Walton, Simeon	SB	-	8	9		
Ward, Ben	HA	Ward, Benj. Jr.	14	16	-	
Ward, John	HA	-	5	6	-	
Ward, Matthew	JT	-	-	1		
Ward, Richard	TBM	-	-	1		
Ward, Roland	EB	Jackson, Stewart	14	16		extremely faded ink
Ward, Rowland Jr.	TBM	-	5	6		
Ware, William	JT	-	1	2		
Warnack, Josiah	PL	-	1	2		
Washbrook, Chas. Jr.	TBM	-	-	1		
Washbrook, Chas. Sr.	TBM	-	1	2		
Watkins, Saml.	SC	-	6	7		
Watkins, Stephen	CH	-	2	3		
Watson, William	PL	Holte, David	17	19		
Webster, Anthony	EBj	Mann, William	2	3		no tithe for AnthonyWebster
Webster, Edward	HA	-	4	5	-	
Webster, John	JT	-	-	1		
Webster, Peter	JT	-	4	5		
Webster, William	JT	-	1	2		
Webster?, Thos.	HA	Johnson?, James	6	8	-	
Weeks, Emanuel	LW	-	1	2		
Weeks, William	JT					see John Gil___
Wells, Richard	VB					see Tucker Hood
Wesbrook, Amos	HA					see Archer Hatchett
White, David	TM	-	?	?		numbers obscured by stain
White, Francis	PL	-	5	6		
White, John	JT					see John Tabb
White, John	TM	Hutcherson, Caner?	4	6		
White, Joseph	PL	-	2	3		
Whitworth, Abraham	JT	Whitworth, Claiborne	4	6		
Whitworth, Claiborne	JT					see Abraham Whitworth
Whitworth, John	TM	-	-	1		
Whitworth, Thomas	TM	Whitworth, Thomas Jr.	1	3		
Wiley, Benjamin	VB	Hutcheson, Wm.	-	2		
Wilkerson, Towns	HA					see John Booker Jr.
Wilkinson, Benj.	PL					see John Wilkinson
Wilkinson, James	TBM	-	1	2		

TAXPAYER	List	Other WMTs	Slaves	Tithes	Acres	COMMENTS
Wilkinson, John's list	PL	Wilkinson, Benj. Wilkinson, Stephen	3	5		no tithe for John Wilkinson
Wilkinson, Jos.'s Est.	CH	Pringle, Oliver	6	7		"Estate"
Wilkinson, Stephen	PL					see John Wilkinson
William, Thos.	PL					see John Thowet (P.G.)
Williams, David	VB	Williams, Sterling	-	2		
Williams, Jno.	TBM					see Richard Jones Jr.
Williams, Phillip	EBj	-	7	7		no tithe for Phillip Williams
Williams, Phillip	TBM	-	4	5		
Williams, Thomas	PL	Shelton, Joel	29	31		
Williamson, Jacob	JT	Sutebury?, John	13	15		
Willkerson, Thos.	VB					see David Greenhill Jr.'s Est.
Willkerson?, William	EB	-	-	1		
Wills, Edmd.	LW					see Elias Wills, who paid his tithe
Wills, Edmd.	LW	-	1	1		
Wills, Elias	LW	Wills, Edmd.	7	8		"To Elias Wills"
Wills, Lau. Smith	LW					see Laurence Wills
Wills, Laurence	LW	Wills, Lau. Smith	7	9		
Wills, Thos. Tabb	LW	-	5	6		
Willson, Danl. Sr.	JT	-	15	16		
Willson, John Jr.	VB	-	2	3		
Willson, Richd.	HA					see Danl. Jones' estate
Willson, Thomas Branch	JT	-	28	29		
Wilson, Charles	PRB					see John Wilson
Wilson, Danl. Jr.	HA	-	9	10	-	
Wilson, George	HA	-	1	2	-	
Wilson, John	PRB	Wilson, Charles	4	5		no tithe for John Wilson
Wilson, John Sr.	LW	-	5	6		
Wilson, William	LW	Tucker, Abel	7	9		
Winfrey, Gideon	SB	Winfrey, Robt.	5	7		
Winfrey, John	SB	-	-	1		
Winfrey, Robt.	SB					see Gideon Winfrey
Wingo, John	TM	Wingo, Joshua? Wingo, John Jr.	1	4		
Wingo, John	TM	-	-	1		
Wingo, Joshua?	TM					see John Wingo
Wingo, Thomas	TM	-	-	1		
Winn, Charles	PL					see John Winn Sr.
Winn, Jno. Jr.	PL					see John Winn Sr.
Winn, John Sr.	PL	Winn, Richard Winn, Jno. Jr.	14	20		

TAXPAYER	List	Other WMTs	Slaves	Tithes	Acres	COMMENTS
		Winn, Charles J_tine?, Jno. W. Overstreet, Wm.				
Winn, Richard	PL					see John Winn Sr.
Wish, John	TM					see Walther Bennit
Wood, Edmund	TM					see John Wood
Wood, John	TM	Wood, Edmund	1	3		
Wood, William	PL	-	1	2		
Wood, William	TM	Wood, Wm. Jr.	6	8		
Woodcock, Isack	TM	-	1	2		
Woodson, Joseph	TBM	-	4	5		
Woodward, Francis	SC	Taylor, Geo.	4	6		
Worsham, Chas.?	EB	-	-	1		
Worsham, Daniel	CH	Robertson, Bridge	15	17		
Worsham, Daniel	EB	-	8	9		
Worsham, Daniel	EB					see Henry Worsham, W.P.
Worsham, Essea?	JT					see "Henry Worsham, W.P."
Worsham, George	LW	Powell, Abraham	4	6		
Worsham, Henry W.P.	EB	Worsham, Daniel	2	4		
Worsham, Henry*	JT	Worsham, Henry Jr. Worsham, Essea?	2	5		"Henry Worsham W.P." (not sure what W.P. stands for)
Worsham, John	SC	-	3	4		4 tithes, but only 2 slaves named
Worsham, Peter	LW					see William Worsham
Worsham, William	EB	-	2	3		
Worsham, William	LW	Worsham, Peter	2	4		
Wright, ???	EB	-	?	?		
Wright, John	EB	Wright, Rubin	7	9		
Wright, Martha's list	EB	-	2	2		
Wright, Rubin	EB					See John Wright
Wright, Thos.	EB	-	-	1		
Wyatt, Thos.	JT					see Thomas Walthall
Yeodaley?, Moses	JT					see John Ford
Young, William	SC					see John Cocke
Young, Wm.	PL					see John Cocke
Zachary, Crawford	TBM					see Thomas B. Munford
Zachary, David Sr.	TBM	Huse, Benj. Zachary, Jonathan	4	7		
Zachary, Jonathan	TBM					see David Zachary Sr.
Zachrey, David Jr.	SB	-	1	2		

SUMMARY OF 1778 TITHE LISTS FOR AMELIA COUNTY

The microfilmed records include summary pages for each parish. These are useful in showing the relative populations of the two parishes. Unfortunately, they don't distinguish between white tithes and slave tithes.

I've included them here, for those who might be interested.

RALEIGH PARISH

Tithes taken by:	Number
Col. Vivion Brooking	403
Thos. Mumford	388
Henry Anderson	365
John Tabb	755
Christopher Hudson	167
Col. Lau. Wills	488
Edmond Booker	621
T.G. Peachey	16
TOTAL	3203

NOTTOWAY PARISH

Tithes taken by:	Number
Stephen Bolling	217
Stephen Cocke	122
Edmond Booker Jr.	208
Peter Lamkin	461
Peter R. Bland	222
Thomas B. Munford	705
T.G. Peachy	14
TOTAL	1949